Listening to Noise and Silence

Listening to Noise and Silence

TOWARDS A PHILOSOPHY OF SOUND ART

by
Salomé Voegelin

continuum

NEW YORK • LONDON

2010

The Continuum International Publishing Group Inc
80 Maiden Lane, New York, NY 10038

The Continuum International Publishing Group Ltd
The Tower Building, 11 York Road, London SE1 7NX

www.continuumbooks.com

Library of Congress Cataloging-in-Publication Data
A catalog record for this book is available from the Library of Congress.

ISBN: 978-1-4411-6207-6 (PB)
       978-1-4411-2643-6 (HB)

Typeset by Newgen Imaging Systems Pvt Ltd, Chennai, India
Printed in the United States of America

Contents

Acknowledgments

This book has been inspired and guided by many informal chats and more formal discussions. It has been made possible through the help and trust of many people around me in my private life as well as in the field of Sound Art, its practice and research. I am grateful for every opportunity I was given to present and debate the concerns of this book with colleagues, family, friends and students, and hope that in return the ideas put forward here will help them to further their own research and practice of Sound Art.

Most of all I want to thank David Mollin who has supported me in so many ways through this endeavour. I also want to particularly thank David Toop who gave me the belief it could be done, and Angus Carlyle and Professor Nick deVille for their close reading and feedback on the text. I want to thank Cathy Lane for our ongoing discussions on sound, and Peter Cusack for his insights and suggestions. I would like to mention the lunches debating the pathetic and memory with Thomas Gardner, and the very useful exchanges on their work with Clare Gasson and Ed Osborn. J. Milo Taylor's immersive database of Sound Art, ImMApp, became an invaluable tool to access work. Ed Baxter and Taigen Kawabe's knowledge on Japanese noise music provided many important pointers, and Rahma Kazham's invitation to speak gave me the opportunity to publicly audition my ideas.

I wish to express gratitude to my sister Dea Voegelin for her help with research, and also wish to thank all my colleagues at LCC (London College of Communication) and the whole of CRiSAP (Creative Research in Sound Arts Practice) as well as other artists who all, one way or another, encouraged and contributed to my ideas on Sound Art over the last few years: Chris Petter, John Wynne, David Cunningham,

Aki Pasoulas, Iris Garrelfs, Jörg Köppl, Helen Bendon, Michael Hiltbrunner, Nye Parry and many more.

Lastly I would also like to mention the Sound Arts students at LCC, whose own struggle with the notion of a critical discourse of Sound Art has in many ways instigated and motivated this project.

INTRODUCTION

When philosophers, who are well known to have difficulty in keeping silent, engage in conversation, they should try always to lose the argument, but in such a way as to convict their opponent of untruth. The point should not be to have absolutely correct, irrefutable, watertight conditions – for they inevitably boil down to tautologies, but insights which cause the question of their justness to judge itself.[1]

The way we think about the world is in no small way influenced by the senses we engage to appreciate this world, and in turn these senses have always already an ideological as well as a cultural function prior to us employing them. The judgement and understanding reached is inadvertently directed by that ideological functioning of the sense employed. If I look at something the information I will gain about that thing is influenced by the physiological mechanism of looking and the cultural interpretation and valuation of seeing. If I notice a concurrent sound, I most likely subsume that heard into the appreciation of the seen: sound fleshes out the visual and renders it real; it gives the image its spatial dimension and temporal dynamic. But these are attributes of the object seen, ignoring the event heard. This impulse to subsume sound into the visual is so ingrained as to blight music criticism and the discourse of sound art, whose focus is invariably on the score or the arrangement, on the orchestra or the performer, the sound source, the installation view or the documentation of the sonic event, in short the visual manifestation rather than the sounds heard.

Sound's ephemeral invisibility obstructs critical engagement, while the apparent stability of the image invites criticism. Vision, by its very nature assumes a distance from the object, which it receives in its monumentality. Seeing always happens in a meta-position, away from the seen, however close. And this distance enables a detach-ment and objectivity that presents itself as truth. Seeing is believing. The visual 'gap' nourishes the idea of structural certainty and the notion that we can truly understand things, give them names, and define ourselves in relation to those names as stable subjects, as identities. The score, the image track of the film, the stage set, the visual editing interface, and so on can make us believe in an objective hearing, but what we hear, guided by these images, is not sound but the realization of the visual. The sound itself is long gone, chased away by the certainty of the image.

By contrast, hearing is full of doubt: phenomenological doubt of the listener about the heard and himself hearing it. Hearing does not offer a meta-position; there is no place where I am not simultaneous with the heard. However far its source, the sound sits in my ear. I can-not hear it if I am not immersed in its auditory object, which is not its source but sound as sound itself. Consequently, a philosophy of sound art must have at its core the principle of sharing time and space with the object or event under consideration. It is a philosophical project that necessitates an involved participation, rather than ena-bles a detached viewing position; and the object or event under con-sideration is by necessity considered not as an artefact but in its dynamic production. This is a continual production that involves the listener as intersubjectively constituted in perception, while produc-ing the very thing he perceives, and both, the subject and the work, thus generated concomitantly, are as transitory as each other.[2] In this way, this project involves the philosopher as listener and it involves the willingness of the reader to listen. A philosophy of sound art thus pursued, can, following Adorno's advice, provide 'insights which cause the question of their justness to judge itself', rather than proposing a truth.[3] This does not make this philosophy irrational or arbitrary, how-ever, but clarifies its intention to embrace the experience of its object rather than replace it with ideas. In other words, it does not seek to mediate the sensorial experience of the artwork under consideration

through theories, categories, hierarchies, histories, to eventually produce canons that release us from the doubt of hearing through the
certainty and knowledge of its worth, which thus render our engagement tautological. Instead, this philosophy seeks to produce a critical
engagement that witnesses, documents and narrates what is going
on in sound art and thus is an aid to develop what is being practised
and how it is being listened to. There will, then, be no real conclusions
but only strategies for engagement and efforts of interpretation. In this
sense this book is an essay rather than a conventional philosophical
text. Again I borrow the term from Adorno to suggest that its formal
enquiry produces experimentations rather than ideology and truth.
The term essay proposes an open-ended enquiry that 'does not begin
with Adam and Eve but with what it wants to discuss', and that does
not produce an exhaustive and total report but a discontinuity of
provisional ideas.[4] In this sense this text writes an experiment and
extends the invitation to read it as such.

Over the course of this experiment, this book comes to consider
listening as an actual practice and as a conceptual sensibility that
raises new questions for the philosophy of art in general and unsettles the perceived certainty of a visual aesthetic, without, however,
proposing a dialectical position. Instead it suggests that a sonic sensibility would illuminate the unseen aspects of visuality, augmenting
rather than opposing a visual philosophy. To achieve this, throughout
this book, different sound works are discussed and this discussion
is articulated in terms of related philosophical debates. It is through
listening that the author gets to the philosophical questions that are
being considered in this book, and it is the listened to sound, the sensorial material, that leads the investigation and makes those philosophical questions and debates concrete and relevant for the reader
as listener. The sonic sensibility put forward in this process re-focuses
philosophical problems around subjectivity and objectivity; it questions the notion of a transcendental *a priori*; and, via the notion of
interpretative fantasies, connects the experience of sound with the
notion of virtuality and possible worlds that are not linked to the logic

and rational of a visual reality but augment that reality through the blind sight of sound within its depth.

In this way, this text contributes to the debate of sound art as well as to that of philosophy. It is about sound art in that it focuses on sound as its 'object' of investigation; and it is philosophical in that it speculates and inquires into new ways to consider art, the world and our position within the production of art and the world through a sonic sensibility. However, the aim is not a philosophy of sound art that explains experience but a philosophy that experiences. Thus it can never be fixed but must constantly evolve with what there is to be played and heard. Any articulation proposed is only a passing theory.[5] A philosophy of sound art must remain a strategy of listening rather than an instruction to hear, and thus its language itself is under scrutiny.

Critical discourse does badly in dealing with sound as it assumes and insists on the gap between that which it describes and its description – it is the very opposite of sound, which is always the heard, immersive and present. Its language relegates the sonic into a position of attribute: sound is loud, clear, silent or noisy, it is fast or slow, but never is it the noun under consideration. Instead it is sublimated to a visual referent, which mutes its particularity. To write about sound as this book endeavours to do is to be engaged in this problem and to practice its own contradiction. Consequently, a great challenge underlying this book is the fact that it is written in language while contesting, through a sonic sensibility, the very principle of language, its visuality. Any attempt to articulate a philosophy of sound art has this paradox at its core, and by revealing this paradox; sound re-evaluates the very basis of discourse and philosophy itself. But in that it also draws out the most far-reaching consequences, beyond sound, for a general notion of philosophy, aesthetics and the sensorial engagement. And so sound reveals the constraints and limitations of the word in language while extending its use in sound. The methodology of investigation is intrinsically linked to its subject: one is investigated through the other.

The ideas of this book are developed in five chapters. The first three, *Listening*, *Noise* and *Silence*, debate the perceptual engagement with sound, while the last two, *Time and Space* and *Now*, examine the consequences of this discussion. The philosophical questions dealt with are wide-ranging but gain their specificity through the focus on sound. In turn the consequences of this investigation are worked out in the specificity of sound, but are far-reaching in terms of a more general aesthetic and cultural sensibility.

The first chapter debates *Listening* as an activity, an interactivity, that produces, invents and demands of the listener a complicity and commitment. It narrates listening to sound work and the acoustic environment and introduces the themes central to a philosophy of sound art: subjectivity, objectivity, communication, collective relations, meaning and sense making. The second chapter goes on to re-consider these issues by listening to sound that deafens my ears to anything but itself. And so *Noise* stretches *Listening* to an extreme and makes a tentative proposal for a philosophy of sound art as a signifying practice of listening that articulates the fragile relationship between experience and communication, and anticipates the meeting of the semiotic and the phenomenological in *Silence*.

In the quiet sounds of *Silence* the listener becomes audible to himself as a discrete member of an audience. *Silence* provides the condition to practise a signifying language that takes account of its sonic base: it embraces the body of the listener in its solitude, and invites him to listen to himself amidst the soundscape that he inhabits. In this sense chapter 3 articulates silence as the basic condition of a philosophy of sound art, and outlines the consequences for a sonic subjectivity and its relationship to the objective world. Thus the chapter discusses silent works and silence in the acoustic environment not as the absence of sound but as the beginning of listening as communication.

Time and Space discusses the sonic subject post *Silence*. The sonic sensibility that found critical language in *Silence* is generated in and manifests the listener's spatio-temporal circumstance. Hence chapter 4 turns to social-geography and its discussion of global networking, to contextualize the listener and sound artworks in terms of their social position and connectivity. Issues of material and imma- terial social relations are illuminated and debated via a sonic sensi- bility. In this way this chapter re-visits earlier issues of subjectivity and identity in relation to belonging and migration, and discovers that a sonic sensibility, since it makes thinkable complex connections and trajectories in time and space, offers a method of engagement and critical evaluation of installation and new media art.

The last chapter *Now* does not constitute a conclusion in the conventional sense but presents a reflection back on much listening. It is in keeping with the central tenet of this book that a philosophy of sound art must remain a passing theory rather than propose a conclusion, in order not to contradict its own methodology. But this constant present passing has a past and a future, and thus the last chapter looks at 'the other time' and 'the over there' of sound and the listening subject. It is through the emotional and personal engage- ment forged by the refrain of the past in the present, that the philoso- phy of sound art proposed so far, becomes useful for an engagement with other arts and in relation to the broader concerns of a socio- aesthetic consciousness and ethics. In this sense, the last chapter articulates how the 'pathetic' invites us into sound and expands the relevance of its philosophy beyond sound art.

The choice of works discussed in this book is unrelated to canonic hierarchies. This is no attempt at forging an alternative history or canon of sound art. There are some known and some lesser-known works discussed here. The emphasis is on the experience of the work rather than its valuation or comparison. A major factor in choosing the pieces was my proximity to them, the possibility to encounter them, to share their time and space. The sonic sensibility proposed can be carried to any works available to the reader, Since, it is the listening engagement and the sonic sensibility thus produced, rather than the production of knowledge or judgement of any particular sound art- work, that motivates this text. Having said this, the works discussed are significant in that they lead to the philosophical issues considered here. It is their particularity that produces the general ideas of a philosophy of sound art that can be applied in the particularity of each reader's own listening practice.

1

LISTENING

This chapter explores listening, not as a physiological fact but as an act of engaging with the world. It is in the engagement with the world rather than in its perception that the world and myself within it are constituted, and it is the sensorial mode of that engagement that determines my constitution and that of the world.

Every sensory interaction relates back to us not the object/ phenomenon perceived, but that object/ phenomenon filtered, shaped and produced by the sense employed in its perception. At the same time this sense outlines and fills the perceiving body, which in its perception shapes and produces his sensory self. Whereby the senses employed are always already ideologically and aesthetically determined, bringing their own influence to perception, the perceptual object and the perceptual subject. It is a matter then of accepting the *a priori* influence while working towards a listening in spite rather than because of it. The task is to suspend, as much as possible, ideas of genre, category, purpose and art historical context, to achieve a hearing that is the material heard, now, contingently and individually. This suspension does not mean a disregard for the artistic context or intention, nor is it frivolous and lazy. Rather it means appreciating the artistic context and intention through the practice of listening rather than as a description and limitation of hearing. This practice follows Theodor W. Adorno's call for philosophical interpretations that,

> . . . answer the questions of a pre-given reality each time, through a fantasy which rearranges the elements of the question without going beyond the circumference of the elements, the exactitude of which has its control in the disappearance of the question.[1]

It is perception as interpretation that knows that to hear the work/ the sound is to invent it in listening to the sensory material rather than to recognize its contemporary and historical context. Such listening will produce the artistic context of the work/the sound in its innovative perception rather than through the expectation of an *a priori* reality. This phantasmagoric practice does not make listening inexact or irrelevant since it is based on the rigour and responsibility of perception.[2] To rely on the pre-given would in any event not make the perceived more valid. It would simply make it more certain within its own description. However, this also means that perception could only ever know the work to the degree to which it fulfils that certainty.

The ideology of a pragmatic visuality is the desire for the whole: to achieve the convenience of comprehension and knowledge through the distance and stability of the object. Such a visuality provides us with maps, traces, borders and certainties, whose consequence are communication and a sense of objectivity. The auditory engagement however, when it is not in the service of simply furnishing the pragmatic visual object, pursues a different engagement. Left in the dark, I need to explore what I hear. Listening discovers and generates the heard.

The difference lies, as Michel de Certeau points out, between the desire for the godlike view, the gnostic drive for total knowledge, satisfied from high above at a distance from the urban text, and the walking of the 'Wandersmänner' down below, producing the city blindly through their temporal and individual trajectories.[3] In this sense listening is not a receptive mode but a method of exploration, a mode of 'walking' through the soundscape/the sound work. What I hear is discovered not received, and this discovery is generative, a fantasy: always different and subjective and continually, presently now.

An aesthetic and philosophy of sound art is based on this discovering drive. This is not a gnostic drive, but a drive to knowing. Knowing as past participle, always now, unfolding in the present, bringing with it the uncertainty of a fleeting understanding. Such a listening does not pursue the question of meaning, as a collective, total comprehension, but that of interpretation in the sense of a phantas-magoric, individual and contingent practice. This practice remains necessarily incomplete in relation to an objective totality but complete in its subjective contingency. Sound narrates, outlines and fills, but it is always ephemeral and doubtful. Between my heard and the sonic object/phenomenon I will never know its truth but can only invent it, producing a knowing for me.

This knowing is the experience of sound as temporal relationship. This 'relationship' is not between things but is the thing, is sound itself. Listening cannot contemplate the object/phenomenon heard separate from its audition because the object does not precede listening. Rather, the auditory is generated in the listening practice: in listening I am in sound, there can be no gap between the heard and hearing, I either hear it or I don't, and what I perceive is what I hear. I can perceive a distance but that is a heard distance. The distance is what I hear here, not over-there. It does not signal a separation of objects or events but is the separation as perceived phenomenon.

The aesthetic subject in sound is defined by this fact of interac-tion with the auditory world. He is placed in the midst of its materiality, complicit with its production. The sounds of his footsteps are part of the auditory city he produces in his movements through it. His sub-ject position is different from the viewing self, whose body is at a distance from the seen. The listener is entwined with the heard. His sense of the world and of himself is constituted in this bond.

The understanding gained is a knowing of the moment as a sensory event that involves the listener and the sound in a reciprocal inventive production. This conception challenges both notions of objectivity and of subjectivity, and reconsiders the possibility and place of meaning, which situates the re-evaluation of all three at the centre of a philosophy of sound art.

This first chapter describes listening as an activity, an interactivity, that produces and invents and demands of the listener a complicity and commitment that rethinks existing philosophies of perception. By narrating listening to sound work and the acoustic environment it introduces the themes central to a philosophy of sound art: subjectivity, objectivity, communication, collective relations, meaning and sense making.

Being Honeyed

In 1948 Maurice Merleau-Ponty was commissioned by the French National radio to give seven audio-lectures on 'The Development of Ideas' to be broadcast as part of 'The French Culture Hour', on each Saturday between the 9th of October and the 13th of November. His series, which focused on the World of Perception, is kept in the archives of the Institut National de L'Audiovisuel (INA) in Paris and has also been published first in French, and now in an English translation, as a small booklet by Routledge.[4] Here I will consider both my experience of the spoken causeries, listening to it by appointment at the National Archive and the statements of the written texts. In these lectures Merleau-Ponty considers the perception of the world not as a passive gazing at its *a priori* attributes but instates visual perception via modern painting and everyday objects an active role. Merleau-Ponty talks about painting and the artistic demand to see beyond the intellectual expectation of a representational reality into the perception of 'a space in which we too are located'. Talking about painting since Cézanne he suggests:

> The lazy viewer will see 'errors of perspective' here, while those who look closely will get the feel of a world in which no two objects are seen simultaneously, a world in which regions of space are separated by the time it takes to move our gaze from one to the other a world in which being is not given but rather emerges over time.[5]

In his descriptions he outlines a phenomenology of perception, a world and art perceived rather than known. He understands conventional, representational and perspectival painting to be polite in that it facilitates a single perception of what is in reality multi-layered and complex. To him such painting kills 'their trembling life' that is perpetually unfolding. Instead he prefers those works that deal with the emergence of being over time.[6]

What he means by this painterly emergence is clarified in his in 1945 written essay 'Cézanne's Doubt', where he articulates the doubt in the singular and habitual veracity of the seen as the prime motivator of the artist's production. He suggests that Cézanne paints incessantly, again and again the landscape before him from the doubt in the referential and prespectival reality of the visible world. This doubt is suspended in the motility of painting out of which the landscape emerges rather than is represented by. He understands such paintings as 'a drive to rediscover the world as we apprehend it in lived experience', and states that painters of that time refused the laws of perspective and instead struggled with the birth of the landscape, the thing, before them.[7] They pushed the body into the mêlé of reality and it is through the bodily experience that that reality becomes real in all its complexity rather than as a detached and firm fact. However, in print his ideas retain the notion of a finished painting rather than the movement of unfolding that he attributes to the sensory material. It remains a description of a work that is the finished product of a complex, bodily engagement; it is not the bodily engagement itself.

What he writes about is the artist's body, his doubt, his need to perpetually rework, to remain fleetingly certain, which evokes in me the certainty of his painting, validated by the painter's struggle and hard work. Cézanne's individual and ceaseless struggle against one point of view is the modernist aura of the painting as a manual fact.[8] The painting remains certain as a painting that I can view from a distance, hanging heavy on the wall. I empathize intellectually but not physically. This is not my doubt being worked through here. It remains the painter's. The multi-layered complexity becomes again one viewpoint in the perspective of the gallery. In the certainty of the museum's context I understand rather than experience doubt. By contrast, through the spoken words of the broadcast the painting unfolds, refolds, from me, as an audio work. I hear and participate in the process of layers, distances, time and separations. The painting emerges over time in my ears. This is not to say that the written text or the painted image really represent a simple and certain unity. But their already-there-ness, their existence before my viewing them and the certainty of their published context, allows my vision to observe rather than participate in the complexity of their unfolding. The physical distance and autonomy of the work as image, as text, allows reading and shapes the interpretation of the read in its own image. This interpretation *is* the work in perception but this perception is spatial and brightly lit. By contrast, the dark serendipity of radio grants no room: its nearness and temporality is not that of my interpretation but that of its own unfolding, out of the dark into my ears, in the physical time of the broadcast. My ears perform the complexity of the work bodily and in some haste. The text as writing is the musical work, framed by convention; it allows entry to scrutinizing eyes that interpret it, while granting it the space for that interpretation. The issue here is not a distinction between music and sound art, but how both of them are listened to. This book includes the discussion of what conventionally could be termed musical works, but attempts to listen to them for the sound they make rather than their musical organization. Since, sound does not allow for an interpretation on top of its work-ness but *is* interpretation as all there is, temporal and contingent. It is the 'unseen' painting as it emerges from Merleau-Ponty's voice that reveals the complex intersubjectivity of its experience. The text as voice is the bodily fragment of its sound, and the painting unfolding in that voice takes that body to meet mine in a dark and transient conduit. Here the painting is experienced in all its complexity rather than appreciated as a firm fact: trembling and in doubt it *is* the motility of being.

What I hear in Merleau-Ponty's *Causeries* is not the body of the text but the body of Merleau-Ponty, whose complex unity, contingent, fragmented and doubtful, meets me in my listening. When, in another broadcast in the series, Merleau-Ponty explains the complex unity of perception through the yellow sourness of a lemon and the liquid stickiness of honey, it is from his voice, the bodily and transient sound of his appearance out of the darkness of the broadcast, that the lemon and honey get formed in my listening as uncertain and complex unities that reveal my own unsure intricacy.

> This is the case with the quality of being-honeyed. Honey is a slow-moving liquid; while it undoubtedly has a certain consistency and allows itself to be grasped, it soon creeps slyly from the fingers and returns to where it started from. It comes apart as soon as it has been given a particular shape, and what is more, it reverses the roles, by grasping the hands of whoever would take hold of it.[9]

Being honeyed expresses the reciprocity of his phenomenological intersubjectivity. The honey can only be felt through my stickiness. It cannot be grasped as a remote object but comes to being in my honeyed-hands as a complex phenomenon of no certain shape but a demanding nature. While the text describes the process, the voice produces it. His voice becomes the honey that drips into my ears and engages me without taking certain shape; it remains a roving complexity that grasps me.

The paintings, sour lemons and sticky honey that Merleau-Ponty talks about in his radio broadcasts are imagined by the listeners, produced in their imagination, invented and tasted through their ears. My cheeks pull together and my saliva starts flowing to the sound of yellow juicy lemon-ness. The image of a lemon sums it up, the sound adds up: adding ever more complex layers that are the object as auditory phenomenon. The adding never reaches a totality but only a contingent realization, which is never ideal but remains the fantasy of Adorno's interpretative process.

While the modernist painter grapples with the multi-perspectuality of the world, in listening I imagine the world: it emerges between his words from my imagination in which I am located. This is not an act of interpretation as much as the fantasy of my audition: it is not the modernist painting nor the golden honey but his voice, his body in his mouth meeting mine in my ears, that shapes the perceived in the sensory-motor action of my perception.

Merleau-Ponty talks about his world of perception in visual terms. The sensibility of his perception however is not that of vision. It is not vision that painting and philosophy has liberated from representation; it is sonic perception, which is free of the visual stranglehold on knowledge and experience. Sound does not describe but produces the object/phenomenon under consideration. It shares nothing of the totalizing ability of the visual. It does not deny visual reality but practises its own fleeting actuality, augmenting the seen through the heard. The sonic reality is intersubjective in that it does not exist without my being in it and I in turn only exist in my complicity with it; and it is generative in that it *is* the sensory-motor process of listening: presently producing one's honeyed-ness from one's position of listening centrifugally into the world.[10]

The listening subject invents, he practises an innovative listening that produces the world for him in a phenomenological sensory-motor action towards the heard, and his auditory self is part of the heard in reciprocal intersubjectivity. Listening as a critical motility practises Merleau-Ponty's phenomenology as a process of doubt: the critical listener himself is full of doubt about the heard, and doubtful in his complicity he needs to hear and hear again, to know himself as an intersubjective being in a sonic life-world.[11] The difficulty arises when this experiential, subjective world is measured and communicated in written language that pretends the objectivity and knowledge of the visual exchange. The transcript of the radio broadcasts gives me a description of the complexity of honey and lemons, the sounds of Merleau-Ponty's voice binds me to honey's sugary stickiness and the lemon's sour flesh. This difference in my perceptual engagement highlights an aesthetic difference.

One intention of *Listening* is to unpack and articulate this distinction through listening to sound work and the everyday acoustic environment, to bring to light the consequences of a sonic perception and subjectivity as a philosophical experience. Another is to bring sounds' particularity to bear on our notion of communication, language and shared meaning, and to celebrate experiential non-sense, Merleau-Ponty's phenomenological sense that comes out of sensation rather than rationality and transgresses the collective through individual sense-making.

To Listen

Sounds constantly enter my ears, bounding around in there, declaring their interest even if I am not listening. As I walk through a busy urban street I try to ignore the incessant hum of thick traffic, the noisy commotion and vocal drone of people around me. However, the fact that I do not listen to them consciously or willingly does not mean that these sounds do not shape the reality as it presents itself to me. Sound renders the crowd massive and pervasive, becoming ever denser and more intimidating, encroaching on my physical space. Their stomping feet reverberate off the hard and shiny architecture. A stampede: emerging from behind my back and stretching ahead of me beyond my visual horizon. They are everywhere, coming closer and closer, engulfing me in their physical presence.

Switch off the drone of hammering footsteps and the aural hubbub of human activity, the crowd shrinks immediately, the frightful beast is tamed. All I see now are people bumbling along, minding their own businesses, nothing to do with me. However, such a visual autonomy does not exist.[12] Listening produces a sonic life-world that we inhabit, with or against our will, generating its complex unity. Sound involves me closely in what I see; it pulls the seen towards me as it grasps me by my ears. Sound renders the object dynamic. It makes it 'tremble with life' and gives it a sense of process rather than a mute stability. Stability is mute, not silent but mute. Silence still involves listening and hearing as a generative action of perception. Muteness by contrast numbs the auditory engagement. It applies a local anaesthetic and disables the hearing process. Stability in this sense is the object minus the action of perception, a state that does not exist but is assumed and pretended by a visual ideology. Sound by contrast negates stability through the force of sensory experience. Listening's focus on the dynamic nature of things renders the perceptual object unstable, fluid and ephemeral: unsettling what *is* through a world of sonic phenomena and audible spirits. Sounds are like ghosts. They slink around the visual object, moving in on it from all directions, forming its contours and content in a formless breeze. The spectre of sound unsettles the idea of visual stability and involves us as listeners in the production of an invisible world. This sonic life-world might be silent but forceful, grasping us as we hear it, pulling us into an auditory imagination even if we mistake if for the thing seen.

Listening in the library draws me into the minutia of human sounds. Every hum, cough, whisper, every footstep, sneeze, paper turn, rasp and throat clearing is amplified. In sound the library becomes an awkward space of fraught physicality: full of bodies, rigid and tense, trying to be silent. Ever so often the restraint cracks under the expectation: a mobile phone goes off, a voice misses the whispering register. In response a reproaching chorus of sounds ensues that leads the offending noise back into the approved sphere. In its rising and falling the sounds of the library invite the imagination of a boundary-less mass of human flesh, heaving in its own rhythm, oozing sighs and whispers and grasping me in its breath: a fleshly monster of which I am part, enveloped, swallowed in its hush as in a faintly murmuring beast. As I look up, I know the people are sitting at a distance, heads in books; their purpose firmly roots them in their own visual world. But in sound they come closer. They become the people of my auditory imagination. They start to breath down my neck and if I do not stop listening I will only be able to hear them.

Listening as an aesthetic practice challenges how we see and how we participate in the production of the visual world. Listening allows fantasy to reassemble the visual fixtures and fittings, and repositions us as designers of our own environment. It challenges, augments and expands what we see, without presenting a negative illusion, by producing the reality of lived experience. Through this generative experience listening revisits those philosophical tenets that are bound to the sovereignty of the visual. Listening, in this sense, is an aesthetic activity that challenges the philosophical tradition of the West, which, according to film theorist Christian Metz, is based on a hierarchy between the senses which positions sound in the attribual location, sublimated to the visual and its linguistic structure.[13] In that position sound is left to describe and enhance but never to do and become. It is a small adjective to the mighty visual noun, furnishing its objects and enhancing its perspective without being acknowledged in that position.

When we start to listen as a critical motility this position becomes untenable. Listening emancipated from the expectation to enhance does something else. It produces, it invents, it generates. It demands that the heard be more than a ghost of the visual, a flimsy figment of the imagination, soon dispelled. However, instead of denying the ephemeral quality of its object, it is the preference for the assumed substance of visuality that needs to be reassessed by focusing on the ephemeral exactly.

Waterlow Park at Dawn (2008)

To listen to Waterlow park at dawn is to generate its morning-park-ness and my morning-self from the midst of its sounds. I merge the city hum with the fresh bird song, the occasional dog walker's call and a jogger's panting breath with the sounds of my auditory imagination for which I cannot name a source. The birds' song, the traffic hum, the runner's breath and the master's whistle recall a sonic objectivity as a residue of all my earlier subjective generative appreciations of such sounds. The objective brings with it the park as cultural notion, and all the parks I have ever visited. Intertwining in my ears this left-over objectivity with my present subjectivity the sounds are produced beyond what they are in a fantastic but plausible reality of what I have them be.

To listen is not to simply know where I am on the visual map that hangs outside the park gates. It is to experience where I am in the park of my own listening. It makes the park real and present for me in the lived reality of my intersubjective self. This intersubjective self carries with it, always already, the relationship to an objective residue of past hearings, but that objectivity too is particular and experiential rather than universal and known. It produces the park as an invented space that is not unreal but phantasmagoric: born out of the reality of experience. Listening here does not enhance but produces the park. It clarifies sound as verb, accounting for its generative facility. But language does not meet it that way. Sound, when it is not heard as sublimated into the service of furnishing a visual reality, but listened to generatively, does not describe a place or an object, nor is it a place or an object, it is neither adjective nor noun. It is to be in motion, to produce. It is an invisible act, a dynamic of production that is not interested to linger and hear its outcome. It is perpetually on the move, making time and tenses rather than following them.

Listening to sound as verb invents places and things whose audience is their producer. In this appreciation of verb-ness the listener confirms the reciprocity of his active engagement and the trembling life of the world can be heard.

Dynamic Things and Places

Our relationship with things is not a distant one, each speaks to our body and the way we live. [. . .] Humanity is invested in the things of the world and these are invested in it.[14]

Sound invites the body into experience and reciprocally makes the object physical. Listening to sound is where objectivity and subjectivity meet: in the experience of our own generative perception we produce the objectivity from our subjective and particular position of listening, which in its turn is constituted by the objectivity of the object as a prior moment of hearing, subjective and particular. It is this particularity of the listening subject in the contingency of his experience that has to be kept in mind, in order, according to Adorno, not to turn the individual subject already into an (objective) universal; in order, in other words, to avoid ideology and hierarchy. It is neither the thing that dominates the being nor the being that dominates the thing. They are reciprocal and equivalent, but in their momentary meeting they are also distinct. They are produced on the spot, together in difference, any prior objectivity and prior subjectivity is invested in this momentary and complex production but does not subsume it.

The subject in sound is an empirical not a transcendental subject and so is its object. It is the lived and concrete experience that constitutes the world as a sonic life-world and the subject reciprocally generated within it. Objectivity and subjectivity are partners rather than adversaries in such a conception. They are concrete and causal, constituted through each other without abandoning their own purpose. And while, according to Adorno, transcendental subjects are more constitutive of a current (visual) society that emphasizes rationality and abstraction over what they are for themselves, they are in that reality always already deformed into the rationality of their surrounding structure. By contrast, empirical subjects are formless, in that they have no visibility or power in that social order, and exist but as beings for themselves, outside the social exchange.[15]

The sonic subject is this empirical subject understood as an experiential subject. Its determination, practised in listening, is formless but not powerless: the sonic object/phenomenon blasts the systemic and rational reality through its insistence on being heard, being experienced rather than abstracted. It challenges the rationality of abstracted relations and its acquiescent ideologies and values and instead insists on concrete experience. The experiential subjects are phenomenological intersubjective selves, who experience rather than abstract social relations. Their formlessness points to a generative (verbial) intersubjectivity rather than to their invisibility and powerlessness.

This emphasis on the concrete formlessness and the intersubjective transitoriness of sound, is the reason for suspending notions of category or genre when considering the following works lest we lose the individual subject in the category of objectivity, or let the subject dominate the contingency of the object. The associations produced might recall things heard, but only through the particular ears of the subject rather than in relation to universal references. The objectivity is as fragile and ephemeral as the subjective moment of listening. The works considered here are discussed from my specific and contingent listening: my subjectivity passing my objectivity in formless but concrete moments. 'For it is only as something definite that the object becomes anything at all.'[16]

matières induites (1975)

Bernard Parmegiani's *matières induites* builds the real object as a figment of my imagination. He attacks me with forceful shrill and insistent sounds that pierce my ears and grate their surface but soon give way to softer, glistening undulations that grasp my listening. Between synthesized sounds I can hear real, visual, attributes, but having lured me into recognition they swiftly move on and transform themselves into things that are experientially, fantastically, real for me, rather than existing as abstracted reality.

Parmegiani builds a whole forest of things, dark, multi-layered, precise, calculated, bursting forth, here, there and going. As a short 3:44 minutes sequence it brings to life and takes away a tiny thing of sound. It is but a snippet, sweet sized, rolling around in my ears. I sense it as a formless shape that fills me with my form. It is a sonic thing that is also a landscape and a narration of things that do not exist. It drums and tinkers, rings and scrapes, flickers and dances firmly around itself. It is a thing that moves through its own production rather than representing it. And yet it remains here and makes me move. We move against each other, in opposite direction circling on the same spot, while moving on. Its time and space is simultaneous and complex. Condensed. Its elements never sit beside each other but produce in four dimensions the sensory complexity of its hearing.

Away from its series, 12 pieces under the title *De Natura Sonorum*, it seems like a little being, lost and exposed to my interpreting ears. And yet it is in itself a pressing thing, with the authority and demand of its own materiality. The composition induces and brings forth its own object, whose objectivity is fragile and passing, but insistent, produced in its composition and generated again and again in my listening rather than as a firm track. It can take any form or shape in the process of listening, growing into what is around, into my ears, into what I hear. Listening means to tempt and encourage the complex object intended in composition but shaped by the listener's subjectivity, bound to the objectivity of prior hearings.

Listening produces the *matières induites* as a subjective objectivity, since its object does not exist before its recording but is produced in its composition that my listening realizes, not as a positivist ideal, but as a contingent interpretation, a fantasy of its materiality. There is no habitual perception that guides this encounter but only a generative attitude that sounds itself into life and whose tones implicate me in its production. I am with the material at its birth, I am attacked by it and my only experience can be that of astonishment and doubt in the heard, because it is not the perception of the expected but the generation of the unexpected.

> Was uns als natürlich vorkommt, ist vermutlich nur das Gewöhnliche einer langen Gewohnheit, die das Ungewohnte, dem sie entsprungen, vergessen hat. Jenes Ungewohnte hat jedoch einst als ein Befremdendes den Menschen angefallen und hat das Denken zum Erstaunen gebracht.[17]

It is the sensorial attack of Parmegiani's *matières induites* and my astonishment which ignites the question about habits of perception that cloak the practice of listening and which motivates my enquiry into the Heideggerian Thing – *das Ding* – through which he grapples with the ontological notion of the *Wesen der Dinge*, the nature of the things, on his way to a philosophy of art.

Martin Heidegger's focus on *das Ding* aims to bring back *das Sein im Seienden*, the being in the object, as it presents itself to *dem Anwesenden*: the human perceiver, who is in attendance. His interpretation of the Thing aims to reinstate experience as a closeness to the being of the things, which has, according to him gone lost since the interpretation of Aristotle by the Romans at which moment, he suggests, begins the *Bodenlosigkeit* of occidental thinking.[18]

By borrowing his philosophical focus I am acknowledging the ontological frame of the search for the nature of things, and understand that sound as Thing responds to that investigation. However, I do not intend to produce a faithful and comprehensive interpretation of Heidegger's answers on the nature of the Thing, his investigation into the nature of objectivity, but want to engage in the question of thing-ness via sound.

For Heidegger everything that is not nothing is a Thing, and his consideration of the *Dingheit* (*Dingsein*) of those things starts with that thought. From there he pursues a discussion of the quality of this *Dingheit*: determining it as firstly *das eigentliche Ding*, just a Thing, in the negative and in the obvious sense of the word, secondly as the *Dingheit* of those initial things, and thirdly as the form and fabric thereof.[19]

To get to the sonic object I make use of Heidegger's *Dingbegriff*, his term of the Thing, and his suggestion of a *Dingheit* that is hidden by the substance of the actual, '*des bloßen und eigentlichen Ding*', just a Thing, and its habitual perception. It is 'das Insichruhende' as *Dinghaftes*, the in itself resting thing-ness of the Thing that is, the formed fabric of the Thing as it is open to and perceived through an astonished sensorial engagement.[20]

Heidegger invests a phenomenological approach to go beyond the naïve consideration of the substance towards the Thing as being in its *Dinghaftigkeit*, thing-ness. He asks, 'als was zeigen sich die Dinge?' and wants us to appreciate the Thing from its-showing-of-itself that which shows itself in the way that it shows itself in its present attendance.[21] In this way he performs a phenomenological reduction from the naively grasped being (*Seienden*) of the Thing, to the being (*Sein*) of the Thing thinging: 'Das Ding dingt.'[22]

The differentiation of the actual Thing (*Seienden*) as *Unterbau*, foundation, of the artwork: just the Thing of stone, canvas, wood, etc. as it presents itself to naïve apperception; and the thinging (*Sein*) of the *Oberbau*:[23] the built of the artwork as *Werk*, as work, as it is reached in a phenomenological engagement, allows for the critical consideration of the Thing heard rather than the Thing composed, performed or recorded, and acknowledges the perceptual process and the *Anwesenheit*, the close presence of the listener to produce its critical hearing.[24]

I take Heidegger's focus on the elemental notion of the Thing in its *Dingheit*, thinging, and foreground the generative possibility of such a thinging thing: not just to be, intransitive and transcendental, but to presently, in a current encounter, impress on the listener its own production. The sounding Thing is *dinglich* through its own sound track rather than in relation to other things. The phenomenological engagement produces the hearing of the material *Unterbau* as its sensorial *Oberbau* without the dialectical differentiation. Since in sound the material is what is heard already in its *Dingheit*, rather than as a secondary motion from a pre-conceived thing. The naïve appercep-tion of the sonic material is not what precedes the phenomenological engagement of listening, but is its visual avoidance.

The Thing as sound is a verb, the thing is what 'things' in its con-tingent production. To thing, it is to do a thing rather than be a Thing. In fact any notion of being as a positive or transcendental existence, in and of itself, is negated in sonic thing-ness. The sonic thing is not perspectival, organized in relation to other things, social functions, or ordered in relation to a purpose. The sonic thing makes the organiza-tion and the purpose, contingently, in passing, and any purpose or social relations thus resounded is equally contingent and transitive. It is empirical, neither formed nor deformed, but formless unless it meets the hearing body. In that sense the thing is intersubjective and only starts to sound in the ears of the thing that is the body encoun-tering it.

The sonic thing as a doing 'substance' is not sublimated to the noun in the sentence. Rather it abandons the hierarchy and becomes the noun as a thinging being. It asks of Metz' critique not to focus on the subject–predicate structure of Indo-European languages and object to its visual organization, but to consider its content: our consciousness of the words thus organized. When the sonic object does not precede its sounding, when the thing is only its thinging, the noun is the location of the verb. The thing is the doing of the individual perception of what it does. It involves the perceiver in the thinging and declares that the world at large is a complex thing generated in our individual and collective listening production of it as such and of us as thinging within it.

By sonic thing-ness we grasp the complexity of the object rather than list its attributes or purposes, and we grasp it in its particular and contingent doing not as a relational being. In other words, the thing-ness is the presence (*Anwesenheit*) of every object and subject as honey: concrete and formless, grasping and slipping away, it *is* the moment of perception as a reciprocal sensory-motor action.

Parmegiani creates a sonic thing that is neither less nor more than the visual object; it does not negate nor sublimate visuality, but builds itself out of its own material to be itself as sound. Its thing-ness is formless but concrete. Its substantiality is the actuality of my fleeting perception, which produces the work as aesthetic moment. It is from this generative momentary-ness that any aesthetic discourse needs to start if it intends to discuss the sensorial attack of the material, rather than allay it with a habitual understanding. The sense produced in this aesthetic moment comes out of sensation. It is Merleau-Ponty's non-sense, which is neither sense as rational meaning, nor is it its nonsensical opposite.[25] Instead it describes a sense that comes out of an experiential sensing of the world as life-world. In this life-world the intersubjective subject produces sense through sensory-motor actions towards this world. This is not the pure sensation of an object's attributes or positive determination, but the sensation of the honeyed thing, involved and complex.

This sense has no claim to generality and shared communication, but remains like the experience a solitary fiction. It involves a sensation of the sensorial thing as well as of the sensing perceiver and its sense cannot divorce the two nor step out of its sphere. The contingent sense of experience brings the object and the subject of perception together in the aesthetic moment that triggers and constitutes the thinging of the work. Our body hears the object as thing and travels the place as thing. Listening to its thinging it produces the place as a transitive location on his way through. The sense of the place is its sensation, which has to be brought to life in a sensory-motor action of listening.

On the Machair (2007)

In Cathy Lane's work *On the Machair* the place too becomes a thing. The Island on the Outer Hebrides of Scotland that the recordings are from is, in its composition, not a place as a certain geographical location, a dwelling place, but a fictional place produced in my innovative listening. It 'things' in that it produces, it maps out, sketches, draws and models people, work and nature, past and present in the space of my imagination.

The place heard emerges from the gusty weather that marks its arrival. It does not stand on a certain site but rushes by. It is made of voices, cows, goats and the sea and encourages in its sonic persistence that you muck-in. The artist's voice welcomes and guides you around the island, narrating stories of the past and commenting on the flora and fauna of the present. Her tentative report offers me a way in: to tune my listening into her production of the place and make it mine. This place is not composed with certainty. Rather there is a sense of a doubtful but intent fumbling in the dark with the microphone, trying to find out where we are at the same time as composing the landscape. This uncertainty is shared with, rather than communicated to, the listener. The artist composes the island, building it as she goes along, and so the listener too builds as he goes along. Memories are retold, plants described and statistics read while walking through them.

This does not mean that there are no artistic intentions nor that there really is equality between composer and listener, because, of course, there is not. But there is an invitation to trust and to commit to the sonic process unfolding in the composition rather than be composed at.

Next to the artist's female voice there soon appears a louder confident male voice and some recorded old Gaelic voices from an archive, dusted down to be heard again. As she explains what it is she is recording, the archive voices are what is recorded, and the male voice meets the two in his confident presence. She is the visitor inviting the ghosts of the past that he retains alive in the factuality of the interview. Together they unfold the consequences of the past in the now.

The voices start to crowd the countryside, bringing facts and memories to the rhythm of the lived and laboured place. They overlap and make clearer in that way how things fit together here in mobile and undulating rhythms, intense and peaceful. The sounds are intimate, not in a feeble way but with great intention, they are tender but not faint, a bit like the gusty breeze that starts it all of.

The spatial rhythm of the island life meets the vocal rhythms of facts and fiction in the temporal space of my listening. At times I am left alone in the countryside with just a faint sound of voices as if in the distance still talking to each other, then I pass the site of music, an accordion and voices probably imagined rather than real, but I move on further into the wind. The artist meets me here again on the top of the blustery hill telling me of an earlier visit to this place.

The three voices meet again, compact on the same spot from different directions. That is the rhythm of the piece, places of solitude interspersed with directions and a sense of crowded observation. As a sound piece it stretches and contracts, condenses and expands, comes close and goes further away, leaving me to my own devices and taking me tightly by the hand. The rhythm of the accordion is the rhythm of the piece, it is its breath that I can hear in the overall composition. It is played by the ghosts of the archive that populate the island still. They are the sonic nature of the place, its thing-ness, hiding from where I have to tease them out in my listening. The land becomes renewed in this rhythm while acknowledging its age and history in its sounds.

The sense I make strides between this listening to the sonic material and the negotiation of the Island's existence as a known, historical and geographical fact. The notion of island, of Scotland, people, cows, goats and hard work, not realized as an immanent outcome but teased out and produced in my contingent and subjective listening. The objectivity of the place follows rather than precedes the sensorial encounter. It is informed and produced by it rather than informing it. This confirms my listening not as a naive and habitual perception but stresses the astonishment and the doubt that motivates its sensory-motor action.

Although, or especially perhaps because, the piece carries the weight of the archive, the foremost symbol of the gnostic desire to store and catalogue information and truth for eternity, the piece does not produce the location or time as fact. Instead it invites a sense making which produces a *practice*, rather than an *apprehension* of knowledge, confirming that listening is a practice, a practice of hearing, inventing, imagining and knowing.[26]

On the Machair produces sense as a sonic knowing, complex, sticky and involved. It is a personal and individual knowing that struggles with language to share it. I would be very hard pressed to tell you an exact knowledge gained, but I could discuss a sense of knowing about myself in relation to the sonic material and the time and place produced in my listening. Listening as such a critical motility produces the statistics and narrations heard as sonic fantasy – as the sense of my sensation. This sense is lonely and isolated as is the island as well as the artist in her pursuit to build the place in a sonic composition. And from this lonely sense of experience, I go and visit the place and other places, and from this listening I find an aesthetic appreciation in relation to ideas of rhythm, category, genre, as well as in terms of political and social issues behind the heard rather than in front of it. This is sense as an aesthetic sensibility of myself as an aesthetic subject and of the material in its aesthetic objectivity as sensorial fantasy.

This solitary, sensate sense meets the notion of artistic sense and its role within the field of practice. The composition reveals not only the thing-ness of the island but also the thing-ness of the work as artwork and as composition. It offers it up to an aesthetic discourse of sound that has as yet no words but lots to talk about. Since, listening as an aesthetic activity, re-evaluates the term art and its modes of philosophical valuation as such. It focuses and amplifies aesthetic issues of experience, identity and materiality, as well as the relationship between the subject and the object of perception.

Seeing is a dialectical act of comparison and differentiation: this chair is not that chair, blue is not black. It is transcendental because it assumes that the seen is there before my spotting it. It produces what Adorno terms a deformed view of the world in that it presents but the abstracted relations of society and reality rather than the groundswell of emotion, individuality and fragility that reality and society is, as an experiential fiction of contingent truths and precarious relations underneath the blanket of visual cohesion.

On the Machair does not support the actual things as they are as transcendental things before perception, in readiness but mute. The composition does not separate between the *Unterbau* of the thing, and the *Oberbau* of the artwork. The piece as artwork, as composition, is the actual thing contemplated as thinging its *Dingheit* in all its complexity. I cannot perceive of the sonic elements, the cows, the wind, the sea or the voices, as actual things before their perception, and in their perception they reveal to me their complex *Dingheit* and mine to me. Any naïve apperception of those things separate from their thing-ness is not listening as production but hearing as recognition, which betrays a visual sensibility. And even this visual recognition can only follow rather than precedes the heard and thus there is at least the opportunity for astonishment.

Listening as a concomitant sensory-motor act of production defies expectations and habitual perception. It builds, in the dark shapes with no form. It is neither formed nor deformed but forms. This process is emotional, binding and contingent. Its involved particularity pushes for the reconsideration not only of aesthetic judgment but also of the methodology of aesthetic investigation, and its resultant notion of valuation as well. It means to consider the aesthetic subject within the aesthetic judgement and to come to sense and valuation from there. It also means to reconsider the relationship between that individual aesthetic subject and a presumed mould of experience that is shared and shareable.

It is the subject who is in attendance at the birth of the artistic object as an aesthetic moment, who himself brings to being the aesthetic moment, who needs to find his way into discourse and bring the work with him.

Critique of a Remote Critic

In his essay 'Freedom of Thought' from 1944 printed in a collection of essays under the title *Minima Morialia*, Adorno laments art criticism's lack of experiential engagement with the work. He talks about the distance of the aesthetic theorist from his object of theorization and blames the displacement of philosophy by science, which excludes experience and mocks the subjective in favour of objectivity that pretends to 'know everything beforehand'.[27]

This scientific objectivism finds in other essays in the same volume a resonance with the war, the war machine: the ideologies of fascism as well as its actual industrial machinery. He understands that it is the scientific and warring machinery of his time that makes a physical involvement in the work impossible and unwanted.

> The Second War is as totally divorced from experience as is the functioning of a machine from the movements of the body, which only begins to resemble it in pathological states.[28]

Adorno's complaints have some currency in contemporary art discourse that often overwhelms the sensorial material with preconceived theories and associations that leave no room for experience and only meet the work in its pathological state. Such criticism still inhabits the same modernity and the same machinery that Adorno laments, and invites our bodies to meet the work after its mediation through language and documentation, rather than before. Maybe our wars, Iraq and Afghanistan, are even more divorced from the body as they are for us but informational wars, fought at a distance, not really fought at all, just watched:[29]

> Total obliteration of the war by information, propaganda, commentaries, with camera-men in the first tanks and war reporters dying heroic deaths, the mish-mash of enlightened manipulation of public opinion and oblivious activity: all this is another expression of the withering of experience, the vacuum between men and their fate, wherein their fate lies.[30]

Art reporters seek in the actual thing of the work relatable ideas from art history as well as from the extra-artistic discourses of cultural, political and social theory, which the lazy writer drags around like suitcases of prior meaning. Intent on their application, he ignores the opaque ambiguity of that which remains of the work: the thinging of its sensorial and physical encounter. Instead he foregoes experience in favour of understanding. However, to experience art is to experience its involved complexity, which is exactly what causes so much grief to the aim of writing. Much better to carry it off in 'oblivious activity' to an *a priori* theory. To categorize it within a canon of artistic creation, or to see in it nothing but a signifier of greater cultural, political and social tendencies and drown it in a sea of quasi socio-political commentary, than engage with its concrete formlessness, and build the work subjectively, intersubjectively, in one's contingent experience. The latter would force the critic towards a writing that is fragile and uncertain of its aim but emboldened by the force of its sensorial experience.

Sound emphasizes this point, which however applies to all art. It is muted in aesthetic description: listening is either replaced through historical or cultural references, or it is contextualized through the quasi visual conventions of the score, the performance set up, the installation shot, the (visual) instrument, the headphones, the concept, etc. The criticism that comes from these visual attributes and reference points of the sonic moment might stand solidly in language but does not convey the sonic phenomenon in its *Dingheit*.

Sound demands to be heard and urges a confrontation of the heard with critical language. Its ephemeral transitivity rebuffs attempts to flatten its immersive complexity from a (visual) distance. It keeps on being demanding and presses for a different criticism. Sound work hits the very core of the malaise of art criticism as Adorno sketches it then and I see it continued now, and issues a challenge to the relationship between the sensorial encounter and its critical analysis in language.

Listening is a subjective task that demands an attending engagement with the work for the time it plays rather than for the time I am prepared to listen, and grasps my being to understand that of the work. I am producing the work in my temporal presence, and that might take a while. This while is lonely and there is no guarantee that any judgement formed will be lasting or communicable.

Sound is the solitary edge of the relationship between phenomenology and semiotics, which are presumed to meet each other in the quarrel over meaning. It raises questions about their relationship, and how one can function through the other without abandoning itself. Does the latter inform and pre-set the experience of the first, or does the experience invite the latter for consolidation? – In sound they just might not meet at all.

Once I submit to the listening process I am alone *On the Machair*. The place produced is mine, the history assembled is mine too: the objectivity reached is constituted through my subjectivity. There are elements, glimpses of communicable sense, but there is the whole mass of sensation, placing, being there, understanding through knowing, where I remain alone in my own making and the place becomes more about me than it is about the geographical location I might find on the map once I am back home.

The art critic who deals with a sonic work needs to listen, which means he needs to spend time and commit to an engagement that is not one of recognition but of making the work in his own ears. He needs to be the generator of the work he critiques, and he needs to understand this double bind. Listening is intersubjective in that it produces the work and the self in the interaction between the subject listening and the object heard. The listener stumbles blindly in the darkness of sound, and is himself revealed in any light generated.

Durational work makes this bind abundantly clear. Sound works of long duration expand the aesthetic moment into potential infinity and thereby stress the question of the relationship between the aesthetic subject and its object and how their meeting might fare in critical discourse. It also articulates the problem of the after the work: The moment when critical discourse starts. It postpones, potentially into infinity, the moment when the sensorial encounter meets language and thus problematizes their relationship.

microscopic trips (2006)

Stini Arn's microscopic trips take time to construct the places she is passing through. Between Los Angeles and Zürich, any place is imaginable. Snippets of conversation at the airport, Tannoy announcements, traffic in the road; incidental encounters meet the sonic infrastructure of place. The focus is on structure rather than content however. She uses sound to narrate not the story itself but the structure of the plot on which the individual narrations of the listeners are to be built. She makes the journey the parameter of the listening time and both are potentially endless.

The events on her journeys are odd enough and ordinary enough to make me hear my own trip. I know she had to have been there as her firm presence is the work, but I do not necessarily know where she is. It all seems rather incidental, the personal overheard, and I am not quite sure I am supposed to hear it. But its temporal insistence, playing on for hours and hours, persuades me that it is okay to listen on.

The work is durational; in fact it is potentially infinite. For all I know it might still go on, unheard but nevertheless recording. This produces not a sense of listening *to*, but of listening *in*. Listening in to the goings on elsewhere that mingle with the goings on over-here, and build the basis of my own journey. Over time it realizes Adorno's demand for experience: The microphone stops being a distant reporter but becomes the present sound and makes itself available to my generative experience. If I refuse to listen the work becomes an archive rather than a sonic piece of work, catalogued and taken note of, but rarely heard. Its sounds never realized it remains mute and inanimate; its space gone, its thing-ness undone. As such a mute archive it meets language easily: chatting about its concepts and processes, its form and structure, but never about listening to it. When committing to its time however a personal sounding emerges that has a more difficult relationship to its own description and critical analysis.

Arn records real places and her trajectories through them, and I produce a sound walk in a space of my imagination, preserving the sounds of my own memory in my present listening: thin lines loosely coming together to produce sheer figments of a composition. No sooner have they arrived they dissipate. I can linger on some incidental stories, ignore others, and forge a relationship with other sounds heard in my own acoustic environment. There are highlights, staged moments, accidents embraced, as well as incidents where she withdraws and hurriedly switches off the microphone. But on the whole moments go by without recourse to the 'exceptional', and after a while her soundtrack *is* my formless sphere of listening. I do not think about Arn's sources anymore as I am moving along her *microscopic trips*: the places passed are constructed in my imagination, and the duration of this journey is mine rather than hers.

This formless duration evokes the 'endless mobility' of Julia Kristeva's fourth signifying practice and directs my enquiry towards her notion of the 'text', through which she implodes the stability of signification. In the *Revolution of Poetic Language* written in 1974, Kristeva outlines our engagement with the world through four related but distinct signifying practices: 'narrative', 'metalanguage', 'contemplation' and 'text'. While the first three work on the basis of a collectively shareable experience, the fourth proposes a more complex, temporal and individual engagement.[31] The text includes a consideration of the autonomy of the subject, working beyond the intention of the author and any stable registration of the artwork, producing the work continually in its perceptual moment.

This signifying practice 'involves *combination*: fitting together detaching, including, and building up "parts" into some kind of "totality"'.[32] Crucially, however, this totality is not a communicative totality, not an objective totality.[33] 'This practice has no addressee; no subject (. . .) can understand it.'[34] Signifying is a solitary practice, which does not function communicatively. Instead, between 'detaching, including, and building up "parts"' an arrangement is proposed which is realized in the composition of the listener working on the arrangement of the author. The 'fragments' that are being taken apart and rearranged are invested in this process. This heterogeneous formation is a continuous passing beyond systemic limits, assuming an infinity of process, which does not seek to overcome sensorial complexity in a higher order resolution of the work as synthetic unit nor does it try to reduce the work to language. Instead, the focus is on the practice of the fragment rather than on a sublimation of the fragments in totality.

Arn's recordings and the fact that they go on for hours enable such an innovative arranging of the heard. It is my signifying listening that uses and transgresses her artistic intentions and generates what I hear on her time line; practising her auditory fragments I produce my sense for me. My listening practice activates her trips in my ears and makes me walk, when otherwise all that would be heard are souvenirs of places passed and moments lived.

This signifying practice of listening, instead of referring to the art historical context of the work, involves the contingent context of the listener. Listening is contextual but its context is fleeting. The time and space of my listening is permanently displaced by the sound heard. I cannot freeze sound, there is no room for contemplation, narration of meta-position, there is only the small sliver of now which is a powerful influence but hard to trace.

Listening to Arn's work I am Kristeva's 'subject in process/on trial': her notion of a generative subject whose sense and identity is produced in the continual trial of articulation that is the signifying practice of the text. In the signifying process the work *and* the subject are on trial: neither of them is pre-given, or in a meta-position, and both are produced in a 'trial of meaning', a 'trial of sense'. I am on trial and so is the material Arn records and by listening our journey is generated intersubjectively.[35]

On the ephemeral map of Arn's journey, listening is practised as a continuous process of what Kristeva calls '*appending territories*': an extensional process working the heard according to the listener's 'rhythm' into his field of experience.[36] As such a textual practice my listening is an extensional process. It appends the recorded world of Arn's journey, centrifugally into the journey of my auditory imagination, which expands me. The signifying practice of listening appends the material into a generative meaning, which is the process of its expansion, and in turn the listener too is propelled into the process of his own expansion, appending his sense of self. The listener activates the sounds in his trial of his sense of them, giving them his own rhythm and expanding his listening territory, understood as his natural attitude or habit.

This notion of '*appending territories*', valid for any sonic work, becomes particularly coherent in relation to soundscape composition, whose conservationist intentions practise a more direct relationship to listening habits and attitudes. Soundscape compositions work to make the listener aware of his acoustic environment, to extend auditory awareness, and stretch the processes of the listener's own sonic engagement.

Listening to the Soundscape Recorded

In many ways Arn's piece is an acoustic ecology, an environment heard. I can hear it in the context of work by the soundscape composer

Hildegard Westerkamp, whose compositions since the mid-1970s have focused on environmental sound, and who uses location sound to produce places that encourage a focused listening while enticing the production of a new place. Such compositions are torn between preservation and invention.

The issue between the two artists' work is intention and the notion of the Real and what it is in relation to the environment recorded. Where is a soundscape produced, composing a fictional place between the intentions of the artist and the perception of the listener, and where is the emphasis on an authentic sense of place, for the purpose of preserving endangered sounds and fostering acoustic awareness? The latter producing a more didactic composing *at* the listener, to make him hear.

Soundscape composition evokes a listening somewhere in-between the aesthetic fantasy proposed by Arn and Lane's work, and the aesthetico-political demand of sound lobbying for a world heard.[37] The project of acoustic ecology pursues the subject directly, willing us to listen and to engage. Soundscape compositions are sonic works that pursue an investigative, research-driven tone, where to listen is a request rather than an ambiguous invitation.

Max Bruinsman in his *Notes of a Listener* from 1985 complains about the audience who does not want to listen . . . and needs to be made to.

Kits Beach (1989)

Westerkamp's guiding voice tells us how the soundscape looks: inviting us to join her on a beach just outside Vancouver through its sounds. The coastline is constructed and scrutinized by her voice. The fragility and ephemerality of its sounds are at first explained rather than heard. She composes the perceptual aspect of the seashore's sounds as she narrates them: she delves into the detail and directs my attention to the tiny sounds of seaweed and barnacles, and expands the work from there. From soundscape research into soundscape composition she starts with a phonographic earnestness and goes on to play with the recordings to make us hear their manipulation, while continually explaining these processes. This sonic shift through registers of reality brings to consciousness the organization of the real, hinting at systems and ideologies rather than facts and truths.

The material slowly unfolds away from her voice and develops the recorded reality into a composition. The work meanders from the apparently real into the real of my personal invention. Following the narrations of her dreams the listener is invited to develop his own fantasies. Now her voice does not guide but becomes itself part of the soundtrack: not narrating it but being it, heard in the same register as the manipulated natural rhythms, clicks and whistles, succulent and bouncy, like the crickety water tinkling that she merges with and makes of both rhythms rhymes.

Her reference to a composition by Iannis Xenakis takes the work out of soundscape composition into an arrangement of another kind: juxtaposing her landscape teased out of its sounds to a 'landscape' composed from granular synthesis. From the vast stretch of the shoreline to the smallest grain of its being and back again, she explores the intensity of the space heard in its all-embracing unfolding. However, *Kits Beach* remains very composed, very intentional. There is no room for the unplanned or coincidental overheard. It is a direct and directing guide of audiel material, that invites a fantastic engagement momentarily only to guide us back to the composed reality of the landscape's sounds: the sheer force of the nearby city in all its sonic monstrosity, big, thundery, and brutal, overriding the little sounds of her dreams in a roaring wave.

By comparison, Arn's construction of place is not a soundscape composition, lacking the poetic intention and educational drive. It is a far more incidental document, somewhat like a sonic diary: a sound walk blog. Oozing with the authenticity of the personal overheard, and the sense of real-time. What makes it sound authentic is its bareness, its lack of focus. Arn's work makes a lot of room for the incidental and only builds a frame of place. The sounds always remain fleeting, ephemeral and endangered by their very nature rather than in relation to an ecological idea. *microscopic trips* simply is what enters the microphone. There is no general undulation between poetry and reality; when the two occasionally converge, it is incidental and experienced only by the individual listener rather than composed intentionally by the author. This sense of the authentic, the trust it inspires, is heightened by the duration of the work. Westerkamp's pieces are short, poem-sized and to a point. Arn's work is potentially endless, unordered and lived.

Eyes work well as an ordering-tool: segregating according to differences and aligning references to build meaning within the field of vision. Even in motion the visual focuses on relationships and differences and derives its meaning from them. Images are dialectical, expressing themselves against each other. They are a chain of differences however mobile.

The ear, when it operates not in the service of such a visual organization, does not order things but produces its own ephemeral order. Sound can give an indication of left or right, high or low, etc. but this is not the orientation of objects and places but of itself. Sonic listening is not dialectical, it works not on differences and similarities but hears cumulatively: it builds from what ever comes at it in a haphazard way shaky buildings whose design is that of sound rather than of its source. It stacks things against each other indiscriminately, hearing whatever is at hand, and it can do so because it operates in the dark, unseen.

Pierre Schaeffer's acousmatic project goes some way to practising such an invisible design: releasing the sounds from their visual association through their reduction to a sonic core.[38] Comparable to Edmund Husserl's phenomenological reduction, Schaeffer's composing and listening performs an epoche, a reduction to the core of [sonic] experience.[39] He brackets the sounds off from their visual context to hear them in all their sonicness as 'objets sonores', and to compose from these 'sonorous objects' acousmatic works.

A visual epoche is a stripping back to the core of visuality, a sonic epoche in Schaeffer's terms, is a stripping away from the sonic anything that ties it down to visuality. However this is not reducing but freeing it and opening it up to a multitude of audible possibilities. Phenomenological listening as an intersubjective sensory-motor engagement is a reduction in order to get to the essence of the perceived, to critically experience and expand that essence; not to reduce the heard but to get to the wealth of the heard through a bracketed listening. The problem of the acousmatic project is the actual reduction after the fact: The re-organization, the structural ordering of the sounds thus heard. Schaeffer analyses the reduced concrete sound objects and illustrates them through a new set of visual symbols that do not relate to the source or to a traditional score but to the sounds heard. However, this visualizing of the auditory object nevertheless brings the bracketed sound back into a structural context. Schaeffer's 'objets sonores' are referenced as signs and symbols of his own devising, yet they are visual and by necessity reduce the heard to their design. Listening as an effort of epoche, in the sense of focusing rather than reducing, without the desire to bring its experience back into the context of language as a structural means of ordering, expands and generates the object as a sonic phenomenon; speechless but eternally resounding.

Westerkamp's work invites focused listening of a kind: a particular microphonic bracketing of the Vancouver shoreline. However, she takes away to make us hear the absent. She posits as lost but reinstates through her intention, and in this way allows the semiotic to enter the work and take over the more fragile sense of it as it is experienced in a discrete audition. In the ideological realm of soundscape research there is meaning that is bigger than the non-sense of the experienced work. There is an educational endeavour of induction and conservation that overrides the dream and leaves us with its aim.

Arn's sonic world expands in my listening from the fleeting context of the heard through my innovative listening, centrifugally into the world, which I am passing. It appends territories. I travel with her and beyond. I jump over the visual referent into an endlessly mobile journey of my imagination. The emphasis is on the experience of the work rather than its classification in an extra-sonic catalogue. This is a phenomenological journey, but one whose essence might remain forever unspeakable hinted at only in the outline of its sonic concept. The phenomenological when it hits the semiotic project, at least in sound, bounces off into the signifying solitariness of the unspeakable.[40]

Focused listening produces this unspeakable, solitary signifying that concentrates as well as expands the material and the subject in a dual but not paradoxical move: it pursues a phenomenological epoche but instead of closing down what it found in a return to the semiotic it continues the endless mobility of listening in the practice of signifying. Sound arts criticism that comes out of such a focused listening confronts the futility of writing its sensorial practice into the text. That does not mean one ought not try though, as it is in the process of writing, as a quasi process of speaking, that sound will find a place when read back aloud, if we can only abandon the quest for a naive substantiality and accept the read as passing reflections, fleeting and ephemeral, like the material it speaks of. On the face of it such sound arts' discourse, given that it avoids certain meaning, might not have much critical value. But it does. When the solitary subjectivity is understood as part of the aesthetic sensibility produced through sound, and when, conversely, this subjectivity is appreciated in its emancipated and powerful generative autonomy, then we will come to understand the radical value of sound to shift not the meaning of things and subjects, but the process of meaning making and the status of any meaning thus made.

Focused listening is radical as it makes us 'see' a different world. The aesthetic materiality of sound insists on complicity and intersubjectivity and challenges not only the reality of the material object itself, but also the position of the subject involved in its generative production. The subject in sound shares the fluidity of its object. Sound is the world as dynamic, as process, rather than as outline of existence. The sonic subject belongs in this temporal flow.

Listening to the Radio

This temporal belonging is particularly apparent on the radio, where the stream of now comes at me out of the dark. Even if I know the radio schedule, the sensorial material heard as focused sound rather than as visual relay, still catches me unprepared. In relation to radio-phonic material listening is utterly blind: a material on trial in darkness it tries my sightless subjectivity in its signifying practice. The sense gleaned comes directly from the heard as my focused non-sense.

The trial of sound on the radio is not different from that of other sound but it is more palpable. I can feel myself working my ears rather than leaning on the visual object provided. The only crutch I can find is the voice, where, at least on a semantic level, sound is temporarily redeemed into the transcendental order of the visual. But no voice is purely semantic. The body speaks in more ambiguous ways and my listening body answers this ambiguity.

If a Voice Like Then What? (1984) and *Langue Etude* (1985)

Gregory Whitehead's radiophonic piece *If a Voice Like Then What?* leads us to the core of the body's communication, its voice. Questioning its sonic materiality while speaking, it turns communication on its material head. 'Do you want a voice like mine?' he asks, while showing you a gaping dark hole that splutters, stutters and avoids cohesion. The voice as messenger is eroded of its semantic meaning as it speaks. It is rendered its own flesh, dissected, infested, rolled around on the listeners tongue. The sounds infect my ears and make me aware of my own mouth and its abeyance quite uncomfortably in the dark. The piece is short and intense, staying with you as you listen to more conventional broadcasts, which are dominated by radiophonic voices that are considered phonogenic: semantic voices without a body to speak of.

Whitehead's sounds resonate with Susan Stone's *Langue Etude* that talks and cuts the tongue apart as it speaks, extinguishing its own trace and constituting the now of radio through forceful and physical intervention.

A lot of experimental radio work is voice-based, playing with the foremost sound of commercial radio: the trusting voice standing in for the unified body that cushions meaning and explains sounds in order to guide you faithfully through the dark on a promise of objectivity, news and information. Instead, experimental work brings us a fleshly and subjective body: the voice visceral and slaughtered. It goads listening out of the heard into the production of the perceived.

The invisibility of radio-sound enables a multiplicity of perception. The listener becomes producer, inventing his own contingent reality between what is heard and the time-space of its perception. This innovative listening uses the darkness of radio as a cave, abundant with sound. Here, no image preserves the listener's hold on an authentic sense of reality, and thus no sense of non-reality limits his imagination.

Radio is a formless stream, emanating from a faceless, boundaryless place. The association of this fleeting stream with a concrete actuality is, accordingly, achieved through a momentary steadying by the individual listener. Sustaining this transitory fact, durationally, as the radio does, broadcasting into our homes and cars, night and day, exaggerates its fleetingness, producing quite categorically a constant stream of now. The sightless box of radio provides no distraction from the durational flow of sound. The demand is endless, and there is literally no end in sight.

This constant now does not produce a certain object, but incites figments of the individual imagination. It does not affirm the surety of a thing but produces its own reality as a reciprocal non-certainty. This is individual and momentary certainty as personal conviction, produced through a contingent and innovative listening to a shared broadcast. The listeners are a collective of individuals, listening all together alone, propelling the sonic materiality into a multitude of private imaginations. This is the paradox of radio: emphasizing the ideology of shared and synchronized sounds, streamed into the non-synchronic ears of a multiplicity of listeners.

To produce a constant flux of sonic pieces that invite individual imaginings, means to implode the parameters of commercial radio:

conventional productions that aim to entertain and inform a collective audience, arranging time and aspiring to create a sense of listenership and a civic identity. Whitehead and Stone's voices at once support and shatter the collective through a visceral particularity. They produce a collective solitariness, a mass of equally but individually alienated people. Their work does not spite communication but makes us aware of its fragility by showing us the dark chasm of its vile throat.

Instead of apparent, knowable radiophonic content, their work involves the structure behind its own medium: speaking and listening itself, the auditory space–time relationship between subjects, and the production of a transitory, invisible objectivity. They foreground the paradox between collectivity and solitude and invite a different engagement in sound production and listening.

Conclusion: Sonic Solitude

Going through the experience of this crucible exposes the subject to impossible dangers: relinquishing his identity in rhythm, dissolving the buffer of reality in a mobile discontinuity, leaving the shelter of the family, the state, or religion, the commotion the practice creates spares nothing: it destroys all constancy to produce another and then destroys that one as well.[41]

It is from the potential of this danger of the ever new and endlessly mobile, against the even greater danger of the illusion of a habitual and total meaning, that the motivation to listen as the motility of doubt and astonishment must start. This might well render all words written here non-sensical in the sense of simply sensate rather than rational, but it does not make them less critical or useful. Since, the engagement with the work, through a sceptical and astounded attitude, is what leads to a re-thinking of the philosophical and aesthetic methodology of enquiry, and therein lies its criticality. If the sense of such an investigation appears nonsensical at this moment, then it is the process of this sensate engagement, which holds the key to its import, that must be further investigated. For now, there is only material ambiguity that grasps your body and guides it into sonic awareness while trickling away from you at the same time, leaving you in this new place, alone. There it is the mobile discontinuity of your contingent practice of perception that destroys and builds to destroy again the heard for joyous non-communication.

The fragments of this mobile discontinuity are generated and seceded in our innovative practice. They explode meaning and lend themselves to 'the most unsayable aspects of our corporeal existence'.[42] The subject of this practice, who is a subject on trial is ideal in its active subjectivity, and the artwork, the object, is ideal in its continual production in perception. A senseable ideality, in the sense of an ideality that is available for sensation, is an ideality of practice, producing sense as sensate non-sense on trial. The centre point is its practical experience rather than a transcendental *a priori*. This process is a constant engagement, peaceful and non-competitive between subjects and objects producing themselves reciprocally.

> In its proper place, even epystemologically, the relationship
> of subject and object would lie in the realization of peace
> among men as well as between man and their Other. Peace is
> the state of distinctness without domination, with the distinct
> participating in each other.[43]

Noise will crank up the volume of solitary listening into complete isolation from where I have to reconsider communication and my participation in shared meaning. For now I can understand communication as the compromise of the experience in the myth of the collective. I can leave it there and listen some more, alone, to appreciate a sonic sensibility, which must by necessity involve me in its trial. Only out of this involved and reciprocal process of *Listening* can the articulation of a philosophy and aesthetics of sound art come.

2
NOISE

Luigi Russolo celebrated noise.[1] He heard in the machine the sounds of progress, liberation and advancement of a people towards a better life that had overcome the imperfection of the menial and manual in the perfection of the machine. His work accompanied and sounded the Zeitgeist of objective ideality, of a faith or doctrine rather that the humanity in mankind should be overcome in the perfection of its creation.[2] After Fordism, Auschwitz, Hiroshima, and into Global Warming and more modern and distanced warfare Merzbow et al. know that that is not what noise can do now.[3] Instead their work celebrates the almost solipsistic intensity of sound when it makes a racket rather than a piece. Noise is the autistic revelation of war, speechless but focused, producing a heavy weight in a fleeting time.

It is as if noise music lives out the trauma of the beginning of the twentieth century: sounding its consequences for community and tolerance. Acknowledging the abject and contemptible consequences of the technological and societal advancements pursued then, noise now, in its quasi inertia, is not about mass movement and progress, but about private and isolated fixity: listening on a heavy spot and pondering that position. Noise pulls my listening down to my feet. It is vertical rather than horizontal, rooting me in the location of my own hearing. Noise is not really inert, it remains strong and pounding, but instead of moving me on it draws a static horizon around my feet. There it develops the locality of hearing rather than the future of listening.

Noise does not have to be loud, but is has to be exclusive: excluding other sounds, creating in sound a bubble against sounds, destroying sonic signifiers and divorcing listening from sense material external to its noise. This can be achieved through tiny sounds that grab my ear and make my listening obsessive and exclusive: a downstairs neighbour's quiet but persistent base beat has enough imperial ability to distract and colonize my hearing all afternoon. Sound is noisy when it deafens my ears to anything but itself. The philosophical experience and consequences of this idea are worked out in this part. Noise of the everyday and Noise-art are debated as extreme sounds that take possession of one's ears by one's own free will and against it, isolating the listener in the heard. In this way *Noise* expands *Listening* to an extreme and exaggerates the issues of communication, sense and non-sense as articulated in the last part, demanding through its uncompromising nature a direct confrontation.

Bad Taste

Noise is other people's music: my neighbours' collection blasting at full volume through the open balcony doors on a hot and sticky summer night. My space starts to shrink as the enjoyment of my own environment vanishes. Other people's musical tastes foisted upon you in a peaceful hour, whatever it is becomes bad taste. The imposing nature of this disturbance does not invite me to listen to the sounds as music but pushes me out of the track, pushes me inside myself, to isolate and close down. Deaf to its music, I hear it as a nuisance, which stops me from hearing anything else. If you like your neighbours their music is less noisy. If you dislike or fear them any sound they make is noise, encroaching on you through the walls or over the garden fence.

My living room is increasingly saturated with *their* sound. This invisible layer litters my room and overpowers the design of my space. Filling it ever more, this noise becomes an inert block of solid auditory material, impeding my movements, my thinking and my feeling, forcing me into internal ruminations of the worst kind. My anger and resentment are intense. Can I reach their backyard with eggs thrown from my kitchen window?

After an hour of faked tolerance I start to turn up my own sound system as loud as it possibly goes. I want to regain control over my auditory space, to be able to listen. This is a defensive rather than an open listening however, practising a pretence of hearing when its focus is unattainable silence. This is not a listening that opens and invents the sound in a signifying practice, but one that closes down, tightly around myself, all possibilities of hearing. The shelter of my noise becomes my prison. Once in a while I interrupt my pretence of enjoyment, get up and turn it down just to hear whether their noise is still there.

My noise interpolates me and within that relationship I am safe. What I hear, however, will only be my defensive listening position. Deaf to anything else my noise-making-listening-effort defends my space but it also sets my socio-aesthetic position. It is the sonic shield in my struggle for space and control. In this particular instance it reveals my non-desire to socialize with my neighbours to share with them in the joy of their barbecue, nor to wish them well with it. In a more general sense noise amplifies social relations and tracks the struggle for identity and space within the tight architectural and demographic organization of a city. In this sense, noise is a social signifier: determining unseen boundaries and waging invisible wars. A comprehensive noise map of London would not only present traffic hotspots and industry, revealing the consequent issues of pollution and congestion, it would also reveal social relations on its fault lines of taste and tolerance.[4]

Noisy Non-sense

The innocent and play-full sensate sense of sound as discussed in *Listening* attains a sharper focus in noise, intensifying its consequences for communication. Merleau-Ponty's phenomenological non-sense that comes out of sensation rather than rationality and transgresses the collective through individual sense-making as a contingent and reciprocal trial of the material is intensified in noise which emphasizes the solitary fantasy of sonic experience.

The last part already acknowledged listening as an interpretative fantasy that generates the sonic object/phenomenon through a contingent engagement with the heard, which renders the heard sub-jectively ideal, rather than receives it as factual relations: objectively ideal and shareable. Listening when it is not concerned with sharing the meaning produced in its practice is indifferent to the failure to do so, and remains focused on the solitary production of what it hears, – whereby, in this phantasmagoric practice, objectivity and subjectivity exist in a close and reciprocal bond. I acknowledged that the sense of such a practice might, for now, appear nonsensical, but stressed that in the process of sensing rather than understanding it, by practis-ing listening itself, the import of its sensate sense on the philosophi-cal and aesthetic methodology of enquiry will be revealed. Since, sonic non-sense as sense on trial forms the meeting point of the semiotic and the phenomenological project without finalizing their relationship in meaning, but by opening possibilities for production. So far, I have outlined only a tentative proximity, a tenuous link between the structure of meaning and its experiential content. Eventually an auditory aesthetics might be formulated from this fragile connection, commending its own formlessness in the concrete frame of a recipro-cal subject–object relationship, which is the basis of its valuation.

The Rave (1993)

Dancing at a loud and dark rave party in a big factory hall outside Zürich in the early 1990s I did not know who was dancing me: my body or the noise. The noise deafened my senses to anything but itself, and funnelled me into its own insistent beat. This was not really hearing music and sounds as much as feeling them through a vague and glorious pain in my ears, entering my body on their way to becom-ing this pain, and moving in reaction to its intensity. I and all the other hundreds of ravers became the visual interpretation of noise: a euphoric mass of isolated movement.[5] The vertical pull of noise inten-sifies listening's solitary experience. Noise exaggerates the isolation of my sensorial engagement and tightens the reciprocity between the listener and the heard. In the non-sense of a noisy life-world my reciprocal intersubjective 'I' is held down to the ground by the weight and exclusivity of the sounds around me. The room to manoeuvre shrinks in my vis-à-vis with noise as it contracts my intersubjectivity, making me one with its sounds, alone.

Rave-nights demonstrate this ferocious isolation produced by noise. While the 1980s disco music allowed for a chat and a giggle at the movements of that guy over there, raves eradicate verbal communication. In its insistence that I hand over my body to its force, noise cuts the cord to the social and produces a euphoria, an ecstasy of freedom in the besieged but autonomous body. The tight reciprocity of this existence is made abundantly clear when I cannot hear myself anymore. Noise does not accompany me but swallows me, in its loud tones or compulsive smaller sounds it reins my sonic self, as I become part of it. My sensory-motor actions become reactions to the intense and obsessive demands of the sounds that command my space.

Noise does not only demand my attention but grasps it literally to the exclusion of all other sensorial possibilities. It works as an anaesthetic in its loud or quiet intensity. However, this is not a desensitized position, but the position of an acute sonic-ness. It is Michel Chion's 'clump of sensation' shrunk tightly onto the body.[6] In noise *I* am the body falling out of the tower block window onto the hood of the car. The clump is felt directly under my skin. The body of the sound has moved so close it *is* my body: I am the host of noise. As if taken over by alien forces noise usurps me and presents me back to myself as the mirror of its insistence.

This tight reciprocity confirms the solitary nature of a sonic sensibility, and the noisy non-sense produced by the individual dancer performing noise at a rave reinforces the fragility of communication. We all do roughly similar movements, but that is just the outward convention: language, so to speak. The communication in the sense of relating, connecting, does not take place. I move alone. Immersed not in the figure of the mass but in the singular body of my own thing-ness as noise-ness.

Noise ingests me and yet it is only noise because it works on my body. When I am not there my neighbour's stereo is not noisy. The relationship between noise and its hearer is uneven but reciprocal. Noise needs me, but demands of me more than any other sound my undivided attention and my abandonment to its materiality. This incorporation of myself into the sensorial material is what makes noise complex in relation to aesthetic discourse. It makes it abundantly clear that distance is not an option, and that joint time is demanded as the circumstance of experience. Noise takes time to unfold and to take a hold of our body and it is meant to do that. Merzbow works over 50 hours to make you his.[7] His sounds assault your senses until they have taken over. The effect comes earlier but the intention is clear: to totally submit to his world of noise that he as its composer has himself submitted to.

Noise is not necessarily an authorial act but an experiential space where the composer submits himself to the noises made. I imagine Merzbow hooked on the noise of his own creation, unable to stop the beast that has taken over his body and only wrestling free after 50 hours and probably not even then. This abandonment is not simply a passive attitude but an active participation in the siege of noise to experience the ecstasy of my own autonomous listening, which gives my formless subjectivity the concreteness of its particularity. Besieged by noise I am concretely the singular body of my formless thinging, speechless but ecstatically me.

Otomo Yoshihide at the Corsica Studios (2005)

Otomo Yoshihide with Sachiko M.'s 2005 turntables, electronics, sine waves and empty sampler performance at the Corsica Studios in London made people clutch their bodies and hold their ears against the fragmenting force of his assault. Meanwhile he remained calm and in control of the attack that shattered ours. Inward and utterly focused, he imposes his noise on us, not to repel, but to make us complicit in extreme sounds that refute distance by insisting you take them here and now. There never is a gap between the heard and hearing, I either hear it or I don't. But in this noise any notion of distance is shattered as his feedback hits my ears. We cannot watch his noise unfold from a safe distance, but are attacked, stunned and physically pinned down by its material assault. A spectacle keeps us together as a mass of voyeurs, collectively viewing but not necessarily feeling a painful act. The immersive grip of noise shatters this distance and fragments the collective to draw tight boundaries around masses of separately contorted ears.

Sound is never about the relationship between things, but is the relationship heard. In noise music of this kind this sonic relationship is not immersing my ears, surrounding them gently to allow me to hear its sounds. Instead it pins my ears to themselves: piercing them to tie them up in the extreme frequencies and volumes of its performance. Unlike eyes I cannot close my ears and so cannot avoid my own physical complicity with his attack. But the assault does not diminish or weaken them but stretches them further and further to hear in Yoshihide's sonic riot inaudible sounds: unable to fight the noise I submit to its demand, gloriously reeling in extreme sounds that verge towards something so loud it is impossible to hear.[8]

The engrossed physicality of his performance renders listening an equally physical practice. I submit with him to the fight with the turntable, bodily rather than exclusively with my ears. He wrenches out of the machine all it has to give, not to overcome human imperfection but to produce extensions, perversions and contortions of the body, with and against the machine. He wrestles until both machine and body are bare, raw and at their end. Yoshihide's turntables and electronic devices make noises that are not part of their perfection but of something else that is much more organic, alive: material rendered formless in the ears of listeners who have lost their form in its assault. I withdraw into the invisible practice of my own concrete noise, contorting my body in the ecstasy of autonomous hearing: I am at this moment nothing but the heard, equally formless and quietly strident. I am a clump of sensation shut off in noise. I am

Merleau-Ponty's sensible sentient, not as two separate sides of one being but as one, now here at the very same time, undifferentiated, acutely my sensate self sensing.[9]

I am held in the spell of his noise. The danger of noise music, the exposure to its physical assault is also its allure. Clasped in its force I enjoy the painful awareness of my body tested and stretched by the physicality of his noise. In the end there is only the possibility of leaving, to escape and nurse outside the performance space internal organs and ears tortured. Organs that have taken on a new shape, that have been extended, dented, turned inside out. Yoshihide performs with a loving disregard for the equipment and the listener. The damage done to the turntables and speakers resembles that done to the listening body. In this way, the body is not surpassed by the machine, its frailty overcome, but is rendered its damaged equivalent, pained and doubled over, standing outside drawing breath.

Charlemagne Palestine at the Queen Elizabeth Hall (1998)

Charlemagne Palestine's piano performance at the Queen Elizabeth Hall in London in 1998 produced such an assault in sound only and another type of noise in the visual performance. When I sit in the concert hall and see him work the piano I can still hear the instrument, I can hear the conventions of its scale, its musical purpose. The body of the instrument is in the way of mine, and the performance: the pounding of the keyboard until the blood stains the keys, is too powerful a spectacle, referencing as well as negating any piano concert ever seen, to let me feel the noise.

The noise Palestine makes in the concert hall is not noisy nonsense in that extreme phenomenological sense of Yoshihide's vertical downpour. Instead it is a theatrical noise that destroys the rationality of the piano and its role in the concert hall.[10] His performance teases and subverts the eminence of the piano, with hat, teddies, candles and all. The inclusion of personal items strewn all over the piano underlines the personal indulgence and sentimentality and yet it is serious in its own aesthetic consideration of the instrument, the performance and the audience. It is serious in the inclusion of bits and pieces and drama and introduces a frail and sentimental humanity in his beating of the keyboard, unsettling the detached perfectionism of virtuoso performance.

Palestine's noise is playful and critical, it needs a visual stage to present all its wares and demonstrate the process of its making. It is the noise of a performance that shatters the idea of performance while playing on. His noise presents the listener with the conventions of its musicality and makes him part of its destruction. Apart from its sounds it is noise as rhetorical device, as a critical faculty, challenging and mocking conventions.

The other noise that of his recording, when it comes at the listener without the defence of a visual performance, is breathtaking and demanding, shattering aesthetic conventions that try to deal in words with the complexity of its material assault. While the performed noise halts conventions, that noise makes me pause in the isolation of my hearing and hang on to the complex configurations of its sounds. Either way, Palestine's noise rebuts the desire for progress in its relentlessly pounding stillness. It negates the cohesion and purpose of mass movement, and retreats from the conquest over human frailty and failure by the machine to the celebration of the incoherent nature of being, in splendid isolation, human.

Such noise challenges the myth of total war *and* of total peace in the realization of sound as incoherent, fragmented, solitary and utterly sensorial. It challenges modernism, its myths and ideals, exploding its aesthetic rationality and sense of progress, with playful dilettantism, personal obsessions, ornaments and sentimentality. Noise is the awkward personal frill in Le Corbusier buildings, 'machines à vivre'. It is the bric-a-brac of sentimental individuality and lots of it, stuffed in from floor to ceiling, opposing with force the professional rationality of the modernist project. Noise is not irrational however. Its rationality is the individual experience of it, grounded in the here and now of a contingent subjectivity. It is the expectation to share collectively this contingent rationality that makes it difficult rather than false or illusionary. This is the difficulty, which, in turn, also holds the promise of a different and more insightful understanding of the volume played.

However noise is not different from other sounds. It simply amplifies the complexity of its reciprocity, tightening its return, and amplifies its demand to be considered in involved contingency, in practice. Noise is not a special case, it is simply more insistent in its sonic particularity. Through this particularity it provokes a more general shift in thinking about aesthetic experience and its position within philosophical discourse: reinforcing the need for a sonic sensibility, a sonic aesthetics, leading towards a philosophy of sound art and the notion of sonic knowing that disobeys the modernist calculation, and invites the unpredictable body into its midst.

It is from the extreme of noise that modernism and postmodernism, and their discourses, need to be reconsidered. This is to make room in the critical discipline for the signifying practice of sound and its contingent non-sense, in order to address the non-communicative isolation of sound, and bring its fantastic reality to bear on aesthetic discourse.

How can you hear it when you do not know what you are listening for? – Noise and Modernism

When training as a classical musician you are asked to identify minor thirds, perfect fifths, major sevenths and so on: sounds are given names and are organized in relation to each other, and it becomes a matter of recognizing what is being played and attributing the right term to the corresponding tonal relationship. You cannot possibly give the right answer unless you know what you are listening for, and the 'listening for' is never its sound but its visual point of reference. On the basis of this knowledge you begin to recognize the structure of a musical piece and start to listen to it with new attention. From this moment on you are listening to the language of music. You appreciate its sonic material in relation to the systemic understanding of its composition.

That of the sonic experience, which finds no acknowledgment in such a musical orientation, eludes its discussion, or under the name of noise, becomes its dialectical opposite. Either way it seizes to be heard.

This musical listening hears sounds according to Hegel's 'pure apprehension': the qualification of the immediate appearance of a sound as the knowledge of its tones.[11] Apprehending listening is the listening of the trained musician who hears, immediately, what he expects within the rules of a (harmonic) system. Sounds in this sense become pure knowledge; relevant and justified in relation to the context they are played within. Such a systemic listening establishes the idea of a 'right' sound and proposes notions of beauty and meaning in relation to a pre-existing vocabulary. A musical aesthetic depends on these conventions to propose its valuations. In this sense musical listening is an *absolute listening* that evokes value and authenticity, producing the idea of an objective ideality as a kind of objecthood in a time-based medium. The composition as object, inspires trust and produces canons of great works of art and their great renditions by the instrumentalist who ceaselessly practises to play the right notes for an ideal performance.

This kind of listening avoids the contingent and fleeting nature of sound by leading any stray tones back to the object of the score: integrating them into the system or rejecting them as their dialectical opposite. In this way it circumvents doubt and speculation. The non-musical equivalent is the discussion of sounds by their object. Either is a modernist pursuit, bringing with it the remnants of an (enlightenment) positivist understanding of the world, where universal knowledge is not only a possibility but is pursued as the ideal goal of the scientific endeavour.[12]

What is Sound? (1999)

Robert Pasnau, in his text *What is Sound?* published in 1999, struggles greatly with sound because he wants to fit it within the frame of a positivist understanding without considering the normative restrictions and ideological limitation of this frame. His project seeks unwittingly to undo what sound artists have tried to progress and establish over the last and since the beginning of this century: the ephemeral complexity of sound that avoids classification and focuses on being heard rather than on being understood.

Pasnau bemoans those who refuse to focus on the object, the source of sound, as illusionists, insisting that its object is all we can know. For him sight as well as hearing are locational modalities that have no sensorial quality in themselves but are carriers of information about the object they stem from. He rejects subjectivism in favour of an objective focus. Any sounds that might be difficult to be perceived in this manner, such as crickets, he excludes as 'a notoriously difficult case', as misfits to his general rule.[13] He decries subjectivism, and belittles any theories that focus on the perceptual nature of sound as 'error theories'.[14] Instead he performs a modernist reduction of the complex and perceptual phenomenon into a certain shape.

He claims that sound has been falsely identified with smell's immersivity and immediacy when it is closer to colour. His recourse is to scientific data, the ideas of waves, equating sound with light. But he forgets that light is what immerses us; we just do not speak about it that way, save in prose. Listening is not a scientific endeavour; it is an experiential fact full of playful illusions, purposeful errors and contingent idiosyncrasies. Listening is not about the physical constitution of sound; as little as seeing is about the physical constitution of the seen, it is the perception of those physical constitutions, fraught with the uncertainty of an erroneous, unreliable ear.

Pasnau represents modernism's quest for rational knowledge, logic and reason: the desire to overcome the individualism of the romantic era and enter a more equitable notion of truth, beauty and reality.[15] He complains about the mistakes of vernacular language and how it talks about sound: naively, from experience. In answer, his language, a philosophico-scientific discourse, reduces sound to what it might be in reality rather than what it is in experience. Consequently, the reality thus discovered is one about objects remote from their experience, which paradoxically is an illusion that sells its reality value on the basis of a scientific truthfulness, which by all accounts is real within its own framework of reality but only exists within its own enquiry. The reality of perception, by contrast, lies in its contingency: it is bodily, fantastic and permanently now.

Pasnau's scientific real is Adorno's deformed reality of a transcendental world, which is always already abstracted into the rationality of the structure that bestows it that rationality. In this way it apparently overcomes the irrational and dangerous edge of experience and finds certainty in the ambit of science and reason, the cornerstones of modernist ideology. In relation to this it is important to remember the well-debated problems inherent in modernist art criticism, particularly in relation to the perceiving body, and recognize Pasnau as a contemporary remnant that ignores the development of a more relevant discourse, which could account for the immersive viscerality of sound.

Cultural modernism of the twentieth century describes an era of change and upheaval in search of the eternal and immutable, certainty and truth. Freeing himself from the emotiveness of representation the modernist art critic turns to the material of production for the certainty of form. The reality that modernist culture seeks is the reality of its own making, away from the vagaries of nature and war. According to Jean-François Lyotard, modernist art theory seeks 'to preserve various consciousnesses from doubt.'[16] Its aim is to establish the artwork as certain and knowable in relation to a transcendental *a priori*. Its vocabulary consequently accommodates the description and judgement of spatial and substantial work: painting and sculpture, at some distance from the viewer. Modernism in this sense is a thoroughly visual discourse, it scans the surface and measures spaces, in search of pictorial essence and sculptural cohesion.

To turn away from the world and seek a truth within the artistic material enables and justifies an elite discourse. It expels the real living body, its visceral complexity: the bleeding, shitting and blubbering of the body dying in the trenches of war and life. Instead it builds metanarratives about life 'whose secretly terroristic function was to ground and legitimate the illusion of a "universal" human history.'[17]

In a sense, the modernist attempt to move away from the sentimentality of living to focus on form reflects and speaks of a time out of (spiritual) content and in that sense it is very engaged and reacts to where it is at. However, the belief in the possibility of distance, of metanarratives, even if those can be read in the plural, and a reverence for the author as well as a slight disregard for the audience makes its principles less useful for a philosophy of sound art.

The difference lies between Emile Zola or Charles Baudelaire's observation of Paris in the late nineteenth century de Certeau's description of New York in 1980. Zola and Baudelaire's moral tales and observations render their protagonists mute, stable and unable to change their position in a fixed and eternal truth about their lot. By contrast, de Certeau's description of New York as a city on the ground produced and challenged daily by the trajectories of the 'Wandersmänner down below' is a city in flux, a sonic city with sonic inhabitants contingently drawing their town with their transient paths.[18] In comparison Zola's people live in a static Paris, immutable, heavy and visual.[19] His quest for knowledge and the idea of universal truths separates his writing from the world as a life-world generated in the contingent experience of perception. It fails to engage the audience in their own particularity and instead, and paradoxically so, creates the illusion of a universalizing reality it set out to contest in its critique of romanticism.

One of the foremost purveyors of this idea of modernism within the visual arts, Clement Greenberg, had very particular ideas as to what an artwork was supposed to do and not do, what the task of painting was, the freedom of sculpture and the rules of engagement in art. His philosophy of art, informed by Kant's *Critique of Judgment*, written in 1790, worked towards the strict autonomy of each art form as it became manifest in the austerity of high modernism. This categorical separation and inward focus of each medium was driven by a belief in a positivist outlook on truth and reality as the chief informant of a contemporary aesthetic sensibility. In his essay on 'Sculpture in Our Time', first published in 1958, Greenberg writes,

. . . the various modernist arts try to confine themselves to that which is most positive and immediate in themselves, which consists in the unique attributes of their mediums. It follows that a modernist work of art must try, in principle, to avoid communication with any order of experience not inherent in the most literally and essentially construed nature of its medium. Among other things, this means renouncing illusion and explicit subject matter.[20]

With this credo Greenberg pleads for a pure art that deals with its material-self: painting that deals with paint and the canvas, sculpture that investigates its own sculptural form and materiality, and for both art forms to avoid an engagement with the perceptual vagueness of an amateur audience. The truth of each work lies in its positive rather than in its perceptual materiality. The viewer is confined to the rules set out by the art critic, the genre, the discourse. Sentiment, emotion, perceptual practice are ruled out in favour of a distanced and intellectual apprehension of form as substance.

In relation to music, it is the score that substantiates and qualifies the work in an *a priori* which is the authority on progress and success, and which binds the temporal sound work to a transcendental substantialism. It is quite confusingly, given his promotion for subjective experience above scientific objectivity, Adorno, who insists on the score as the arbiter of the aesthetic judgement of music. The actual, temporary, quality of music, which could be seen as its critical edge vis-à-vis spatial art practices, is for Adorno a problem, unless it is compositionally controlled; the temporal sounds fixed in the *Notenbild* (the image of notes/ the score).[21]

It is according to him the score that substantiates and qualifies the work and on whose visual materiality is judged the immediate, in the sense of the apprehensional, success of the work. The score promotes the quasi objective relationship between tones in harmonic intervals in relation to the compositional totality of the work that renders the musical work ideal. For Adorno music is a thoroughly temporal art form whose spatial orientation is merely an outward characteristic. It is the ideal temporality of the score, not the fleeting temporal space of its performance, that allows for a complex organization of tone material. Improvisation and score-less performances can according to him not achieve the complex criticality of the scored work. The improvised work lacks critical rigour and musical achievement, it is lax and lazy.[22] The critical temporality of music, which he insists on, is thereby paradoxically confined within the certain, quasi-spatial, temporality of its written organization. The score visualizes and thus arrests the individual performance in an ideal temporality. It demonstrates the work's visual complexity, is proof of its existence and determines its value above the improvised performance as well as guards against the potential fallibility of the human player.

For Adorno the score does not negate experience but allows for the appreciation of greater complexity. He wants to follow the thread of the composition and immanently realize the read in the tones heard.[23] This allows for interpretation whose practice however is determined within the overall goal of the realization of the total composition. It is the means to realize the objective musical structure of the audible.[24] The instrumentalist remains in the role of the interpreter, and the listener retains the responsibility of apprehending his rendition.

Rosalind Krauss identifies the Grid as the quintessential modernist preoccupation. She explains the abundance of the grid in modernist practice to demonstrate the mapping not of reality onto art or vice-versa but, the mapping of art onto art; form without content. It is the space where the aesthetic object and the physical object become one: 'considered in this way, the bottom line of the grid is naked and determined materialism.'[25]

For her the grid promotes silence as a refusal of speech. Its visual mesh denies anything exterior any involvement in its contemplation. The grid is impervious to language, anti-referential and denies a narrativation of the seen. It is the artwork in its absolute purposelessness from which according to Krauss it gained its autonomy.

Understood as grid, the score does not represent or enable sound but mutes it, silences its articulation in a dense net of horizontal and vertical lines that purport distance and closed-ness. 'No echoes of footsteps in empty rooms, no screams of birds across open skies, no rush of distant water – . . .'[26] The modernist score is autonomous of the sounds potentially produced, which would drag the lines and dots back to life.[27] Instead, relative to the score the sounds only become its ideal realization, the listener simply the means of their fulfilment. The actual sounds are uncontrollable, feeble and human, involving the fleshness of living that the score avoids.

The question of the origin or ideological investment of the criteria that set the (positivist) modernist understanding is never raised, it is a given, a fixed a priori, immutable: painting has to be flat to support the essence of the pictorial surface, sculpture has to be three dimensional, sound has to be organised in intelligible sequences. To fulfil these criteria means aesthetic progress on the path to absolute high modernist beauty. It appears at least according to Krauss, that the grid, the score, embodies this path, at once denying history and negating interfering articulations for the purpose of artistic purpose-lessness and autonomy.

In relation to such philosophical attitudes noise simply manifests the failure to communicate, it becomes the negative of what is beautiful, permissive and harmonic. In that sense it is in modernist discourse because it is what has to be excluded, as it is counter that which fulfils the demands of the medium to reach its own autonomous ideality. But it is not listened to. It is unclean sound, not treated to reach its positivist purity. It is a bad realization that questions the trustworthiness not only of the producer as interpreter, but also of the audience who apprehend it.

The material in contemporary noise art is tainted by extra-musical reference. It lacks autonomy and its obsessive nature refuses intellectual contemplation. Instead it grabs the listener and holds him hostage to his own listening, if it does not do that it is not noise. Meanwhile the subject in noise is the abject, non-progressive subject who lacks taste and aesthetic sophistication. It is a subject without historical consciousness and artistic finesse, a subject who does not understand the artness of art: its autonomy, and who is unappreciative of its formal concerns and instead submits himself viscerally to the sonic charge. This subject does not contemplate but is taken over by sound possessed in a primitive abandon that is the nemesis of modernist restraint.

The hefty sound of a sub woofer compresses your diaphragm and hollows out every cavity until you feel your eyes might bulge and you cannot draw breath anymore. This physical noise crowds your body, and when it is suddenly switched off you feel emptied out and hollow. Switched on and off rhythmically it directs your breathing and makes your body move to its will. It does not so much enter you through the ears but squashes you all the length of your body. Its physicality overwhelms you and changes your shape. There is no question about your physical engagement, noise is realized on your body.

Noise understood as radical sound has no place in modernist discourse.[28] Or rather, and this possibility should be tried out in practice: we do not listen to modernist work not because no noisy visceral and impure work has been produced within its time, but because the discourse surrounding and contextualising the work has not dared to listen. If we bring the sonic sensibility of noise, its extravagant demand for involvement, its sheer insistence on the body and its referential messiness to the modernist oeuvre and forget the conventions of its criticism maybe we would see something else entirely. The question here is how can I hear something when not only do I not know what to listen out for, but have in fact been categorically told not to listen? – Noise crashes those barriers of obliging politeness and hears what cannot be seen. The artwork as sensorial material cannot set boundaries of experience only discourse does that. Noise re-asserts experience over modernist reserve, and gets the body moving.

Records 1981–1989 (1997)

Christian Marclay's *Records* sounds like such a failure and invites abandon. Not only can there be no score to this work, it abuses genres, stretches references, mixes history into the now and repeals it all.

I am not sure what I am listening to most of the time and this 'acoustic blindness' allows me to hear anything I can imagine.[29] I fall into the sensorial rhythm of the work and abandon any attempt to summarize or judge it. It is there to be heard.

It is as if Marclay had invited me in and presented to me his entire record collection at once, in space rather than time, without frame, without titles, without censorship or judgement simply to have me hear it and do with it what I will. There is undoubtedly artistic intention, but there is no shame and it all blurs into a big thing of sound that kills historical and generic particularity in its noisy non-sense. At times I recognize voices and sonic vignettes which only serves to draw me in closer to compulsively listen to sounds moving well away from the meaning first assumed, leading me to the sounds of my own imagination. There it becomes my record collection of songs never written. At other times he seems to physically demolish the records played through their own sound tracks. The sensorial material is forcefully fused to evoke its own sonic destruction.

His work produces an experience in my hearing that is complex and dynamic and that is not confined to the length of the tracks played but only to the imaginative space of my listening. This is contingent sound close up, and any gap between the work and myself is subjectively rather than objectively overcome through my sensory-motor movement towards its thing-ness.

What remains recognizable all through the work is rhythm. Rhythm is the only universal that remains, but even that is contingently practised rather than collectively and intellectually assumed. This is not the rhythm assured and expected at the beginning of notational bars, something to clap to. Rather this is a contingent rhythm, changing all the time. It is the rhythm of my unexpected moves, Lyotard's *coups inattendus*, that carry me along.[30] Rhythm as a concept is a modernist universal, the contingent practice of that rhythm however demands another engagement.[31] Its transitive persistence and immersive presence challenges postmodern theories to find some words in the midst of its racket and anarchic thumping, because the modernist insistence on perception as the ideal realization of a transcendental objectivity from a distance is defied by its noise.

Noise and Postmodernism

Lyotard offers a clear explanation of how he understands the relationship between the author, the work and the spectator after modernism. Discussing the sublime, which he understands as 'perhaps the only mode of artistic sensibility to characterize the modern' he states that,

> Henceforth is seems right to analyse the ways in which the subject is affected, its ways of receiving and experiencing feelings, its ways of judging works. This is how aesthetic, the analysis of the addressee's feelings, comes to supplant poetics and rhetoric, which are didactic forms, of and by the understanding, intended for the artist as sender.[32]

In an attempt to answer the question on the nature of the postmodern, Lyotard replies that 'postmodernism thus understood is not modernism at its end but in the nascent state, and this state is constant.'[33] His postmodernism is thus not something in itself, but is simply the condition of present-ness, continually transitive and potentially anything as long as it is here and now. This condition of present-ness problematizes, in his terms, any attempt to legitimize and validate the now through a meta-discourse established in the 'grand narratives' of the Enlightenment. According to Lyotard the notion of knowledge legitimization in grand narratives leads to a unification of knowledge in the 'Idea' (the emancipation of humanity) and in the Idea, knowledge is posited as an ideal and objective totality. Totality, however, is a notion that Lyotard considers as 'violence to the heterogeneity of language games.'[34] Instead, in place of the 'grand narrative' comes a local and *petit récit*.[35] This 'little narration' is not produced nor legitimated by an (enlightenment) metadiscourse, but is discourse, not without rules, but those are always contingently and locally determined.[36]

Postmodern art criticism refocuses modernist idealism of totality and unity via the consideration of perception; challenging modernism via a temporal and individual dimension. In this sense postmodernism does not present a break with modernism but rather is a logical interpretation and development of its principles thrown into doubt. According to Lyotard postmodernism puts forward that which in modernism remains 'unpresentable'.[37] I interpret his unpresentable as the moment when the modernist objective vocabulary clashes with the momentary perception of the individual listener and fails to account for his experience. This clash is the aesthetic moment the art critic has to account for rather than write over. Consequently the postmodern reading reflects not the understanding of the work as supplying or representing one total and ideal artwork. Rather, it discusses artistic experience as 'real' and 'ideal' in the sense in which the audience connects it to a personal and individual experience of the real, constructing a multitude of re-presentations.

In this sense postmodernism is to modernism the noise of heterogeneity, working outside and across disciplines, squandering its systemic valuation in decadent centrifugality. The postmodern is a radicalization of the modernist understanding of the artwork. However, in the overall context of modernity the postmodern excursion into decadence is ultimately redeemed. Lyotard's interpretation of the postmodern as language game highlights this state of affairs. As a game it is ultimately halted or at least paused, and its players go back to the pragmatics of everyday living, where homogeneity is produced in order to get on; any noisy non-sense recuperated within a solid consensus of meaning. In fact postmodernism never abandons the notion of shared meaning, good taste and form, in the first place. It queries the nominalism and homogeneity of those who participate in the meaning-making process, never however the possibility of meaning making *per se*.

Postmodern production embraces fragmentation, diversity and anarchic openness. However, the postmodern critic and cultural observer work tirelessly to bind even the most idiosyncratic, contrary and ephemeral thoughts and actions together into one picture of postmodernism.[38] Discourse closes the gaps and ties together the fragments ripped forcefully from the bosom of modernism.[39] Any proclamation against meta-discourse becomes in fact a new meta-discourse. In language the fragments become signifiers of fragmentation unable to produce the experience of fragmentation proposed by the work. Postmodern fragmentation is a practice that for discourse is but a temporal abandonment of reason embodied in criticism, which is tied to modernism by its recourse to the same language base. It is paradoxically, or logically, the unspeakable fragmentation and anarchic confusion of the postmodern work that hands power to the text, which consolidates it. For when Lyotard talks about doubt he frames it in the certainty of theory rather than expose it in the fragility of experience. Postmodern philosophy, as long as it remains a philosophical theory that explains rather than practises experience, does not abandon the presumed certainty of language but still insists on distance from the production process to establish its criticality.

Postmodern criticism sets out to embrace the body, to lead him back into the work, to make him an imaginative reader, a player in Lyotard's language game. However, postmodernism insists on rules of engagement, even if Lyotard allows the individual player to come to the rules through play, rather than as an *a priori* set of parameters. The rules are there to be found. 'The artist and the writer, then, are working without rules in order to formulate the rules of what *will have been done*.'[40] The rules and the game are posited separately from each other. And it is this separation, which allows him to come to a *'have been done'*. Thus, aesthetic judgement and systemic knowledge position the game as plan, even if after the event. The game plan renders the *coups inattendus* (unexpected moves) of the individual players, relative to each other and in this relative unity they are negative to an 'outside', another realm where the grand narratives validate the work. The term 'game' sums up the postmodern condition. It allows the critic to marginalize playfulness as perverted or decadent, asocial or simply silly and to consolidate it in the higher order synthesis of the critical text.[41]

Like modernism, the postmodern ultimately avoids the sensorial, but for a slightly different reason: instead of universal objectivity, what is sought is a shared heterogeneity. Anything shared however has to compromise the individual sensorial experience on a base of meaning. Language, even the post-structuralist dérive and différance, halts for breaths of meaning and clings to a framework within which its differences move. In language that posits meaning, rather than purposeless utterance, the artistic phenomenon remains a structural object however mobile. Post-structuralism replaces the identification of an object's origin with the identity of its shifting shape. Identity is not abandoned however. In fact the removal of historical similarities through an insistence on absolute and mobile differences promotes rather than abandon the system as the guarantor of meaning. Its language changes in time but remains concomitant in space. It is this spatial agreement that flattens the true experientiality of the object, the work, in language.

Noise, not as a temporary abandonment of taste and good form, decadent, asocial or simply silly, imminently redeemed in a new (visual) referential framework, but radically and always just simply noise, upsets not only a universal homogeneous (modernist) meaning and the possibility to produce shared heterogeneous meanings (postmodernism), but also unsettles, the infrastructure of the game plan per se: the plateau on which postmodernist meanings slide and melt.

Noise breaks with the language base. All I can do is stutter, swear, switch my own sound system on or at best dance. I won't be heard anyway through this racket. Noise can only find its way to language in the acknowledgment that it can't. The thing discussed is the body that heard not the work that played. Noise forces the listening subject into the critical ring and turns the work into moments of experience. And that is the true criticality of noise. The fact, stated above, that noise is not different from other sounds but simply amplifies its demand to be considered in its immersive contingency rather than in relation to a system, pre-conceived or established imminently in its realization, makes these observations relevant for sound art at large.

The consequence of this in relation to auditory practice is that postmodernism, as a critical framework for artistic production and perception, is not radical enough for sound to be heard, nor indeed for the postmodern artwork to be experienced in its transient and fragmented complexity. The real issue of the postmodern work, when it is not just a game with modernist conventions, is the experiencing body and the constitution of his aesthetic subjectivity rather than that of the work.

Sonic Noise

Juliane Rebentisch in her book on the *Ästhetik der Installation* from 2003, reflects on the current malaise of art criticism that avoids its sensorial object. Her investigation into the aesthetic of installation art is motivated and framed by the problem of how the philosophy of art struggles to embrace the complexity of its phenomenon. A lot of her complaints echo the concerns of Adorno and his foregrounding of subjectivity and experience, but her discussion also includes a consideration of the reality and limitations of his perceptual engagement. She accuses art discourse of closing installation work off in criticism rather than opening it up for a more practical contemplation, and challenges the critic to re-engage in the work's experienced reality.

> Indem sie durch die Verletzung modernistischer Formbildungskonventionen zentrale Probleme des modernen aesthetischen Diskurses aktualisieren, bündeln und zuspitzen, fordern Installation besonders nachdrücklich zu einder anderen, einer zudem, wie sich zeigen wird, entschieden nachmetaphysischen Form der philosophischen Reflexion auf den Begriff von Kunst – und den ihrer Erfahrung – heraus.[42]

For Rebentisch the formal complexity of installation art challenges and actualizes the notion of art per se in that it questions its claim to autonomy, whereby she does not simply refer to a modernist autonomy of category but acknowledges a more complex aesthetic autonomy. For Rebentisch, without autonomy the notion of art is conceptually empty, and it is into this conceptual void that art criticism rushes with political and social theories rather than engaging in the present complexity. She understands aesthetic theory and practice to be implicated in each other and warns aesthetic philosophy from becoming irrelevant if it loses contact with its object: the aesthetic practice.

Sound art equally challenges conventional methods of critical and philosophical contemplation. The complexity of installation art and its challenge to theorization and pictorial representation, which Rebentisch understands to particularize and focus the philosophical consideration of the notion of art per se, is even more acutely relevant for sound art and is particularly foregrounded in noise. Noise is formless yet spatial in its concentration on the listening body. It avoids the autonomy of category by being its dialectical opposite, but demands aesthetic autonomy in its sheer insistence on being heard, alone.[43] In noise I hear nothing but the phenomenon under consideration. I cannot even hear myself but am immersed in a sonic subjectivity, more felt than heard. This is aesthetic autonomy understood as the autonomy of the work as an aesthetic moment: when it is produced by the listening subject, transient and reciprocal. Noise renders any sensory-motor action a reaction held in a tight reciprocity by the vertical weight of its downpour.

1930 (1997)

Listening to Merzbow's album *1930* in a closed and darkened room I enter this tight reciprocity willingly. It is a direct hit, right between the eyes. The shards of glass enter my ears blinding me. The bit of light that manages to come in through the blinds only emphasizes the sharpness of the sound: piercing and enveloping me at the same time, weighing down on me and lifting me up into a most acute hearing.

Nobody would be able to hear me now, and neither am I able to hear the outside world. This is my world, my noisy life-world tailored tightly onto my body. I take its rhythm and run, and run. I am getting tired, sleepy even, submitting to his sounds. Maybe this is what it is like just before an alien abduction. This is the preparation before being beamed up by their own beam of light. It is the aesthetic effort of carving me out of the mould of collective humanity into a solitary existence ready for takeoff. This preparation takes an hour. It is durational, slowly unwinding my own sense of self to become its noise.

Short, quieter, but not less noisy spells form a small reprisal from the sonic assault. They are checking that I am still breathing before the next wave of loud material hits my body. The visual room I am in is grey, carpeted, still, the sonic room is vibrating, undulating, porous, moving in and out. My listening practice goes into non-sensical overdrive. The sensate material that pounds in on me demands of me to produce, to stay at pace: to process the trial of the material, in order to enter its complexity.

The sensate material crowds in on me and digests me. I am practising the trial of my body through the signifying engagement with the sonic material. The sonic fragments and rhythms are trying me and I am trying myself through them. I am as porous as the walls now, moving in and out with them. The noise pours into me and makes me burst into its inundation. My listening performs the noise as it enters me and implodes me, scattering my body all over the room: centrifugally into space, propelling ever further outwards, onwards, away from here. I am fragments, everywhere, fast, distinct, rhythmical fragments that fragment me.[44]

I am not passive in this rhythm but deliberately merge with the thinging of noise to become a noisy thing myself. The centrifugal force of the sound meets the desire of my generative fantasy to verge to the fringes of my body, to move towards the outside of myself, and finally to let go and become a visceral body that has left the sense of material objectivity to live in the dense ephemerality of sound as itself.

Once Merzbow's noise has come to an end I fall back to earth, heavy and with a great clunk, full of another sense. I wont be able to tell them what happened. The proof that it did is on my body, the body that heard, who bares the invisible after-image of its experience as a sonic sensibility. It is this aesthetic body, sensible of the sonic material that is at the centre of a philosophy of sound art. The artwork as aesthetic moment binds the sensory material onto the body. Aesthetic criticism has to enter this relationship, unpack it carefully to present it tentatively and with lots of caveats to discourse. Any critical analysis of the aesthetic moment has to start in the listener's fragmented-ness and needs to proceed from his astonishment to meet his doubt in the networks and mechanisms of a shared and consolidating communication. It is the body that listens and hears and then tries to find language that holds the key to the language sought itself. As fragments this body has abandoned habitual language, it has shot past the collective towards an alien utterance.

> This is why Cézanne's people are strange, as if viewed by a creature of another species. Nature itself is stripped of the attributes, which make it ready for animistic communions: there is no wind in the landscape, no movement in the Lac d'Annecy, the frozen objects hesitate at the beginning of the world. It is an unfamiliar world in which one is uncomfortable and which forbids all human effusiveness.[45]

The body in noise is silent, not mute but silent. Momentarily stunned by the force of experience that impresses on him a sonic sensibility, he is estranged from his assumptions. After noise it is this body that needs to try and speak again to find a shareable voice and become ready for communication. But in the midst of this racket there is no language base to make his point. The body in noise can scream but not talk.

Keiji Haino at the Drake Hotel Underground (2006)

Keiji Haino shouts and wails at me. High pitch and squealing, low growling and howling: urgently, fleshly, covering the walls with his noisy breathe. It does not matter one little bit that he probably shouts in Japanese. He means to exclaim rather than be understood. His vocal assault is shocking and raw. He squashes lyrics and words that dress the body in formal clothing. Instead he is naked, unclothed, shielded only by the voice of bodily fluids that destroyed his gown. He spits out any vocal sound possible, with great velocity and design. This is punk beyond the swear words: sexual without a body to have intercourse with, it challenges not desire but the raw idea of the desired itself. He works with feedback pedals to resend himself his unutterable voice, to speak back to it even less understandable and even more fleshly sounds. These bodiless voices fill the space, adding ever more invisible organs without bodies. This self-reproduction puts his real body in question. Symbiotes take over, swallowing and masking the performing body in their flesh. The social body has broken down, collapsed and given in to the inner necessity of its cravings. This is not anti-dialectical, but the dialectical stripped bare of its idealizing cloak. It is that which we are rather than that which we might become.

The sheer force and weight of his exclamations collapse the distance of language and converge our bodies beyond speech. His noisy voices crowd and digest my listening body in his body, as subject, rather than as object. They get to the point of the subject–subject relationship without communication, through our flesh. My whole body becomes the receptacle of his as his symbiotic voices penetrate beyond the polite reserve of an ordinary encounter. I am exposed as he envelops me, bears down on me with the weight of his open body, fragmented and transformed. The tight reciprocity of noise is made fleshly by his screams: intimate, erotic, scary, breaking the boundary between social relations and language once and for all.[46]

The less he is language the more I am noise. As noise I am his scream, the means of his centrifugal extension into the world, thrusting away from his own body, into mine and beyond. His scream brings about an explosion within my hearing, triggering the production of my own bodily fantasy. This fantasy is generative: casting in his screams intertwining bodies that do not speak. I do not listen to recognize and understand but experience total non-understanding as the spontaneous place of my body vis-à-vis his. This is not lost language but the meeting before all language. It calls for it but does not provide its framework.

Noise urges us back into communication not as translation but as a transfer between sensibles. It pushes on the door of language, from the sensibility of isolation, without reaching the infrastructure of meaning. The signifying practice of non-sense tries my body by trying his. His noise becomes my noise, it meets if not my scream exactly then my capability to do so. His noisy voice enters my vocal cords as a tangible possibility that finds speech at least in my ears. It is through this voice that thought hits experience and questions its articulation.

Conclusion: Noisy Voices

There is no doubt that within the era and cultural ideology of what is termed postmodernism more and different voices have been allowed to speak, although they have not necessarily always been heard. Postmodernism answered the imperialization of an enlightened modernity that presumes to speak for others by setting up groups that can speak for themselves.[47] However, the promotion of such groups is in many ways neo-imperialist owing to its own parameters of choice and publication. It pretends the homogeneity of the group and supports the principle of sameness and relative difference implicit in the notion of groupings and identities. Moreover, these other identities have to speak in the dominant discourse to be listened to at all. Anything of their reality that does not correspond, or cannot be expressed within the parameters of that discourse becomes a noisy voice and is suppressed by the very channel of its liberation: language, the infrastructure of communication.

The noisy voice is the thing-ness of the subject, in turn; the subject listening becomes its thing-ness in its voice. They are both on trial producing their own non-sense, sensitive to the intersubjective process that generates them both in simultaneous isolation. The sensibility of noisy voices questions the ideological interest of groupings by doubting the viability of *a priori* communication within those groups even. Instead the sonic subject grasps sense as the non-sense of his own sensate experience through formlessness in isolation, and then practises a language that is itself signifying contingently and nonsensically. This language is framed by doubt in the perceived *and* the possibility to share its sense rather than the certainty of its meaning, but motivated by the desire to communicate because rather than in spite of it.

Haino's voice meets mine in my ears. It produces the desire to communicate without recourse to a system of communication. We are totally other, without a system of relative differences and substitutions; defined in the noise that bears us both down and lifts us both up into the centrifugal subjectivity of a sonic sensibility. As sonic sensibles we constitute each other reciprocally without definition: formless, fragmented, up in the air. His screams produce the meeting of two silent bodies. Back to back we know each other in knowing rather than in talking. As sonic subjects we produce a sea of engaged misunderstandings from which by coincidence and good timing, passing understandings will form formlessly without the pressure of intent.

Any notion of *a priori* communication in cohesive groups and identities excludes or at least compromises this personal experience that by necessity is at the base of language as the desire to speak. While an *a priori* language might possibly empower the cause of the group it disempowers the individual subjects within and outside that group. In other words, whereas the modernist framework lives with universality and postmodernism considers us and others, the sonic understands there only to be engaged, but absolute, others. A philosophy of sound art consequently must follow the idea that any identification of groupings, however well intended, is sonically impossible, since it supports the principle of *a priori* sameness and difference, that legitimizes hierarchies, exclusion and discrimination, the very things its material dispels.

The voice as noise pursues no legitimation in language. It is thinging in its most provocative fashion. Embracing me in its breath, it is the sensible sentient, the sensing body as thing, that senses my sensibility in its sensorial production, as my own sensibility senses it. It is the noise of Haino's voice through which I hear the body as a sensible thing in all its *Dingheit*. My voice meets his voice not through language but through both our fleshness: screaming, screeching, yelling and croaking, shouting the corporeality out of our bodies to expand into the formless shape of sound. This frees us from the prejudice of objective materiality and makes the body raw and fragile; its relationship to communication hesitant and cautious. This relationship to language literally embodies our doubt in a transcendental world. It is the tentative approach of our naked bodies to the civilization of speaking for which we have to invent ourselves as fleeting associations by making our own noise.

The body is central to the contemporary artwork, but it is still not central in the language of its discourse. Since language prepares and frames the experience and subsequently leads it back into discourse, this relationship hinders the work from being the sensorial practice its material tries to entice us into. Theory arranges and calculates the complexity of the work in order to find a form for the formless and avoid emotional confrontation. Contemporary discourse aims to account where there are but the vagaries of experience and a sea of unsayables.

Lyotard's nascent postmodernity as the condition of present-ness, continually transitive, and potentially anything as long as it is here and now, vanishes into the weight of language. The postmodern now is cemented in letters that confer academic authority, professional autonomy and legitimacy. The real now is long gone. What was termed postmodern practice has long moved on into a formless shape without a name. This is not post-postmodernity, altermodernity[48] or any other modernity, since it is the 'modern' rather than its prefix that cannot take account of the true heterogeneity of a global practice without considering it through the dominant discourse. However, this formless practice is not a dialectical reaction either, but it knows its histories through the complex and reciprocal relationship between subjects and objects in their contingent pasts. And so it is simply practice now as it unfolds and confronts. Such practice speedily pursues its endless mobility, detaching, fragmenting and forming in parts, while the theory lags with a heavy leaden foot, clomping into the perceived gap between the work and its critical perception. To account for this mobility the signifying practice has to be kept up in a theory that is as practical as the practice that it theorizes. It must know its responsibility to the present and accept the fact that it might only ever produce another practice rather than theoretical conclusions. Any such conclusion would suppress the signifying practice of the work: to sum up the now instead of to invite to produce it continually without a reason for justification.

Noise leaves no space for a theoretical or philosophical foot to lodge itself between the heard and the felt for language to assert its right over the work. Noise *is* aesthetic simultaneity. It demands a consideration of itself in its sensorial complexity without recourse to art historical, political, relational, social, etc. theories that present it with a language that precedes its encounter and immobilizes its present production. Instead it demands listening. It is the body listening that is at the core of the aesthetic autonomy of sound and who through his thinging meets the thinging of sound and gives it speech. This listening body is a solitary subject who practises rather than assumes the work. He does not group himself but passes others with a noisy voice. This voice does not make sense but reciprocates with its body any passing body and is not reduced to the prejudices of its face.

> They have a name in all languages, but a name which in all of them also conveys significations in tufts, thickest of proper meanings and figurative meanings, so that, unlike those of science, not one of these names clarifies by attributing to what is named a circumscribed signification. Rather, they are the repeated index the insistent reminder of a mystery as

familiar as it is unexplained, of a light which illuminating the rest, remains at its source in obscurity.[49]

The semiotic and the phenomenological meet each other in the obscurity of this noisy voice. Back to back, they feel each other's weight and outline, and shape the desire to practice a signifying that meets occasionally and lights a sparkle in what are misunderstandings turned understandings for the expediency of a nominally illuminated visual communication. Noise cannot speak, but knows there is a fragile relationship between its experience and the system of communication and longs to practise that relationship. It taps into the dense ephemerality of subjective objectivity. It fragments its fragments that fragment it ever more. It reduces to open up, it expands to be more precise, and it disperses to hold back. In this way it practises a signifying practice that finds no signification but continually builds a bridge between the structure for the articulation of meaning and the process of its experience, on which eventually and tentatively such a meaning might be formulated in its own formlessness.

Silence provides the condition to practise such a signifying language that takes account of its noisy base: that embraces the body in its formless solitude and invites him to listen to himself amidst the soundscape to become ready to speak and find his vocabulary. What we can share in *Noise* is the desire to communicate, to seek and practise signifying, not however its meanings. Those are practised in silence, contingently, reciprocally, centrifugally out of the sensate material out into the world to strike whatever shared meanings occur. The basis of the critical language of a philosophy of sound art is personal conviction, which arises out of the practice of listening rather than social contracts that precede it.

3

SILENCE

Barry Beach (2008)

On a dark and stormy day at Barry beach, a pebble beach in the south of Wales, the sea is deafening. The wind cuts my face as the sea bruises my ears. The waves pour vertically down on me, engulfing me in their harsh sounds. I am entrenched in the location of my own listening, heavy and alone. Only the screeching of the seagulls' piercing pitch penetrates through the wall of noise, adding a layer of extravagant pain. I get dizzy and disorientated and cannot feel myself in the cold noise. It isolates me from my surroundings as it carries me off into its ephemeral weight.

Later on, when the tide is out and the wind died down I come again; walking over the pebbles in the moonlight I can see some fishermen with their lines in a calm and steady sea. The wind is a breeze now, still cold but no more than a quiet hush. The wall of sound has turned into a delicate and differentiated soundscape. The pebbles crackling as if laughing quietly as the water draws in and out. This rhythmic whisper is almost tangible, tingling the palms of my hands. Faint and much calmer seagull cries syncopate the sky, and the odd invisible dog walker calling his pet punctuates this sonic carpet.

In this quiet I can hear myself. My shoes slipping on the larger and smaller pebbles in the dark and my cold breath are at the centre of the sonic scene, which engulfs me still but does not carry me off in its deafening roar, instead it opens my ears to hear myself listen. After the crashing clamour of the afternoon I come back to silence. From the intense isolation of noise I join the quiet of the fishermen and start to sense the possibility of speech.

Conceptual Silence

The discourse on silence is dominated by John Cage's work and ideas, particularly of course by his *4'33"* (1952).[1] There is no doubt that *4'33"* is a seminal work and as important to the development of twentieth-century sound art and music as Marcel Duchamp's *Fountain,* a porcelain urinal inscribed 'R. Mutt' (1917) had been, 35 years earlier, to the practice and discourse of the visual arts. In many ways like Fountain, *4'33"* is a 'ready made'.[2] It brings silence, an extra musical sound concept, into the concert hall, and thereby asks comparable questions of musical materiality and its conventions of performance as Duchamp did in relation to the aesthetic content and exhibition of visual art works by bringing a urinal into the gallery space.

Both works introduced new, everyday, material into the realm of art and broadened the artistic process, proposing new aesthetic possibilities. They defied conventions to contest what was artistically doable. Many musical ideas would not have been realized without Cage's dedication to the liberation and expansion of the musical scope through the inclusion of silence. However, Cage as well as Duchamp's 'ready mades' were primarily concerned with expanding the possibilities of music and the visual arts, respectively. Their proposition works within their respective aesthetic framework, contesting and criticizing its conventions but remaining within and confirming even its domain. The silence of *4'33"* is a musical silence not a sonic silence. Cage's interest in silence lies in establishing every sound within the musical register. It does not invite a listening to sound as sound but to all sound as music. The framework of the concert hall guides the listener towards that aim.

The Museum establishes Duchamp's *Fountain* within the aesthetic concerns of visual art, which lends it authenticity and makes it readable and available for assessment in discourse. Similarly *4'33"* too is framed by the concert hall, which makes it audible and admits it into discourse, which eventually re-establishes it in relation to musical conventions. This is the silence of the musical work: it echoes harmonies and intervals, and opens musical possibilities while filling the room with the expectation of its oeuvre rather than the sounds of the everyday.

In the concert hall Cage's *4'33"* is musical silence, and as such any sound heard is practised in relation to the expectations and conventions of musical performance and musical listening. When we have not heard it but only heard about it, as is the case for many, no doubt, *4'33"* becomes a conceptual work. Its description is potent in its theatrical evocation and invites our imaginations to engage in it through the time stricture *4'33"*. What we experience now is the outline of silence rather than its materiality, which is locked into rather than freed by the time code.

As an idea, Cage's silence can be related to Conceptual Art and its concerns with dematerialization of established forms of objecthood and authorship. This relationship is particularly evident in a comparison between Cage's *4'33"* and conceptual artist Mel Bochner's *8" Measurement* (1969): a black ink arrow on empty graph paper indicating its length of 8". Whereas Cage's *4'33"* outlines a silent time in music, Bochner's *8" Measurement* draws an empty space on paper. Both works depend on the discursive context of their respective practices to frame this emptiness, to render it visible and audible. This conceptual dimension does not free the page but makes its limits available for contemplation. Equally it does not free silence to participate in the musical work but instead makes audible the parameters of musical scoring and counting. The dematerialization of the object of composition, emptying the score of its musical sounds, does invite new sounds but at the same time confines these new sounds in the tight space of musical conventions and expectations.

Silence, in a contemporary context, is not about opening up all sounds to the musical scheme or locking them into a musical time frame. Silence is about listening, listening to small sounds, tiny sounds, quiet and loud sounds out of any context, musical, visual or otherwise. Silent sounds can be loud, as much as noisy sounds can be quiet, but they do not deafen my body to anything but themselves, and instead include me in their production.

This third part foregrounds the material perception of silence outside the musical realm. It explores silence as a sonic condition that engages my listening in sound rather than in music, and that implicates me in my hearing through its quiet demand to be heard. Such silence shifts the responsibility of production from the conventions of the composition/the artwork onto the individual audience member, who becomes audible to himself in the contingent context of his listening practice. This is a formless silence inhabited by the formless listener who just came out of *Noise*. Having been weighed upon heavily by the blast and exclusivity of capacious sound, besieged by its volume, he gets himself back in *Silence*. The sensible is at the centre of noise but deaf to himself. In silence he comes to hear himself and comes to speak about the heard from that central position. In this sense this part discusses silent works and silence in the acoustic environment as the basic condition of an aesthetics and philosophy of sound art, and outlines the consequences for a sonic subjectivity and its relationship to the objective world.

When there is nothing to hear you start hearing things

> Behind the work of any creative artist there are three principal wishes: the wish to make something; the wish to perceive something, [. . .] and the wish to communicate these perceptions to others. [. . .] Those who have no interest in communication do not become artists either; they become mystics or madmen.[3]

After the fragmented loneliness of *Noise*, *Silence* turns to the notion of communication and collective sense, and visits the idea of madness too.

I am sitting in the mountains with snow all around. It is the preseason and hardly any tourists have yet arrived. It is dead quiet, pressing down on me, heavy and dark, but not unpleasant or exclusive. This weight is inclusive, all encompassing and abundant. All that could sound has been quietened under a blanket of snow, but vibrates gently in its possibility. The dynamic of life appears less fast here, unhurried, just trembling quietly. The movements are slowed down by the landscape and the weather; the sounds are muffled and contained. Even the murmur of the river has been suffocated under a heavy sheet of ice, leaving no sonic hint of its former vitality. The house itself, covered in a thick layer of snow, surrounded by snowed-in trees, feels dense and compact like a thick carpet. I am inside this carpet, listening.

When there is nothing to hear, so much starts to sound. Silence is not the absence of sound but the beginning of listening. This is listening as a generative process not of noises external to me, but from inside, from the body, where my subjectivity is at the centre of the sound production, audible to myself. Silence reveals to me my own sounds: my head, my stomach, my body becomes their conductor. This is not John Cage's anechoic chamber, where the vacuum denies external sounds a path to the ear and the sound of blood pumping through the body and the tingling of the nervous system starts to be audible.[4] Instead here the external sounds are so small, embalmed in the white silence of snow that they come to play with my body, close up and intimate. The rumbling of my stomach becomes the gurgling of the water pipes, my breathing relates to the humming of the house, inside and out take on equivalence. The muffled outside soundscape morphs with my inner soundings. I become the soundscape in me and from me. The explosive centrifugality of noise finds a centripetal motion to match – silence occupies their undulation.

Silence is possibly the most lucid moment of one's experiential production of sound. In silence I comprehend, physically, the idea of intersubjective listening: I am in the soundscape through my listening to it and in turn the soundscape is what I listen to, perpetually in the present. Silence confirms the soundscape as a sonic life-world, and clarifies the notion that sound is a relationship not between things but just a relationship, passing through my ears. The quiet sounds do not belong to a visual source; they sound out of silence the being of the house and myself as being within it. I cannot encounter them vis-à-vis myself but only through myself. Their autonomy is not spatial, distanced, but aesthetic: they sound the autonomy of the aesthetic moment.

In silence the visual perspective vanishes into sensorial simultaneity. The sound field is compact but potentially infinite. The tiny sounds are close up and real, to the point of being hyper-real: shiny and sharp, quasi-tangible, heard through the surface of my skin. They do not represent the real but produce a reality all of their own. This hyper-reality is local to my body wherever *I* am listening; it calibrates the little sounds on my flesh. Silence is everywhere near, and I am in that abundant silence all it sounds. In its hushed nothingness I am the simultaneity of listening *and* sound making. After the whirlwind fragmentation of noise I am an open sonic subject, ready to reciprocate sound with my fleshly body and to practise myself in that relationship. I am a sensible thing, thinging in the midst of sonic things, thinging with me in silence.

This perspective-lessness is the basis of all sound but for the most part it is masked by the ordering facility of the eye and visual expectations with which we orientate ourselves in a noisier environment and which take the listener away from his complicit relationship with the soundscape into the 'illumination' of visual comprehension. Perspective is not a sonic but a visual trait, it organizes and hierarchizes what I perceive. Sound, by contrast, enjoys the obscurity of non-sense and celebrates the simultaneity of hearing. Listening organizes not the source but sound itself, not through a dialectical differentiation but in a cumulative fashion, immersing me in ephemeral buildings whose construction I am part of. Silence emphasizes this fleeting simultaneity of listening. It brings me back to the aesthetic moment of sound, its autonomy, where its materiality is exposed to the ears in an acute way without offering a visual referent, and where my hearing is linked directly to its production rather than guided by an extra-sonic point of reference. Sounds in silence are what I hear.

The sounds in snow are microscopic, amplified in my perception. The quiet creaks, trickles and gurgles of the house pierce through me. This is not really hearing but sensing sound. Sounds are tangible in this dense quietness. I am feeling through my body whole clumps of sensate material. The quietness enhances my perception; I take notice of every whisper, hum and buzz. I feel them as phenomena filling the room and me, defining our contours as one without knowing what we are.

There is a potent tension between each creak. Individual morsels of silence are extended in my hearing to produce micro narratives that stretch around me in the compact hum of nothing. The dripping of an icicle on the balcony becomes a persistent pulse that accompanies me into the next room. I start to hear a different quality to each drop, high and low, big and small, coinciding with a trickle and a buzz from elsewhere. The lack of perspective allows me to mix them all in my perception that has long left the icicle behind. The inhaling and exhaling rhythms around the house evoke the bells of a grandfather clock heard earlier. I continue to hear it developing its narrative and add to it a base tone from a hum and a whistle from a creak I can hear, and so the story goes. The line between what really sounds and what I hear is faint in the snow. At times I hear things that I fear are not here at all, but who can tell, there is nobody else around who does not hear it too. These sounds are not about the visual source they are about themselves and how I hear them, sharp and insistently so.

This acuteness focuses the mind and alerts me to myself. The disconnection from a noisy, populated city soundscape is in equal measures liberating and anxiety inducing. In the daytime quaint sonic narratives fill the house inviting me to invent a cheery sense of self in their midst. At night however when sleep will not come worldly burglars and more abstract monsters start to inhabit the silence unsettling my listening self. Steven King's *The Shining* makes sense in the snow as I lie here in the dark. Since, what I produce in this nightly stillness is not tied to recognition. Instead, what I hear are internal demons; freed from the noise of a busier soundscape they jump at me in this silent solitude. There is a salient pull to break the silence, to shout into the icy night.[5] Or I can stay quiet and organize the heard into an order, an *a priori* language that dispels its tension. The will to hear musical qualities in this terse silence manifests such a desire to overcome the unease of hearing nothing in particular by giving it a frame of reference. However, to impose any framework and expectation onto what I hear in this stillness negates the opportunity to listen. To discover the musical in the sounds of this hushed environment destroys the audible. Instead I want to listen to quiet sounds that strain my hearing and experience the pressure of its materiality. Since, even when the whispers of the silent house do not bring forth monsters and horrors beyond all visual imagination, silence produces a burden of hearing and compels me to work out of its compact materiality into sense and meaning to be shared and spoken.

This pressure is akin to that experienced when going up a mountain. Closing my nose and breathing through it won't clear the sensation. The tension of hearing tiny sounds that pierce the ears remains, causing unease. There is anxiety in the isolation of the dark white landscape tightening the window frames. It was a strange relief to hear somebody else's child crying through the baby phone on channel A. Somewhere within radio distance is another family, hearing nothing as well. Stranger still though, when on exploring the next morning, I discovered that none of the nearby chalets were occupied.

This is a different isolation than the one produced by noise. Noise pushes vertically down on my body, compressing my chest, and propelling me outward into my breathless bodily fantasy. Silence by contrast enters me and pulls on me, inside out, stretching my nervous system through thin layers of skin, hooking my inner flesh to the very outskirts of my body. While noise roots my body on the spot to propel my listening outward, in fragments that fragment the heard in the fantasy of the listening body, silence captures my body within itself: horizontal, thick and all-inclusive. Listening to silence practises the noisy fragments *within* the body.

Noise goes towards language, from the sensibility of isolation, without reaching its infrastructure of meaning. It remains non-sense, sensate sense, contingent, passing and discrete. What we share in noise is the desire to communicate, not however the system of speaking: we meet in the dark, back to back, and know each other as sensibles, reciprocally constituted in our bodily fantasy. Noise is there before language, when we try each other in the trial of ourselves on the way to a contingent and passing self that passes others of the same temporary constitution. It is the necessary basis of language as the desire to speak, not however its lexis. Silence provides the condition to build understanding from within the compact materiality of sound: to produce a passing vocabulary from the dense quietness of its intersubjective life-world. However, silence's path towards communication does not demonstrate an opposition to noise. Rather it arises out of noise's sensitive solitude and its acute and bodily understanding of one's responsibility towards any exchange. Chief among which is the responsibility to suspend all habits of thought that shroud the practice of listening. In many ways noise is concealed silence rather than its opposite. It compels the listener to develop the sonic sensibility that silence demands to be heard.

On the other side of noise, silence promotes listening as a way towards language: not to fragment but to hear the fragments fragmenting. It works from the signifying practice of non-sense towards communication, not to abandon and deny the individual's acoustic reality in a noisy life-world as was discussed in the previous part, but to try its passing and contingent listener in a collective exchange. Working from the intense isolation of noise back into language, the sonic subject in silence is sensitive to the fragility of his belonging and knows that he deals in misunderstandings that meet in occasional and fleeting moments of shared meaning rather than with an *a priori* language base to make his point. Silence is not the language base but a basis for language to develop as a contingent and passing mode of exchange.

The communication thus proposed does not translate but produces meaning, fragile and full of doubt, as a tentative transfer of sensorial experience between sonic subjects. It uses language not to talk away from and replace the experience but to build temporary and delicate bridges between sonic sensibles offering one another their solitary non-sense. The non-sense thus communicated has no entitlement to be understood as such, these are instructions to hear and engage rather than conclusions of perception.

Quieting (2000)

Christof Migone's piece *Quieting*, created from and around a canon that is fired every day at noon from the Citadel in Halifax, Canada, composes silence. The work starts with utter stillness that bids you into its quiet materiality, 34 tracks thereof, through the sounds of its mediator: the *zipzipzip* of the CD-player. That is all the proof I have at first that something is actually playing. From there I listen to the tiny sounds soon heard that extend what I hear to all that is present to listen to. This is the fullness of silence that grasps everything as it goes along: the *zipzipzip* of the CD-player, the humming of the road outside, the faint ticking of a clock, a distant siren, all get embedded in its tracks.

At track 18 the canon is fired. Its shot snaps me into the readiness of listening, and I become aware retrospectively of the intentionality of the faint hushes, bubbles, voices and crackles that punctuated my soundscape for the last 15 minutes. The canon shot is like the clap of the Zen master readying you to fight. The fight is the phenomenological focus of listening to the work as a sensory-motor production. The canon brackets the silence and reveals the intention of the work: to make you listen, to quieten yourself and hear your own process and location of engagement. Within this intention the work is not arbitrary but full of rhythmic and purposeful encounters with the material on and off the tracks.

Quieting reduces sound to the core of its experience. It produces a shiny surface of little trickles of tiny sounds and small tactile rhythms that mirror my listening and show me my own expectations. Sound is percolating, bubbling up under this surface of quiet that covers my walls horizontally floor to ceiling. I am bound to the sonic materiality produced in my own listening imagination. The reciprocity is reflective, sharp and fast. Unlike in noise this is not a reactive intersubjectivity; the material does not digest and fragment me or make me bear its heavy weight. Instead I hear myself in this quiet soundscape, I am the centre of its weightless sounds: called by its faintness to listen and recognize nothing but myself in the heard.

Silence is at once reflective and encompassing: taking into itself all that is audible to echo back to me my own listening engagement. It provides a thick surface in which I hear myself listening to my surroundings, to gain a knowing about these surroundings from myself within them. Silence binds me into its sensorial materiality, and I start to build my own narrative between the heard and the anticipation of what there is to hear next. This next is not transcendental and certain, always already there before hearing it, but experiential and doubtful, produced now in my contingent signifying practice of listening to Migone's composition.

His work is not slight but bare. He bares sounds in silence to produce the force of anticipation that produces the work. *Quieting* makes the condition of sound audible by taking away the soundings and quieting the space as well as the listener, inviting him to hear. I am still listening when it is all gone, and my surroundings have become his tracks. In the spell of the canon shot I have attained a sensibility that lasts at least for a little while. There is a silent after-sound that vibrates the room for a moment after it has passed. It is a silence you have to write about with a soft pencil in order not to erase the quiet sounds and come to write about the motion of writing rather than the sounds of listening.

Silence frees the work to embrace the soundscape and make it resonate in its composition. Composing silence is to build an infinite frame around the experience of these sounds. However, this frame is the contingent act of listening rather than a particular instruction to hear. It happens on the composer's wish but the desire of the audience to hear fulfils it. The composer of silence composes not only auditory materiality but also stages listening as the invention of sound. In this sense silence places the composer and the listener in corresponding locations: he is the composer as producer and I am the composer as listener. This equivalence explains the responsibility of the listener and his centrality in any exchange about the heard. And thus it renders silence critical in respect to aesthetic discourse, since it shifts the focus of writing about the work to writing about its production in perception.

Migone composes his silence that enables mine. The sensorial material however is not the same at all. What we share is the canon shot as a call to listen. It is our moment of understanding in the midst of a much more solitary and personal production. The work is realized as the aesthetic moment of my subjective silence. It is ideal in its contingent ephemerality and becomes material through my fleshly encounter: hooked inside my body its silence tugs on the surface of my skin to hear it as a whisper all over my body. We share listening, not however the heard. Our meeting point is more poetic, fleeting and full of misunderstandings. Our silence is fragile, passing around a canon shot in Halifax. Communicating what we hear in this silence is like talking about thin air. It is to discuss something that is invisible, ephemeral and fleeting, but substantial in its consistency, surrounding us all the time.

This embedded parity between Migone and me has a more general application however, since it is at least the conceptual starting point for any composing and listening, even of a noisier piece.

Talking about the silent snowed-in night feels like groping for words in the dark to describe what I hear, and when I am talking the very thing I am describing is erased by my voice. This makes for a very tentative sensibility. I start to speak with the knowledge that I obliterate what I talk about with every word, and that my meaning is as fleeting and microscopic as the sounds I am trying to discuss. 'It made a certain faint ticking sound' I insist, trying to explain my fear and inability to sleep. 'I definitively heard a quiet creak in the empty house, listen. . . there. . .' My partner in communication despairs. 'You are mad' he shouts, chasing away the silence monsters. As it gets quiet again I start again, trying in whispering tones, afraid to chase away the tiny sounds, to narrate what I think I can hear, so he would hear it too.

To Have Done with the Judgment of God (1947)

Antonin Artaud's voice arrives at silence from the horrified astonishment at the noise of war. His piece *To Have Done with the Judgment of God* manifests the will to communicate as well as the insight that we can't understand each other. That what I hear in his mad rantings and ravings is my understanding which only maybe and only momentarily so coincides with his meanings, and on the whole we remain alone. Silence points out that we are working from a position of singular non-understanding towards fleeting congruence in the midst of incomprehension. Rather than expecting to be understood on the basis of a visual, substantial vocabulary and a sense of belonging in groups, we have to try and hope that some words meet in the flesh.

His voice is not speech as language, but the *zipzipzip* of the CD player audible through the tracks of Migone's piece. It is the media babbling about what cannot be said but has to be felt body to body: fleshly in the thick and glutinous simultaneity of silence. It sounds like language but is the body that comes out of noise spitting out sounds into the silence of the space before language. It is the physical reminder of the perspectivelessness we inhabit all together in our bare fleshness before language and vision tidies things up a bit and brings with it the substantial transparency of ideology. He says the unsayable in a whisper that pierces my body and makes sense within me rather than through an external vocabulary.

It is not surprising that the French authorities banned the broadcast and it did not come to its first airing until 30 years later.[6] The idea that we actually do not understand each other but only pretend to do so for expediency's sake undermines the foundation of a post-enlightenment humanism of modernity and therefore of the whole principle of the nation-state as a territorial unit of cultural and political communality: absolute similarity in relation to total difference as the basic principle of exchange and identification.

However, when we focus on the desire to be understood out of incomprehension and isolation, in utter astonishment, we can build an understanding that accounts for the sensorial complexity of the thinging (*Dingheit*) of the world and its things, objects and subjects alike, which is not constraint by national and cultural boundaries. We can be estranged to ourselves even and find to ourselves in the fleeting encounter with others in silence. This silence is not dialectical; it does not build identity out of conflict and antagonism. It is the absurd but peaceful simultaneity of subjects and objects totally other but intertwined through the trial of themselves in each other. But this understanding is not pragmatic and does not lend itself to the affirmation of identity and aesthetic judgement or to political borders. It is a fleeting understanding, produced on the spot and instantly revoked. No prerequisites of national belonging and racial identity frame it in certainty.

Artaud's sounds signs us at total others same only in our capacity to experience. However, Artaud is neither Auden's mystic nor his madman. It is not that he does not have the desire to communicate his perceptions to others, but he knows that the way through language is barred by the ideology he seeks to critique and therefore he needs to wrestle with the body. The critic who grapples with his words has to enter this position to sense experientially rather than intellectually Artaud's quiet words in order to transfer any strategy of listening to his reader. He has to work the material, inside out, connecting his fleshly encounter with the nervous skin of his visible body, to reach from his experience into a language that carries and encourages the engagement of his sonic subjectivity.

The silent 'I'/ sonic subjectivity

This sonic subjectivity is drawn in silence. It is fragile and tender and full of doubt about hearing and the heard. My 'I' hears within the quiet soundscape, through its silence, my sounds. My subjectivity is produced in this intersubjective act of listening to silent sounds that meet me in the snow. It is this fragile relationship that sounds, neither me nor the silence, but our continual and fluid embrace. This relationship is complex, intertwined and reciprocal, we produce each other. Silence shapes the subject in his sonic form. In a sonic life-world, the 'I' is produced as ephemerally as the sounds that sound the world perceived. The reciprocal intertwining of the 'I' with the sonic life-world produces a transient and fleeting subject, en par with the sounds of its composition. This intertwined 'I' is not a solid identity but an ever passing and evolving subjectivity that drifts in and out of certainty from the doubt and experience that form it continually and contingently as a formless sonic self.

Silence is a mirror that shows this formless subject to himself: echoing back from the shiny surface of ice and snow he hears himself as listener in his surroundings. All sounds I hear include my own and I am always at the centre of all the sounds heard. Silence is the place of the 'I' in the listened-to world. However, this is not a confident, territorial 'I' but an 'I' in doubt about his position, for ever awkward about being in the middle of the 'picture'. This middle is stretched out all over my perception, centripetally into me and centrifugally from me, transparently covering the perceived with its shiny materiality to reveal it and reflect myself within its quietness. This transparent cloak that bares what it covers is silence as the call to listen to the world and to myself, as things in the world.

I am not just a thing, however, but I am thinging with other things to whom I am the agent of their thinging. I am intertwined with the world of my own perception, equivalent and yet in charge through my doubt in its always-already-thereness, bound to it by the generative nature of my perception that also generates myself. What silence reflects back to me is myself as my agency in the world, as life-world.[7] Silence in turn, is not an *a priori* location or materiality but the dynamic locale of the agency of my perception. It is the locale of anticipation through which via doubt in a transcendental *a priori*, the agency of perception starts to produce both the silence and the sonic subject as complex intertwined things (*Dingheiten*).

Listening produces me as a dynamic subjectivity intertwined with the dynamic things that are thinging the life-world rather than in relation to a substantial and permanent vis-à-vis of a transcendental world. Any connection of myself to another thing or subject ensues in this dynamic. The sonic self finds the collective from his solitary agency of listening through his body rather than through language, because of it rather than in spite of it, and it is his effort to communicate, to belong, that *is* the belonging rather than an assumed and preordained position of national or cultural identity backed by an *a priori* language.

This is a political position or rather a political positioning. Not in the sense of a political identification but in the sense of a political and ideological sensibility that understands the visual substantial sense of 'I' and 'You' and 'them' to be an illusion and prefers to work on the basis of fragile 'I's passing in the dark. Silence makes apparent the consequences of intersubjective listening and politicizes sound. What is reflected by the mirror of silence is the listener's agency with which he hears the world and himself within this world generated in his signifying practice of listening. From its reflection he so grasps his listening position and eventually establishes *his* language through his body thrown into the ring of communication.

Artaud's work is political not only because of what he says but also because of what cannot be understood. His political is a sensorial political that involves the listening subject and produces the political on his body rather than talks about it. It is the aesthetico-political sensibility of sound, when it is silent or loud, that hems the political onto the experiential body and compels him to his voice rather than gives him one. The sound artist who works from the understanding of the self in silence composes a political position. He does so implicitly rather than explicitly, not about the great issues of the day made sound but about the position of understanding the great issues of the day via a sonic sensibility. The understanding of silence as the basic context for hearing politicizes composition as a process. The understanding of the self, born out of silence, politicizes the process of listening and the sonic subjectivity.

Contours of Silence (1994)

Hildegard Westerkamp's *Contours of Silence* tells the story between silences, noises and speech. All elements are equivalent, narrating through their sonic materiality rather than their acoustic properties or semiotic meanings. This is a silent piece in the sense that it is quiet, nothing at times, leaving me alone in the sparse sounds of its arrangement. The material sounds out of silence and brings me into the silence composed and talked about.

This silence is the guideline of the work. My listening happens from this line: I am in the silent moments in stillness, the noises develop around me. The silence makes me listen, imagine and try to understand the man talking about his childhood memories, the horses . . . I am trying to meet his recounting from the silence that engulfs us both again and again. The understanding I reach is the exception rather than the norm. I exceptionally understand him, most of the time I only understand myself. Our subjectivities however are not pitched antagonistically against each other. We happily exist together in the framework of Westerkamp's silence. Its moments allow me enough time to build my own contours in the space on which his narrative is built.

The meaning comes from this aim to understand rather than the expectation to know. I do not desire to know his life but get to a knowing of my own story through his narration. This is a public aural history in the sense that the main protagonist talks about events in a particular time and place. This is a private aural history in my listening. I am hearing my own life, in my time and place, through his: passing the story on, re-telling it as small narrations (*petit récits*) without emphasis on the bigger relationships and grand narratives evoked. The listener is an *écoutant* as in Roland Barthes' *écrivant*, amateurish but productive.[8]

This *écoutant* is a transitive listener, who produces the work in his subjective hearing, disregarding conventions, and who is unambiguously individual. According to Barthes it is the task of the *écrivant* to write without hesitation what he thinks: '*le fonction de l'écrivant, c'est de dire en toute occasion et sans retard ce qu'il pense*'; and in this urgent and subjective doing lies his criticality.[9] As *écoutant*, I am listening, I am a participle, a verb, like the sounds I hear. I meet the sound as verb and we are both doing: playfully walking through a geography of time and place producing a fiction of our own which establishes a temporary authority in the conviction of our urgent perception. The *écoutant* listens with unashamed fervour, hearing what he thinks, as an act of his unimpeded imagination.

This fiction does not undermine the authority of the author but reconsiders the authority of authorship. Westerkamp is the author as enabler of my own narrative, rather than the authority of his. He tells for me not to know but to participate in his narrative that I will retell and you will retell and so on and so forth. It renders both our subjectivities fluid, since paradoxically by telling his story he loses his past and gains a new one in my imagination, and my own life also is narrated in this interpretative fantasy: new highlights and memories are uncovered through his narration in mine.

The *écoutant* does not come to understand the work as transparent totality, but builds it, with the zeal and urgency of an amateur but not his naivety. He is a phenomenological subject, intent and focused, he builds from silence the core of sound. However, his aim is not the outcome but the doing, again and again, intentional, engaged and committed, not held back by conventions but prompted by his own anticipation to produce, through doubt in the listened-to the heard.

It is the plentiful nothingness of silence that mirrors him from which his anticipation generates the sonic narration as well as his subjectivity urgently, unconventionally and with conviction. What is revealed in his *récit écoutant* is his agency in the world as life-world, which produces both the dynamic condition of his hearing, as well as his dynamic subjectivity of his speech, complex and intertwined. As *écoutant* I keep on walking together with Westerkamp's narrator, through his into my own stories. The sounds are not about the listened-to but are what *I* hear in the contours of silence.

Crickets

Silent Landscapes No2 (2008)

Robert Curgenven's *Silent Landscapes No2* moves around me while I am still. His steps animate the long dry grass in the garden that stretches out before me in the dark summer night. Sitting on the terrace I can hear him wandering around out there. His crickets combine with mine, quiet but piercing, covering the surface of my stillness.

His sound track augments my own. It doubles my acoustic environment and melts with my surroundings. The horizontal layer thickens and vibrates in this encounter until his landscape encompasses mine and I take his to be my location. The narration between his and mine expands the possible and provides an entry into my bodily fantasy of where I want to be without questioning where I am. Our spaces are not conflictual but complex. I am in his space that extends from me around myself and engulfs me as it is grasped by me. I am its agency and it is a mirror of myself whose surface thickens into the place of my location.

The landscape is alive, full of things thinging in the dark. Electronic buzzes meet the occasional car driving by. These sounds lose their source in the dark of the nightly landscape. They emerge and merge in my invented space and give it rhythm and pace. They are sounds that pass what they become in my fantasy. Curgenven walks as Land artist in the solitude of his own footsteps, which offer me his landscape as my experiential reality. His wanderings through the long grass guide me into my landscape.

The piercing sounds of the crickets create the carpet to this silent landscape, outlining its contours in the dark. They sing all day but shine at night. They are the metaphor for silence as the base-tone of sound that is only heard when you listen. Cricket sound falls out of Pasnau's positivist modality as it refuses to affirm its source. He dismisses it as the exception to his rules, when in fact it is the base of sound that destroys his rulebook. Its locationality is my ears. As source it remains invisible, slipping out of the audible when seen. The locational modality of its sound is my body as transitive thing, thinging with it from its sensorial silence into its sonic materiality. Crickets are the cornerstone of silence that gets uncovered in the night. The tension of listening to such silence leads into the compositional act, producing the landscape before me in my embedded parity.

The sound of crickets announces the silence of the imminent and remains silent when all else starts cranking up the volume. Curgenven's silence is my space of anticipation of what has not happened yet. This is sonic waiting that generates continually the expectation to hear something and makes for a very focused listening. In this expectation I practise a new listening and therefore generate a new hearing of what appeared obvious before. This is not the gap that language assumes, but the gap that prepares listening. It is an obscure gap not illuminated by words, but tended to in the darkness of the contingent and private anticipation of the *écoutant*. It is the place of sound, where it gurgles in anticipation before it blurts out: it is the layer of ice on the river that holds the imminent gush of the spring thaw, and the quiet space of the library that holds the sounds of talking bodies. This sonic gap is the holdall of the voices that break it and accompany me through my listening while encouraging my own hearing.

Silence is not the space left by sound but the space at the basis of all sound. It is the basic chowder within which we meet any sound and thus it sets the space for the aesthetic consideration of any sound work. Silence is what guides me into both Westerkamp and Curgenven's work. It is their compositional condition. The art critic

and philosopher dealing with sound must understand his embedded-
ness in this condition and bring that involved subjectivity to the
listening and judging of any sound work. Being a critical listener
is listening to silence and being able to bare to hear yourself. If I cannot listen to silence I cannot really listen to anything but only hear
stuff, as just a thing of Heidegger's *Unterbau*.

Silence confirms and provides what Rebentisch and Adorno
demand: experience as the central and initiating factor of aesthetic
judgement and discourse. The ephemeral and fragmented sound work
can only be aesthetically experienced and judged if the aesthetic sensibility comes out of silence and understands the fragility and experientiality of its judgement rather than aspires to a visio-ideological
continuity and substantiality. In this sense silence is an experiential
field as well as an ideological positioning. It beckons the critic to
listen and to formulate his speech as *écoutant*: urgently, individually,
talking from the contingency of his embedded position, tentatively,
day by day a new, without certainty but perpetual astonishment at
the moments of understanding that pass his voice, and aware of the
authority of his agency. In this way a philosophy of sound art offers a
tentative critique, aware of its contrary nature of erasing what is being
discussed and conscious of the fleeting and solitary nature of the
sensorial experience which occasions it.

I can stand in front of a painting and discuss it loudly and confi-
dently with my fellow gallery visitor, when I speak during a sound
performance I obliterate what I talk about. This paradox is at the basis
of speaking about sound. That and the fact that we do not hear the
same.[10] – 'You are mad' he insists as I tell him again of the monsters
that surely must live in the attic. We do not share the same hearing
and cannot overcome this fact by placing our perception in assumed
agreement in an object in front of us.

Vision affords the space to talk and write as *écrivain*, an author
within the sturdy walls of history and conventions. It takes its space
and certainty from the alphabet, which allows it to expand beyond the
now into a substantial permanent meaning of concepts and ideas.[11]

By contrast, sonic communication is based on the fragility of time: continuous time that assumes space and is assumed by it in the unfolding of its temporality, always now. The essence of auditory meaning lies in the effort of its production rather than in any ideas produced.[12] Sonic letters are bendy and formless and do not allow for conceptualization on top of their fragility but are the concepts themselves.

Metz states that culture needs the permanence of the image and evidences this pre-requisite in the philosophical pre-occupation with vision in the West. But aural stories preserve too. They preserve not only the story, but also the access to that story by making me complicit in its narration again and again. Sound evokes the permanence of participation and production. Paradoxically, going against the bias of an enlightened humanity with its pre-occupation with the Idea, historical identity and the conventions of the nation-state, sound rather than the image preserves the human subject as a maker of culture, and therefore preserves culture as a dynamic production, rather than as concluded artefacts. The critic of sound is invited to consider the dynamic of perception rather than the monument of its materiality. He does not conclude the story but keeps on narrating and enters rather than observes cultural production.

Silent Duration

Durational work highlights this participatory permanence. It extends the effort of the material's dynamic production and renders it the core of the work. In turn the subject listening durationally is extended in his dynamic agency, producing the work and himself in an extended signifying practice of listening. This is a temporal and contingent permanence, a paradox that challenges the notion of permanence as quasi substantiality outside the process of perception. It binds the subject and the thing into a fluid embrace, permanently, for as long as it plays, and gives the listener access to the production of the work as permanently intertwined sonic self.

Piano and String Quartet (1985)

Morton Feldman's *Piano and String Quartet* recorded by the Kronos Quartet with Aki Takahashi in 1993, comes at me tentatively at first but soon swathes the whole room. Its tones are drawn out, precise and full of compositional tensions, which remain unresolved. These are not harmonic tensions that seek the proper chord to calm things down. These are sonic tensions that build anticipation towards the sensorial material outside the work in the silent space of listening. The close of the piece does not resolve this tension but foregrounds the taut silence all around, inviting an unending listening.

The work is sparse but demanding. Its tones emerge out of silence, singularly, one by one as if pulled along a firm yet invisible string. These singular tones are not buffered in the harmonious sounds of a musical structure but are suspended above the work, on a tightrope. From there they drop into the listening space, existing not chronologically but in complex simultaneity: filling the space with their precise tension more and more. This tightrope suspends the sensorial material as well as my musical expectations. I listen breathlessly holding each fragment in my open mouth, while it enters me and fills me also. The work is produced between my breathless anticipation and its sonic tension in the innovative practice of my listening. As I glide along on its swaying motion, I have to hold its fragments together on my listening body. Without that effort the work collapses, it topples down and ceases to exist as a durational suspension but assumes a sequential temporality that defies its spatial complexity. It becomes trivial and known and my body slackens into the attitude of habitual listening.

However, when worked on the body, like the drops of the icicle, it expands as a distinct but changing sound from this room into the next, soon quietly covering the floors and walls of the whole house. This cover is not opaque but translucent and iridescent, letting the architecture shine through while reflecting me. It covers its territory not its character, which it brings out. The space is silenced by the sounds of his composition but not muted. It is an abundant silence that suspends habitual perceptions and allows me to hear my space anew. In the signifying practice of my listening this space becomes a sonic room, with sonic walls and a sonic time, suggesting a sonic materiality that is invisible but produces space and time as a space and time for me. This sonic room finds its architectural permanence in my contingent listening and I find my bodily duration within its temporal walls.

Piano and String Quartet shares with other durational works the fact that its rhythms become my rhythms, however, it is more particular about my place within its duration. Feldman's quiet sounds come out of silence and clarify what silence is through my bodily experience. I can hear myself as I expand into the work and the work compels me to open my body and let it expand into me. The sounds swaying motion is taken on by my body who undulates between the centripetal motion of the discrete sounds and centrifugal motion of the work as taut fragments straining at the surface of my skin. Over time I produce a silent sense of time remote from clock time. It is the fleshly time of my swaying and undulating body. Back and forth, in and out, gently progressing ever deeper into the work's materiality. His sounds fill silence with silence to show it as materiality rather than nothingness or its conceptual frame. It is thick and plentiful, and stretches out translucently over surfaces, over me, embalming us all together in its reflective materiality, forcefully calling on my hearing to produce its suspended space.

Such silence is not a no-tone and it is not a baseline on top of which sound is produced. It is the baseline of all sounds that brings us to listening and reflects our position in the listened-to world. It is every sound as ephemeral object, fleeting and compelling, drawing us out to bring us in, permanent in our engaged temporality. It is the endurance of sound in that it is, even if inaudible, continuously what we hear. As such it focuses the listener on the basic material and experiential nature of sound, and offers the time to engage in its horizontal demand for a generative listening. Durational silence is the condition of listening to Feldman *and* to crickets. It suspends the heard and produces my own listening and what it is I hear after a while. I slip into the sound's long duration and merge with its translucent materiality which stretches me along its reflective surface. This silence does not organize itself into an idea, but enables its audition which opens hearing to an infinity of possibilities forever. It is the basic condition of the soundscape. It assumes its time through which it merges with my acoustic environment and is produced by my body drawn towards as yet inaudible articulations.

Symbolic, Semiotic and Social Sound

> Parmis nos articles de quincaillerie paresseuse nous recommandons le robinet qui s'arrête de couler quand on ne l'écoute pas.[13]

Duchamp's verbal pun rotating on a black and white spiral hints at the authority of one's own listening. It confirms listening as invention, as an interpretative fantasy that draws inwards to pull outwards, moves slowly and seems fast, and whose vigorous non-hearing is as much part of the heard as is the heard: both are invented rather than relate to an actual source of its sounding. Silence is at the base of such inventions, it enables and nourishes it and gives it a hold in the world, which as life-world is produced through the agency of listening that it echoes.

This agency of listening, which suspends habitual experience through doubt in always-already-thereness, and performs a continual production of perception, is also the agency that will ultimately drive silent experience and bodily thought into speech. Silence is the dynamic locale of the agency of perception and it is also the locale of anticipation that wills experience to speak. On its way to language experience meets the symbolic in the thick materiality of silence and searches for words in its sensorial depth.

In Kristeva's terms the symbolic constitutes the basic condition of things: it positions the subject within a socio-historically fixed subjectivity and constitutes the necessary basis of (consensual) meaning as it presents the order on which its processes depend. The symbolic in this sense is a lexical register within which meaning gains its universal halt. In the movement of language the symbolic is breached by the semiotic and in this transgression the symbolic is activated, moved on, and ultimately a new symbolic is constituted.[14] For Kristeva it is the primary status of symbolization in the thetic, which makes the heterogeneity of this process possible without it threatening (consensual) meaning.[15] It allows for the diverse and slipping nature of post-structural language while still assuring collective comprehension. Art, poetic practice, disrupts the thetic by introducing an asocial drive into the symbolic order. However, it does not truly destroy meaning but only moves it on in semiotic motility, since, at the basis of things there exists a symbolic order, which ultimately offers a replacement. The gap that is opened by such a practice invites the fetish to replace the loss of the understanding of the object as real.[16] The artistic rupture is thus identified as relative to the thetic, the artistic drive is positioned as a negative to a social system, and both are re-assured in the poetic. The poetic remodels the symbolic rather than really breaking with it. Only 'the residues of first symbolizations' are removed, the symbolic order remains intact.[17]

'Aesthetic fetishism' stops the asocial drive. It does so 'in order to keep the process signifying, to avoid foundering in an "unsayable" without limits, and thus posit the subject of a practice, the subject of poetic language clings to the help fetishism offers.'[18] Fetishism is a displacement and substitution, which assures collective signification and presents the asocial drive that produced the gap as a negative to be immanently overcome in poetic meaning. Such a fetish replacement performs an aesthetic stoppage, which arrests the generative process of perception and consolidates the complex experience in a poetic system rather than allowing for it to exist continually in contingent but engaged temporality. Aesthetic criticism as stoppage does not take account of experience and does not build a bridge between the phenomenological encounter and its description in (structural) language but simply replaces and re-organizes the fleshly bits that stick out, with material from its register of pre-existing ideas.

In sound the object does not exist before its perception and thus can never be posited as lost and no replacement can bring the breach with the symbolic back into a poetic meaning constituting a poetic aesthetic. An aesthetics of sound art has to be found elsewhere: through a sensory, engaged and solitary relationship with the symbolic in silence. Here, tiny sounds can play on my body and reveal their symbolic quality in a private encounter. Listening, as a signifying practice that embraces non-sense rather than poetic meaning, does not find to language through replacements and substitutions but through an engaged practice on the back of symbolism as a tendential quality. The language found will thus never be a poetic aesthetic or critical discourse as meta-language but a temporary signifying practice always yet again.

For Kristeva the fourth signifying practice of the text ignores the symbolic and sweeps past it in an endless mobility that is the dynamic of its dialectical *Aufhebung* (sublimation). Sound shares its endless mobility but not its dialectical dynamic: it does neither stand apart from language as its negative opposite nor does it sweep through it in endlessly synthesizing motion, instead it has an engaged and fluid relationship with symbolization. Listening does not ignore the symbolic but it does not read it as the apprehensional knowledge of a lexicon, instead it produces symbolization from the tendential quality of the sounds heard. In this way it does not breach an existing symbolization but produces a symbolic, contingently and temporarily from the tendency of the material to symbolize. What we share collectively is the awareness of symbolic quality as the symbolic tendency of things and of us as things thinging that in our agency of listening we activate towards speech. In other words we share the tendency towards symbolism, not its lexicon. This symbolic quality does not produce a consensual replacement meaning ensuring collective language, but offers the access to the production of meaning as the tendency to speak.

The sonico-symbolic subject is not a socio-historically fixed subjectivity, held in place and grouped in relation to the lexicon that governs its articulation, nor is it its negative opposite of a foundering subjectivity, solipsistic and asocial. It is a solid subject that fluidly and contingently practises its grouping, its language, as sense from the non-sense of the phenomenological engagement through the symbolic quality of sounds in silence, towards a language that meets sense at least tendentially: that is an 'expression of experience by experience'.[19]

Silence is the place where the symbolic quality of things can be heard by me: where sense and non-sense undulate and sway on my body. The symbolic quality of myself meets the symbolic quality of the things around me and we are brought together under the transparent cover of silence that reflects us both. As such silence constitutes the basic condition of things without being an *a priori* baseline. It is not always already there but is produced in my signifying practice of listening that takes it as the base of the heard, always now. It offers the subject a grip on hearing while grasping it, and constitutes the necessary basis of meaning while refuting an easy consensus. Instead it invites the ceaseless practising of a symbolic tendency from within the material heard. It presents the order as the condition on which the processes of meaning depend without constraining these processes in meaning but only enabling their contingent production which reciprocates with the production of the subject generating them.

The drips of the icicle quietly dropping into the layer of my snowy silence are symbolic not through their vertical relation with a symbolic lexicon but in the suggestive quality of their sensorial materiality stretching out horizontally, densely filling every room. My motion of language (the semiotic) does thus not breach that register to make new but still consensual sense. Rather, these sounds are symbolic as a tendency, which through my engagement with its symbolization as an interpretative fantasy unfolds and leads to language. On my way to language I pick up its symbolization as my effort of engagement with its symbolic tendency. This does not assure shared meaning. What is shared is the effort of interpretation involved and the sense of a symbolic quality experienced, not however the register of symbolization. Conversely, the language produced is a tendential language.

It does not lean on the conceptualizing power of the alphabet as the building blocks of a (post-) structural language but produces from the tendency to speak, on the taut back of tendential symbolism, words that produce a tendential sociality, a sociality that knows that understanding is the effort rather than the result of language. The history and authority of the subsequent speech is contingent: the subject drawing subjectively on his own objectivity.

Feldman's *Piano and String Quartet* suspends the sensorial material and our ability to speak about it in silence. It produces anticipation that urges towards speech and at the same time suspends the access to structural language to share the said. The silent tension that anticipates the sounds of the work are not the gaps that the authority of structural language assumes from its object. Rather their tension forms the experiential baseline of a tendential language from which individual articulation starts. The articulation produced on that tense stillness is language as a phenomenological act, words in physical action. No aesthetic replacement and substitution articulates the distended body of the listener who sways open mouthed but as yet silent along the tight configuration of its sounds. Listening on the tense precision of Feldman's swaying tightrope, we are torn out of the habit of language into the experience of speech, whose sociality depends on the effort of listening rather than a register of hearing.

The relationship between the symbolic, the semiotic and the social are distended over the chasm of silence. This is a hanging bridge suspended by tight ropes stretched over the thick nothingness of silence. It is the wobbly and swaying bridge that connects the phenomenological experience with its semiotic articulation. This is a bridge without pillars, without an ontological ground on which its words move upwards towards the illumination of meaning. Instead the horizontal slats are fastened on the sky of my own imagination as it swings from side to side to make its fragile structure sing. The connections are tendential, fragile and a matter of my own effort rather than held in the social contract of a lexical semiotico-symbolic relationship. The history of each articulation is similarly contingent, expressing a subjective ideality that is my contingent conviction rather than an assumed objective totality. Silence mirrors my agency of listening back to myself and shows me the language of my conviction.[20]

This is not everyday language but the focus of critical language, the language of philosophy and art criticism. It is the equivalent and circular continuation of phenomenological reduction: focusing language to its bodily essence. If, according to Merleau-Ponty, speech accomplishes thought, critical reflection, rather than translate its object, then critical theory needs to achieve this accomplishment too.[21] It needs to make that effort of production and invite to be read in the same embodied effort as the work perceived. And the writing needs to contain the body of the critic who met the work bodily, as *écoutant*, and struggles as *écrivant* to narrate that meeting as an aesthetic moment. This is critical language not as a structural system but as a sensorial material, which becomes the signifying moment of speech itself. This signifying moment of speech is tendential language, nascent in silence and desired out of noise. What we bring to this silence is the desire to speak and our own tongue, thick and stunned from noise it stirs in silence and finds the movement and space to speak: fleshly and bodily articulating its movement through its contingent experience rather through a shared lexicon. This fleshly speech is critical language as experience that generates the form as formless and passing experience again and again.

There is no pre-linguistic, naïve, unspoken moment, the aesthetic moment is always already in language but this language is tendential rather than full of words. Silence is the suspension of language and the condition of its production urged on by noise. This language does not work on the habitual, but utters out of shock and sensorial isolation the words afresh by stepping tentatively over the wobbly bridge between the phenomenological experience and its semiotic articulation. It emerges from anticipation out of silence and draws on the symbolic tendency to come to achieve the tendency of speech that marks us as social beings.

Tendential language is not unsaid or indirect. It is the condition of words in speech. There is noise before silence and silence before noise, again and again in circles the speech is found and lost to be found again but never the same. This language does not allude to but produces the said. Its speech does not get better, its motility is not dialectical working towards ideal pronunciation, but remains always practice: it is directly my experience of the heard. This practice of language accounts for the complexity of experience through its own complexity and can only be experienced in the same way. It is the body in Artaud's judgement not its ideology, nor its intellect. It is the body as it wrestles through the boundary of ideology towards an understanding that is physical and urgent in its uncompromising articulation. Such language is a generative extension of experience; it transfers and induces rather than translates meaning. It is not a metalanguage, which is language as the pretence of the permanence of cultural artefacts. But is language as fluid production swinging on the hanging bridge of the semiotico–symbolic motion. It is contingent speech, tendentially social experientially alone. It does not give us the grand Idea but makes us participate, and this effort of participation yields meaning as little ideas.

Silence, at once covering surface and reflective mirror, takes and gives, and entrusts my subjectivity with this same responsibility of taking and giving as the basic condition of a communicative subjectivity. The sonic subject is not assumed as a naïve, non-ideological, natural being, nor is he solipsistic, mystic or mad. He finds the tendency to be social in the grasp of silence and brings with him the awareness of himself within this grasp and the understanding of his responsibility in any exchange.

Such a sonic exchange and ultimately sound arts discourse bring out the stunned astonishment of noise in the fragile condition of silence. From centrifugal fragmentations the sonic subject finds a centripetal weight in the thick materiality of his own sounds. It is the bareness of myself in silence, the sense of hearing myself amidst sounds, perspectiveless in complex simultaneity, which engenders doubt and suspends habits, while offering me the condition to speak. This speech accepts probable failure of communication as a good position to begin language with as it avoids assumptions and pre-emptive understandings in favour of a sense constructed on the spot, again and again, however unlikely the meeting of meaning might be. Consequently I know that I will not necessarily understand my fellow men nor be understood. That does not mean I will not try, it just means that I work from the acceptance of misunderstandings into the occasional understanding, the 'moments of coincidence', that is humanity in its dynamic production rather than as historical ideology and artefact. There is meaning but not necessarily a shared sense of perception thereof.

> But as soon as one goes beyond the circle of instituted opin-
> ions, which are undivided among us as are the Madeleine or
> the Palais de Justice, much less thoughts than monuments
> of our historical landscape, as soon as one reaches the true,
> that is, the invisible, it seems rather that each man inhabits
> his own islet, without there being transition from one to the
> other, and we should rather be astonished that sometimes
> men come to agreement about anything whatever.[22]

Moments of Coincidence

The brief instants I meet Artaud in the narrow corridor of his ramblings are moments of coincidence. Our bodies pass in the tight space of his words, rubbing against each other, linking briefly to combine our non-sense in a momentary sense for me. At those moments we bind our little islands of meaning together to produce a tentative territory, a land that is not a nation-state and has no national language, that passes and leaves but a gobbet of spit on the floor. It is the astonish-ment of meeting his body in that space that draws my breath and creates our meaning rather than the certainty of a language that precedes it. The sense produced is bodily and only meets language in passing my mouth on the way up from my stomach into my head. It is speech about me and my body emerging from the coincidence with his.

Migone stages this moment of coincidence in his canon shot. The symbolic quality of its thundering noise makes us meet in astonishment. We jump in unison, suddenly aware of the solitary nature that precedes and follows this moment of collectivity. We are rendered speechless together alone, all the better to hear silence with.

Curgenven I meet in the long grass of nightly silence. That is all we share, the sense of dry grass rubbing our legs, and legs. The rest is his, and mine distinct and equally different, all heard by me. I have to want to make that encounter. This moment of coincidence is a matter of will and effort to meet in the dark beyond the safe space of my patio. Without that willingness I make no connection at all and hear but what I think must always have been out there and thus the crickets will have stopped.

Entre Chiens et Loups (1995)

Erik Samakh's piece *Entre Chiens et Loups* sounds the space of twilight when all cats are grey, and distinction is found in oneself rather than in the dimly lit road ahead. The work is a sound installation in the trees at the Crestet centre d'art, Vaison la Romaine, which comprises of autonomous acoustic modules that are triggered by solar panels. They sound the closing of the day and awake the sounds of the morning. I am responding to an excerpt of the work that sounds the dawn, when everything is nothing yet, and yet everything appears ready for its encounter. I hear in anticipation the sounds fragility as they emerge in the morning dew. I have to want to engage with these sounds, quiet, coming out of a soup of thick early morning nothingness for me to inhabit them and for them to pass me in moments of coincidence from which we both emerge and disappear into again. The symbolic tendency of the sounds, the almost somethingness and yet not quite there-ness, and never-there-before-ness, engages my listening in the new dawn.

Samakh's work invites acousmatic listening. The sleepiness of its sounds refutes them easy recognition and instead offers them as pure sounds: urgent and raw. Not quite awake yet they rest on my locational modality to find their distinction as I start to hear in them my own particularity. The work produces a knowing not only of another time but also of another place, the place of listening that is mine as the coincidence of my hearing. Small sounds spread far on the silent surface of the early morning, covering me, embedding me in the depth of their distance. A bodily knowing emerges from this blanket of quiet sounds. Knowing through sound, the sound of the quotidian as it leaves the night. Not from a symbolic lexicon but from a symbolic quality through the body that inhabits it and which it stretches in its distance.

As the piece goes on the soundscape unfolds out of the dark, the sound levels rise and organize themselves into the order of the day. I am increasingly surrounded by an uninterrupted arrangement becoming ever denser, maturing out of sound the morning breaks. A rhythm emerges and complex relationships begin to arise that take me with them and shut me out. From the sensorial dim of the earlier hour a map of the day starts to emerge. The composition makes the purpose of waking audible as more and more sounds find relationships and bond to formulate the day's geography. The sounds start to respond to each other, forming layers of motion, work and purpose. I stand in the middle of these connections; increasingly located by a more distinct acoustic environment that ruptures the sleepy bond I had with the sonic world at dawn.

The silent landscape at dawn affords me the space of anticipation: to find to the language of its sounds without a pre-conceived vocabulary; to meet them momentarily in my perception and produce a sense about myself within their silent density rather than about them. The about comes later, when purpose and order work themselves out during the day before quietening down again for the night. For now, the murmur of voices in the morning fog, the rhythms of quiet clattering, bubbling, humming and whizzing in the thickness of the dawn's silence offer a symbolic quality that I use to build my own sense of things. Responding to this symbolic tendency I get to language that is not yet structural but tendential, veering towards speech on its own track.

I can hear my agency in my listening. It reflects back to me my own position in the work and urges me towards articulation. The aesthetic moments thus produced are moments of coincidence that I work out in an effort of *bricoler*[23]: I make do with what I hear and build with whatever is at hand to come to an articulation that is critical language as practice. Out of the night's shadow a passing theory emerges from my contingent conviction in the symbolic tendency of the material towards my speech that gets swallowed by its structural companion, language, by daybreak. Before that happens however, the sounds, their materialization on the surface of the night's silence, grasp me in their emergence and bond with me in a private moment that is my moment of coincidence with the work which realizes the work as an aesthetic moment. This is the moment when my subjectivity meets the body of the work fleshly and we share a glimpse of meaning, but on the whole I am alone in our simultaneity, hoping for and producing rather than using a social bond to find to sociality in the practice of speech.

Listening to the radio stresses the solitary sociality of sound as the buzz of its tuning embeds us into its social radius alone.

Radiophonic Silence

All radiophonic sounds are born from silence and die into that silence.[24]

Analogue radiowaves present a silent surface for an abundance of sounds to cross the sightless space of its medium publicly into the non-place of private listening. This is a non-place in the same sense that sensate sense is non-sense and that silence is nothingness: the non-place of radio is its site-specificity in my living room, your bedroom, his car; it is every space embedded and reflected by the serendipitous silence of its medium in the transient time of its contingent audition. It is everywhere and no-where, manifesting the omnipresent nature of radio, while highlighting the specificity of my listening to it. Radio builds a silent territory: opaque, thick but reflective, mirroring my own contingent sociality in the public space of its invisible transmission.

The radio generates an invisible social network that weaves and bounces on the silent airwaves towards a shared sense that can only ever be a passing moment of coincidence. We share, if not the content of the material heard, the symbolic tendency of the medium. This symbolic tendency conditions listening to the radio as it at once facilitates and contextualizes its sounds. It offers the surface for the soundings and grasps them within its particularity as it stages their centrifugal dispersal as well as binds them to the centripetal weight of our discrete and private encounter.

Listening to the radio we listen to airwaves that in their basic configuration are empty, silent, but full of promise. Turning the dial on an analogue radio guides us through the buzzing of this emptiness towards moments where sound covers a frequency and exploits the depth of its transmitting nothingness.[25] The listeners are bound to this silence, even if listening to a noisy channel. It is the thick soup of potentiality on which radio emits and disperses its sounds. This silent buzzing is the metaphor for a sonic sensibility: it manifests the dynamics of a sonic sociality through its invisible trajectories and fleeting connections, and inadvertently presents the difficulties of communication: of sharing in critical language the solitary experience that emerges from anticipation out of silence and causes doubt in the heard.

Commercial radio avoids all moments of silence with a three second cut off point. This prevents the space of anticipation to extend into doubt about the heard. The sounds of commercial radio build a formidable wall, solid and permanent. Belying their own fragile emergence out of silence, they assure us that all is well. However, in doing so commercial radio also denies us an aesthetic position within its materiality. We remain distant, quasi viewers, understanding the music and voices as structural artefacts and as meta-language, not as the sensory material of a signifying practice. Radio as a signifying practice does not hide but amplifies the shared nothingness of its medium. The empty stage is furnished with voices, sounds and noise, which in their turn are audible only because of the emptiness that surrounds them and through which we gain access to them. In that sense radio exemplifies the sonic sensibility of the everyday. The buzzing of analogue radio is the cricket in my garden, which zirps all day but is only audible at night.[26] It provides the basic condition of listening and offers moments to meet coincidentally with a transitory and invisible co-audience.

This invisible co-audience becomes a vital part of my imagination when radiophonic silence becomes audible due to a military emergency, when radio stations have to stop transmitting in order for their frequency to be used to send out homing signals or to transmit secret military positions. This radiophonic silence puts a space on hold in the midst of all of us in the event of an attack. It is the bus line or the hard shoulder of the airwaves that allows a distress call to get through. Held at the edge of this silent airspace, we hover in fear, trying to glimpse its cause and listen for its conclusion and the swift continuation of the broadcast. Anxiety binds us into this silence. We are held in anticipation and trepidation, longing for a signal to make things clear and alleviate our fear. This emergency silence exaggerates the solitary and anticipating position of listening. We are really waiting now, braced for the astonishment not of a never-there-before event, but a never imaginable event even, whose distress call we will all hear alone.

The invisible paths of the radio waves outline the visual community, but the horror of the unexpected underlines the fragility of contact and the isolation of the individual listener regardless of that visual collectivity. The radio is a lonely box, it encourages the desire for communication and social connectivity but ultimately reveals their near non-attainability. Radio edges the listener on to participate, gives him a sense of belonging without however truly being able to realize such a connectivity. Instead anxiously we listen alone and are glad for the moments of coincidence that pass our ear in the mouths of invisible strangers. The opaque fog of radiophonic silence makes us listen to what might occur with anticipation and trepidation, but without the prejudices of a visual encounter. What we hear on the radio is not already there before we hear it. Rather it emerges out of its blind box, envelops us and produces an anxiety that encourages an invisible sociality and a sightless effort of speech that is sonic rather than not visual:

> I don't know what happened to Antonio Bay tonight. Some-
> thing came out of the fog, and tried to destroy us. In one
> moment it vanished. But if this has been anything but a
> nightmare, and if we don't wake up to find ourselves safe
> in our beds, it could come again. To the ships at sea, who
> can hear my voice. Look across the water in the darkness,
> look for the fog.[27]

Listening to the radio we come to understand the unease of our own loneliness motivating any communication and do not presume that there is a way to mitigate this angst. Maybe we come to accept instead that we build communication, again and again, from the anxiety of unshared fantasies, through a contingent imagination, as fleeting understandings. Radiophonic silence is a significant nothingness, signifying the social as an invisible practice of relating, tentatively from the extreme outposts of solitary listening through the effort of a tendential language.

Conclusion: Silence as the Context of
Auditory Aesthetics

Back in the snowy mountains the tourists start to arrive. The village fills up. One by one the chalet lights are turned on and gradually the noise levels rise. Now I can hear real people, rather than hyper-real monsters, walking about above my head. Their presence, their real noises, divorces me from my own sound making and listening. The tiny sounds hush away, underneath the carpet, back into the radiator, out through the chimney and down the icy drainpipes away into the snowy landscape. Now I do not bond with these tiny sounds anymore. They no longer combine with my own sonic presence in the bed of silence that covers and reflects us both. Instead they are subsumed into an extraneous soundscape, and have become truly quiet, mute. The tiny sounds have distanced themselves from my listening. My acoustic environment expands away from me and gains a perspective, its sounds slowly moving into the visual sources that sweep them up. They belong to the sound makers around me now, who penetrate through the cover of snow into my ears, disowning me my own quietness. The silent tension is broken and with it my focused listening.[28]

What remains is a sonic sensibility through which I remember my sonic self and which reminds me to bring it to any listening. I now understand that listening starts from that silent context of listening to the self in the midst of tiny sounds. I am aware of the way sound implicates me in my hearing, and sense the ideological dimension of this position even in this 're-newed' noisiness. Silence even when inaudible affords me a sonic sensibility that is the starting point of any listening and the basis of an auditory aesthetics of art and the everyday. It is the point from which listening starts and the consciousness on which a philosophy of sound art can evolve.

The understanding of oneself in silence is a pre-requisite for composition and its criticism alike. The ability to listen to yourself and to hear yourself fleshly within this audition is an aesthetic position that produces the work as aesthetic moment, continually now. The understanding of this bare and fleeting reciprocity affords the critic the sensibility to listen to the thinging of the heard and provides him with the condition of critical language as the urgent anticipation of his practical speech. This practical speech in turn does not sum up and ascertain experience, but extends it into the thick distance of silence.

The critical language of this speech comes out of silence into the passing ears of strangers whose relationship *is* their identity as fluid subjectivities. They whisper at each other and tentatively use the bridge built in silence between the phenomenological encounter and the semiotico-symbolic infrastructure of meaning to produce a tendential language and thus a tendential sociality that reflects the will and effort to communicate rather than the lexicon of communication. Silence prepares this willingness, and anticipates its release in words that come out of the doubt in the already-thereness of things and language as thing thinging, contingent and passing.

Silence elucidates the responsibility of this critical articulation as the effort of listening and speaking, taking and giving, as the basic condition of communication. A contingent sharing of one's own perceptual fantasy is achieved at the intersections with other such fantasies and depends on one's willingness to realize such relations. The sociality (shared sense) of a (non-dialectical) sonic subjectivity is ensured by the *desire to share* rather than a *shared order or lexicon*. It is the contingent desire of the individual subject to exchange the solitary experience that moves non-sense towards a momentary and passing consensual sense in a moment of coincidence. This sense is only ever contingent. It is constructed the moment we desire to share the fleeting material experience in a committed individual and generative interpretation. In this moment the tendential sociality of sound is being practised in a tendential language that articulates the symbolic tendency of the sensorial encounter and establishes a sonic sociality.[29] Thus it is the contingent relationship between the subjects encountering the artwork in the silence of its aesthetic context, rather than the relationship between artworks in their (temporal) historical context, or between the listener and the work geographically in their spatial context, that ensures a shared sense. This sense is passing and the relationships involved are complex, wholly dependent on the subjects taking on their responsibility for the effort of engagement and possessing the awareness of the fragility of their exchange.[30]

Critical language cannot corroborate sonic meaning. For a philosophy of sound art language too is a practice, is a thing thinging rather than a transcendental *Unterbau*, just stuff. It is language as the tendency to speak, to make sound, rather than language as structure. It is language not as score, as *Notenbild*, that fixes visually, in space, the temporal performance. Rather, this language comes to the thing thinging itself, and tunes in with it in silence to extend its experience in speech. That speech is not built on time and space as a dialectical baseline, but evokes time and space as they emerge out of silence: honeyed, thick and viscous; producing a deep nothingness that realizes all within it as it is realized by those within. The urgent and necessary relationship with language in *Silence* guides the listener into *Time and Space*. To hear himself there between the vertical downpour of noise, and the horizontal expanse of silence thinging his subjectivity and propelling his own voice into that place to bounce around the spatio-temporal outline of social relations.

4

TIME AND SPACE

This chapter considers space and time as they are built in our ears and unfold in our auditory imagination. It focuses on the generation and manipulation of place through sound, and pursues the production and perception of time and space in sound art work, as well as in the everyday acoustic environment.

Time and Space discusses the sonic subject post *Silence*. The uncertain but communicating subject who tries to relate because of his doubt, rather than in spite of it, does so in time and space. His aesthetic sensibility is generated in and manifests his spatio-temporal circumstance. One aim of this chapter is to observe time and space and their relationship to reflect on the subject at once generating and inhabiting a sonic place. Another is to re-consider existing philosophical ideas of time and space through listening: to hear the relationship between space, time and the subject, in the dynamic in which they unfold, refold and overtake that which seems to be already there. The sonic sensibility established in relation to noise and silence resounds space in time and time in space. Its tendential language, which, in the practical tendency of speech comes to the thing it describes thinging itself, meets the thing of space in the place of the thing of the time of its generative perception. This speech is not built on time and space as a dialectical baseline but evokes time and space continuously as they emerge out of sound: local and momentary. The listener things his subjectivity momentarily in the locational modality of hearing and propels the heard into the place of his voice to bounce around the spatio-temporal locale of his own making. In these local moments, the tendential sociality of sound is being practised in a tendential language that builds rather than describes the circumstance of its own production. This tendential language builds the time-space of listening that leads towards a tendential sociality in the practice of speech. In this sense, time and space are at once what speech builds as well as its building blocks. To take account of the complexity of this relationship, the subject in the 'built' sonic environment and his part in its building and consequently his intersubjectivity, bound to the build thus built, is one key aspect of a philosophy of sound art. The listener encounters the work in a space and in a time, which pretend to be always-already-there before their encounter, while the sonic work, due to its temporality and effusiveness questions such *a priori* situations and invites their playful production instead. This play has no purpose. No ideal objective guides or precedes the action that it is. Equally, the building thus produced is not a projection of my extension into space, but is my extension as space in time.[1] It does not produce a building but is building, continuously in the present. In this way it escapes its own *a priori* as well as the dialectical opposition of its building blocks: time and space.

The interrelationship between time and space in sound challenges the possibility of a dialectic definition that purports their autonomous discussion and pretends them as stable absolutes (*Gesammtheiten*): time exclusive of its spatial manifestation, and space exclusive of its temporal dimension. The notion of 'time' in sound is neither time as opposed to space nor is it time *plus* space. At the same time the sonic idea of 'space' is not opposed to that time nor is it space *plus* time. Sound prompts a re-thinking of temporality *and* spatiality vis-à-vis each other and invites the experience of ephemeral stability and fixed fluidity. These are not terms of contradiction or even paradoxes. Rather they reveal how time and space extend each other and produce each other as immaterial composite[2] without dialectical conflict in agonistic playfulness.[3] Listening to sound art and the sonic environment engages in the playful tensions of spatio-temporal productions and highlights the critical equivalence between spatial and temporal processes.

Pre-empting the sonic dynamic of this non-dialectical play I remove the dash between time-space and bring time and space together in the term *timespace*. This avoids the possibility of separation and subsequent return to exclusivity, and instead joins them in one complex sensory concept. The discussion of different acoustic environments and sound artworks that deal with, produce and negate spatio-temporal relationships engages in this play-fight: listening builds, trashes and connects places in time, and tracks and diverts times in space; listening hears space as sonic dynamics and produces a reciprocal time that is full of thickset materiality, and both are mutually generated rather than separately constituted.

Timespace in this sense is not a simple agreement or similitude, but an equal difference, a monistic ensemble that appreciates the individual element, time and space, and brings them together in their particularity. In this sense they '*do not accompany* (nor even parallel) each other, but function *as elements of equal significance*'.[4] According to Eisenstein, in a monistic ensemble, the individual elements, in his case sound and image and in my case time and space, complete each other without abandoning themselves.[5] Listening produces such a monistic value similarity between time and space, whose differences are worked out in a signifying practice by the 'inhabiting' subject. This experiential practice is guided by the subject's generative and complex, sensorial simultaneity with the sounds heard rather than from a meta-position, outside the motion of being in timespace. He inhabits the time and space of his own making by building it from distinct but complementing elements, to sense through their difference the particularity of place. Sound is the complex monism of being in timespace. It is the dynamic of their incongruous congruity that produces them both as a sensible, distinct but transient materiality: one builds the other in the fleeting locale of its perception from the skin of the self in the shape of the other, and so they are one as dynamic modalities produced locationally in the passing ears of the listening subject. The listening subject builds this sensible ensemble around himself to enable his voice that finally shatters his built to meet that of others, at least momentarily in his locale.

In this chapter I trail this listening body through the dynamic mound of sonic materiality and follow him into his inhabiting of sonic timespace, to rethink listening from within the time of its spatiality, local and passing, and to come to deliberate timespace as the 'process' of listening to sound. Heidegger, Hegel und Merleau-Ponty's own space and time are debated in this part of the book, to propose through affinity and criticism a timespace of sound.

Sitting in Rooms

Heidegger sits in his hut. It is a 6 meter by 7 meter wooden homestead located in the Black Forest in southern Germany. Built functionally according to the needs of his living and the traditions of the land, it is a home that extends his own body, as the body of his inner necessity, into the space, to work and live according to the order and functions of his thinking. It is the ground on which he writes and the grounding which he writes. In many ways this hut is the firm building block of his thinking that he extends into an equally solid ground of language as ontology and symbolic register. Everything is solid, familiar, located and builds the purpose that he expects to live. In his first recorded radio address and later published as a newspaper article, translated as 'Why do I stay in the Provinces?'[6] Heidegger excites about the land, nature, the conventional living as the background of his polemic:

> The gravity of the mountains and the hardness of their primeval rock, the slow and deliberate growth of the fir-tress, the brilliant, simple splendour of the meadows in bloom, the rush of the mountain brook in the long autumn night, the stern simplicity of the flatlands covered with snow – all of this moves and flows through and penetrates daily existence up there, and not in forced moments of 'aesthetic' immersion or artificial empathy, but only when one's existence stands in its work. It is the work alone that opens up space for the reality that is these mountains. The course of the work remains embedded in what happens in this region.[7]

He writes there, rooted in and surrounded by the order of nature, which he extols as the authentic experience of being. It is this Heim:

the ground of the homeland and the mother tongue that gives his world stability and the desire for which extends into his writing. He builds a place made of functional time on symbolic space, anchoring himself in the lexicon of being as identity, fearful of the pull of migration and the loss of belonging.[8]

I Am Sitting in a Room (1970)

A great number of sound artists have produced and manipulated rooms. Sitting in them as Alvin Lucier does and producing them through his sitting in there by telling us that he is indeed sitting in there. In 1970, Alvin Lucier sits in a room and records himself telling us 'I am sitting in a room, different from the one you are in now. I am recording the sound of my speaking voice.' He records this voice and plays it back into the room exploiting the distinct resonances of that room he is sitting in to erase slowly, through repetition, the semantic meaning of the words that tell us of his location. And with this expunging of his voice's semantic function the symbolic function of the room is eroded too. The repetitions erase its architectural certainty rather than stabilizing it. In the end he is not sitting in a room at all anymore. Instead he is sitting in pure sound; the reverb and repetition having performed an acousmatic reduction to the core of sonic timespace: *that* of his enunciation and *that* of my listening.

The place of performance becomes the place of listening, the timespace of production coinciding with the timespace of perception and yet a multiplicity of places are thus produced that erode the notion of an authentic room while offering me the experience of my own temporality. Sound shatters spatial certainty and builds time of fluid rooms. Lucier's voice builds a room that knows no outside and yet it has no boundary. I am in it or it does not exist. It belongs not in language and architecture but in the body of the listener, who takes up the extension of Lucier's body to extend his own. Lucier's voice does not extend into a space that is already there, realizing the inner necessity of his body, but builds the space of his voice in the time of my perception. This space is not authentic or rooted, it does not offer function or order. It is the unordered timespace of the voice as sound, which does not follow language to build a room but erases the notion of roomness in the concrete experience of words as sounds erasing their own meaning in the timespace of their building.

Washaway Rd. (2008)

Clare Gasson's work *Washaway Rd.* sounds not only the rooms but also the connections between the rooms of two people speaking on their mobile phones. One sitting still in his studio, the other running frantically through the interior of the Royal Opera House's car park, desperately trying to find the exit. The listener is positioned in a third room, the imaginary and voyeuristic room between the two, the one neither of them will ever inhabit, otherwise their relationship would have worked out or they would have never embarked on one in the first place.

The sound is set in scene by a physical installation: an old fashioned chair, as you would have it in an artist's studio, some brushes and a packet of fags, a bare light bulb hangs extended from the ceiling and a brick is cushioned on a velvety blue shelf. These items may seem incidental but they start to come together through the sound. They move towards each other outlining the timespace of my listening and witnessing the place produced by its sound. The sound does not animate this furniture but furnishes it, fills it with live, lived now, that I observe in the duration of my listening, without being seen. The sound makes the time of these things apparent without being limited to their physical appearance. In turn, in their stillness they grasp the sound, and are the listeners when nobody else is there to hear the work. They are here not as just the thing but as things thinging the room in its time.

Outside this mis-en-scène is an antechamber, a shrine of things left behind. This is the baggage both refuse to bring to the table but that we all have. They are placed there with a careless precision, full of purpose but not owning it. A mirror, some books, some pebbles.

They remain mute, as in stable, as in sitting there stubbornly and unflinchingly, responsible for the mess but not admitting it. They are the memorabilia left behind, thoroughly visual memorabilia, disconnected from the present event unfolding inside, left at the door.

The voices draw me in, and not just through the narrative but also through their intimate separation: they resonate closely in their respective rooms. These are not visual rooms but sonic rooms, which stream into the place seen and hover in its mis-en-scène. They add phantom tracks for absent voices that take their places when the conversation collapses into monologues, which it often does: not because just one party speaks, but because the listener is elsewhere. On these vacant tracks I am caught in a cross fire of patronizing care and desperate melancholia, in a space of my own making.

I cannot remember in detail what either said but I remember their invented bodies in a space between my imagination of their private places, the virtual space of the mobile phone network, and the actual space set up downstairs at Gimpel Fils Gallery in London. The bodies multiply, become other people, other voices. The work is not then about this conversation, but about conversations across spaces that do not meet, or only do so incidentally in fleeting moments, easily missed. Reflective of sound in general, it is fleeting and intangible, and what one party mourns and the other seems to run away from is but an illusion of togetherness, of one space and time shared, when probably they never did. This sense is amplified in the silence that follows. Drawn out and empty, the broken mobile phone connection slows the pace of the space until it stops momentarily in my ears: freeze framing the chair, the brushes, the fags, the light bulb, the brick on his soft velvety cushion, in the incredulity of my own listening. Gasson's work plays with and destroys virtual connections and leaves you acutely alone to rebuild them again and again, from the shreds of what is left in the room of your own time.

The space of the mobile phones becomes tangible in this present quietness. This is the solid timespace of silence, vibrating on the spot rather than moving on ahead, it produces a heavy burden of hearing.

Forced by this burden into hearing myself listening I am acutely aware of my voyeurism. I am still there, hanging in for more. I listen on for a repeat of the conversation, seeking to hide myself in the spaces between the voices, to loose myself in these invisible rooms and remain in them some more. This compulsion to remain is created by spaces and times, virtual and actual, colliding down here at Gimpel Fils. These times and spaces are not continuous or consecutive; they do not formulate a narrative path but produce a multiplicity of places within which to hear the stories. These places vibrate time and resonate space not as a series of absences and presences but as a network of concrete inventions expanding from my body as fantastic interpretations. I could be anywhere, my visual hold is tenuous. Glared by the bare light bulb, distances lose certainty and come to measure themselves on my body that is seduced by its invisible centrality. From here I build places and connect times between heard locations and my own locale. The chair, the light bulb, the fags and even the brick for all its cushioned substantiality is not an anchor but only a pre-text: a slim contour of a place that is formless and unordered timespace colliding in sound.

Resonating Places; Sounding Time

Installing sound to resonate spaces, to enter into conversation with their architectural parameters, their visual identification and everyday use, to extol their histories and expand their present circumstance evokes Gaston Bachelard's *Poetics of Space* (1964). The nooks and crannies of a dark abandoned house are opened by sound; memories and narratives replayed and invented. Sound re-invests and invents spaces; it plays with its contours and shapes it into its own time. However, Bachelard's dwelling is not Heidegger's *Heim*. The first considers memory to find the visceral body of a present inhabitant; the latter lives up to the function of the house. The listener who enters sound installations is made to inhabit the visual space bodily. He gets to its spatiality through its sound, and comes to query the place through its sonic temporality. This is not an orderly or meaningful pursuit but a physical process, a building from the murmur of the being of sound.[9] In this sense installed sound, playing at us from loudspeakers hidden in corners or openly displayed, produced by our presence, or present without us, brings to perception, and makes available to all of us the personal poetics Bachelard is excavating from his old family home.

The Dark Pool (2009)

Janet Cardiff and George Bures Miller's work *The Dark Pool* installed at the Oxford Museum of Modern Art in 2009, can only be entered six at a time. This ensures intimacy but also makes you acutely self-conscious as a member of a small team of explorers excavating an old and dusty and by all accounts long-abandoned artist's studio. The place is filled with old things: books, pictures, gramophone horns sticking out all over the place, clothing rails and wooden crates, box shaped and coffin like, staked up against the wall and sitting on the floor; little things that seem precious even in their neglect while other things were just abandoned, left without another thought. Part of it is a studio setting another part resembles more a cabinet of curiosities whose peculiar collection disabuses the mind of the familiar. The retro-look of the magazines and book covers stands not in contradiction to this statement. While the visual analogies to a past are undoubtedly there, almost stylized, the sonic elements, blurting at you from the ominous phonograph horns and singular bare speakers, retain the space solidly in an ephemeral present that broaches no past.

The voices that come at you from these smaller and larger funnels are half-overheard/ half-directed at you. They seem to narrate something long past while ordering you in your present action, an action you already committed to by activating them through a clunky sensor set up: going past with an unambiguous step and swinging your arms in an obvious effort of engagement you keep them alive while being shouted down by their own arguing voices. The voices are in dispute, never agreeing on what they see, they quarrel over the past through misremembering it and insist on its presence. The clunky slowness of these interactive devices is the dust that settles on all these items over time while the voices maintain them in the now, dark and unordered.

Merleau-Ponty's notion of space, which emerges out of Heidegger's phenomenology, accords space a universal power to connect things as place, and gives the subject the agency to perform these spatializations. However, his place is a visual space, brightly illuminated, not a dark pool of things. This visibility affords him the ability to order and arrange, to bring Heidegger's functionality to bear on the place, even if with caveats of the phenomenal. Merleau-Ponty's subject performs the unity of space through a synthesis of things experienced not as discrete objects but as distinct viewpoints, which are connected through the agency of perception producing a visual realization of place. The dynamic of this perceptual synthesis is based on the given that is its primordial ground. This ground is not Heidegger's *Heimat*, but it is a given nevertheless that weighs down heavily on present perception. And so while all else appears up for grabs, the primordial ground it stands on makes Merleau-Ponty's space struc-tural, collective and ordered.[10] It is only when faced with the night that another space emerges, one that more usefully articulates a sonic sensibility.

> All space for the reflecting mind is sustained by thinking which relates its part to each other, but in this case [the night] the thinking starts from nowhere. On the contrary, it is from the heard of nocturnal space that I become united with it. The distress felt by neuropaths in the night is caused by the fact that it brings home to us our contingency, the uncaused and tireless impulse which directs us to seek an anchorage and to surmount ourselves in things, without any guarantee that we shall always find them.[11]

Merleau-Ponty's night is, like his invisible, the space that sound makes.[12] It comes at us from nowhere opening a dark pool through which we wade, unsure but immersed, distressed in isolation but willing to find, not at its ground but within us an anchorage from which we might, in moments of coincidence, establish a passing and contingent collectivity. Merleau-Ponty's daytime space is transcendental; it is always already constituted, while the night time holds the formless body of the experiential subject.[13] It is as a formless body that I walk through the artist's studio in the dark. I cannot see to make sense but hear to understand, contingently, the meaning of my place. Sound is the invisible depth of the spectacle. It is depth not achieved through a visual synthesis but depth inhabited. In sound I am in depth. I am in the dark pool of Cardiff and Bures Miller and make sense of it as the non-sense of my signifying practice of listening.

In this depth of place my time is not guaranteed in its linearity, but is shaped in the formless motion of my excavation of it.[14] It rings out in the dark as the time of my movements, through which I activate the devices that are the triggers for the building of my space in the time that the darkness gave to my body. For the experiential rather than the transcendental subject time is not pre-ordered but concrete and formless. The dust is my dust, is my sprinkling of myself all over the place that is the artist's studio, now abandoned and at the mercy of my interpretative fantasy. No shouting and arguing will make me see their point of view. The moments of coincidence are more benign and voluntary. The chronology of my present perception is neither *abgeschattet*[15] nor phenomenally continuous, but simultaneous and vertiginous: I build in rickety shapes all manner of things from my bodily memory through which I understand the present dust, the particles of which are built from this hierarchyless past and whose authenticity or ground I cannot see.

Transition is the form of time but the sense of time is space as a thing of things thinging their own temporality, not from one event to the next but in a simultaneous drawing out of a non-chronological fantasy all that could ever be. The nooks and crannies of this studio are mine not Cardiff or Bures Miller's. The architecture is the stage for my own artistic anxieties: bottomless and in temporal vertigo. If the lights went on I could see all the fragments and tidy up, give them a function, extend their physical form into an ideological purpose to create a home in the sense of Heidegger's hut. In the darkness of this room it is only the sound that illuminates such functions and that relationship is tenuous and ephemeral, not distinct or purposeful at all. The installation erases objective time in the dark folds of its sounds and expands space beyond the physical walls of its mis-en-scène. This is subjective time embodied by the listener who has left the hold on clock time on the door. He does not synthesize this time out of its fragments to build a social reality, but squeezes a place, without greater purpose or ideal aim, out of the thing of time and the thing of space provided.

Shapes for Statics (2008)

Brice Jeannin, too, works with the thing of time and the thing of space to play with the time of their transition, which is the space that his sound builds. His piece *Shapes for Statics* was installed at The Royal Saltworks of Arc-et-Senans near Besançon in France in the summer of 2008. Up in the Jura most of what I hear is nature, but this nature is not used by Jeannin to ground us in an originary authenticity but to play with the subjectivity of time and the permanence and certainty of space. In one of the smaller building's of the Saltworks, open to the front, sit brightly lit four dozen box-like objects of various sizes, placed all over the stone floor. Some of them are silent, just sit there, but many of them are linked by thin black leads to a small cupboard of a room to one side of the open building. The door slightly ajar, I can see computers working, thinking, glowing. This is the engine room, the laboratory of the operation that is Jeannin's wonderfully weird fabrication of time through movements in space. These small objects, by all appearances made from polystyrene and MDF, emit sound matter coming from radio signals that are generated by multiple electromagnetic activities in the atmosphere. And so the thunder storm, which was meant to hit the village the next day was here today, and when it came again tomorrow I did not believe it anymore, until the rain drenched me and brought back to me the physical reality that the soundwork played with yesterday. Jeannin transports places in time with a playful disregard for reality and authenticity. His work renders senseable, in the sense of available for sensory contemplation, the idea of time not as an abstract concept but as 'a dimension of our being'.[16] However, his listener is a being that is not grounded in continuity, past, present and future. He is not anchored in the un-broken river of the flow of time but in the deep infinity of silence. In silence, time does not move but vibrates gently on the spot, it is slowed down on my body whose time it has become. Silence is not so much the base of sound as its possibility. And from this silent possibility the listener builds out of the fragments of sound that come at him in the dark the temporality of his environment. This building effort is not a synthesis but a rickety stacking of time from the middle, anyway up. In this way the listener produces a broken passing that is non-linear and whose spatialization is multiplicities.[17]

Shapes for Statics builds the passing time of the place by manipulating the temporal locality of its sounds. Jeannin brings me the other-time by making it audible in this-time. The place sounding is not here and its time is not now, it is a timespace all of its own, produced somewhere between the site, the computer room, and my auditory imagination. It is an invisible timespace created by little boxes that gather the inaudible sounds of the thunder that is yet to come, and shift time into spaces that are produced by its sounds only. In this way it plays with the stasis of visual architecture and produces visual contortions: visual spaces are expanded, invented and denied; time and space are made audible as a dynamic arrangement whose elements are equally different and generate each other not against but through each other, without a baseline, but from the subjective ground of my body. Timespace articulates a spatiality that knows it is the temporal movement of sound, and a temporality that knows it is such spatial motions without sublimating one to the other because it is so purposelessly: there is no necessity that drives thought to synthesize the motion of the two. This purposelessness is not absurd and irrational however. Rather, it is the sense and significance of the signifying practice as the concrete experience of the formless subject who does not work on the 'primordial thickness of pre-objective being' but produces from within the depth of the material a contingent interpretation.[18] This signifying practice produces neither an objective nor an ideal realization of the work, but generates a contingent effecting of the work as interpretative fantasy. Any prior objectivity and prior subjectivity is invested in this momentary and complex production but does not correct itself to its shape.[19]

Both Cardiff and Bures Miller as well as Jeannin's sound installations produce a formless place through sound. While *The Dark Pool* immerses me in its clutter and disarray, which I inhabit purposelessly through their disagreeing voices, *Shapes for Statics* pulls me into a time that is its place, just not yet. Both pieces connect times in spaces and play with spaces through time, and bring to perception invisible connections to playfully sound places that defy ideologies of separation. They interfere with one's natural attitude of perception to make one's invisible routines senseable. The weird and quaint is lit up by sound to propose a fluidity of space and remind us of a fixity of time that is not absolute but locked on our body. In this way they both release place from an objective orientation and instead produce locations on sonic maps: timespace mapped out through listening, continuously from my body into the world that I encounter through my mapping of the path trodden rather than the direction taken.[20] Such maps pronounce a different notion of geography, one that is not captured with a compass and guided by meridian lines, but that starts from my body wherever I am. Indeed this geography cannot result in maps but is a constant mapping: building and taking apart, a mobile practice of individual existence as motility.

Geography of Timespace

Early contentions of the network age and digital virtuality have, very usefully for this discussion, reinvigorated the debate around time and space. Often referring back to Heidegger and Hegel to evoke an originary, authentic sense of place and time, they retrace and update spatio-temporal theorizations, freed and challenged by the virtuality of computer worlds. In particular the discourse of social-geography that traces human interactions rather than map its territories, has contributed to the discussion of digital virtuality and the networked world in a way that makes it relevant for the discussion of sonic time-space. Socio-geographical theorizations of the relationship between time and space in the sensibility of global connectivity consider online (informational, immaterial or virtual) as well as offline (material, 'real' world) dynamics of connectivity for their discussion of place, identity and communication. They investigate social relations by taking account of virtual and actual movement, and by considering invisible relations rather than mapped correlations. Social-geography's focus on human activity rather than the abstract stability of maps, and its deliberation of material and immaterial social relations resonate with the notion of a sonic sensibility practised between sound as sensorial material and its contingent perception. It is the subject inside sound, listening, and reciprocated in its soundings, whose place and identity is tried on the fluid maps of a 'sonico-social-geography'. This reference allows me to debate sound in the context of a networking sensibility: to foreground sound's ephemeral transitory-ness; and to sketch the fluidity of sonic relations, rather than insist on abstract notions of association and cause.

Much early writings on the network age express extremes of euphoria and doom. David Harvey describes the fluidity of the network as crisis. In his essay 'From Space to Place and Back Again: Reflections on the Condition of Postmodernity', he talks about the terror of 'time-space compression'. He understands the technological and organizational shifts in the networking age, to 'annihilate space through time'.[21] For him the fluid ephemerality of the networking age threatens spatial belonging and thus produces a reactionary 'territoriality of place'.[22] Promptly staging such a reactionary ideology he goes on to suggest that 'deprived of such roots [in a native soil], art is reduced to a meaningless caricature of its former self'.[23] His fears echo a Hegelian sense of space as immediate externality, indifferent and continuous it is but a container, sublimated to time through the idea of motion; as well as a Heideggerian obsession with *Heim* as the functional dwelling that realizes the purpose of being and stands in opposition to migration and flux.[24] The dialectical basis of both their argument, and the identification of fluidity generally as crisis standing in opposition to a spatialized certainty, does not lead to a more differentiated and critical understanding of place in the network age. Rather it confirms the dichotomy between temporality as producing an inauthentic and uncertain place and space as the arbiter of its substantial and certain authenticity.

To avoid such a dialectical foreclosure I turn to Doreen Massey, who, in order to articulate time/space relations in all their complexity, considers time and space not as dialectically opposed absolutes, but discusses them in relation to their perception and conceptualization. In her sense, time and space are concepts rather than absolutes. They are a matter of perception, and also a matter of belief. Not, however, in relation to a dominant ideology but in relation to an individual ideology, or what I call a contingent conviction.[25] Their status depends on the position of the subject perceiving them rather than on their relation to a symbolic authentication. In relation to this she considers the relationship between time and space in the perceived fluidity of the network age to come from a privileged position. It is according to her ironically the White Male Anglo Academic, for whom movement always happens in relation to nice hotel rooms and the certainty of a home to go back to, and hence whose discourse does not take into account the real, experiential and individual timespace of those for whom movement means flight and the uncertainty of non-belonging.

In an elaboration of this critique she proposes a differentiation of time and space according to its 'inhabitant'.

> For different social groups and different individuals are placed in very distinct ways in relation to these flows and interconnections. (. . .) Some are more in charge of it than others, some initiate flows and movement, others don't; some are more on the receiving end than others; some are effectively imprisoned by it.[26]

Thus she distinguishes between those with control over the networking fluidity, those who move and those who are fixed by the fluidity of others. Consequently different places are produced which are dependent on the particular subject's status within time and space. There is, then, not one condition of network sensibility, not one here and now of postmodernity. Rather, this here and now is dependent on the *who* of its practice, and at the same time, the place (the here and now) thus produced *is* the practice of a subjective and contingent perception.

Je n'ai pas le droit de voyager sans passport (1968)

Julian Beck's repeated mantra 'Je n'ai pas le droit de voyager sans passport' is ambivalent. He has no right to travel without a passport, but does that not give him the privilege of place? The lack of a passport thus announced scrutinizes the notion of fixity as privilege as it denies the right to fluidity. At the same time it suggests that the fixity has to be authenticated through the power of official agency, which could give him the right to fluidity as privileged movement, officiated through a purpose and the visual documentation of identity.

We can only guess from the sound of his voice that the consequence of imposed fixity is feared, and the right to move is wanted, maybe even if it won't be taken up after all, but needs to exist as a conceptual freedom, to make his fixed space a fluid concept and to assume power over the movement of his body. Beck's repeated exclamation encapsulates the contingent and practical complexity of timespace. He exposes the illusion of a substantial belonging and lays bare the complex spatiotemporality of being in timespace as a place produced by my circumstance and my power over the mapping of my physical confines.

Moving the responsibility away from the authors of place, those with the authority of spatial agency, to the individual inhabitant, does not eradicate the threat and fear of instability, but it acknowledges that the real uncertainty lies not in a universal anxiety of fluidity, but in the individual experience of place.[27] According to Massey its 'form *is* process': places are generative, created by interaction, 'they do not have to have boundaries in the sense of divisions' and 'they are full of internal differences and conflicts.'[28] These conflicts and differences are not dialectical, they are not conflicts between absolutes, but generative and subjective differences that at their intersections produce a place for me. The process of Massey's place relates to sound's spatiotemporal complexity, while its non-dialectical conflicts identify its dynamic as agonistic and playful, rather than antagonistic and pressing for a resolution in a higher order absolute: the ideal place of the hut. Playful differences trigger the production of similarities in agonistic relationships produced in the particularity of their perception as moments of coincidence. In turn the inhabitants of these timespace places are intersubjectively produced in the agonistic practice of their perception. They meet each other in moments of coincidence that form their identity and their social connections as processes of interaction.

Inhabiting a Playful Agonism

In his report on knowledge, *The Postmodern Condition: A Report on Knowledge*, originally published in French in 1979, Lyotard identifies agonistics as the founding principle of an informational society and pursues the question of its legitimacy through narratology.[29] The narrative knowledge he considers for this purpose is not that of the grand narratives of history, politics and science, which are legitimated through *a priori* notions of truth and authority, but that of more local, contingent narrations (*petit récit*) of language games that do not seek truth but find legitimation in a practical competence. The individual interlocuters play the game through their utterances, *coups*, which are the moves of the game. 'Great joy is had in the endless invention of turns of phrase, of words and meanings, the process behind the evolution of language on the level of *parole*.'[30] This game is not without rules however. At its base is a contract, the contract of the profession, the set of people with an interest in a particular game, that holds even the most unexpected moves (*coups inattendus*) to the game plan, which ensures that play proceed without destroying its own rules.

Although agonism describes a certain sense of adversariness, conflict and the idea of progression, Lyotard's use of the term does not to set up an explicit conflict, which needs to be overcome in a higher order ideality. 'This does not necessarily mean that one plays to win.'[31] Rather, his agonism is the condition of change and exchange in the heterogeneous society of postmodernity that does not seek a singular ideality. What is pursued is not the Idea, the continuation of the enlightenment project towards universal freedom. Rather and in distinction to the dialectical conflict of Hegel's *Wiedersprüchlichkeit* (antagonistic conflict) that aims towards a total and ideal objectivity it suggests a multiplicity of playful positions *within* discourse.

Lyotard's notion of agonistic playfulness is useful to articulate the amicable difference, what was earlier in relation to time and space described as equal difference, of sound art work: the playful conflicts of the sensorial material. Agonistic compositions produce a playful conflict between monistic value similarities, the differences of which are worked out by the 'inhabiting' listener in his signifying practice of listening: parole's counterpart in sound. This agonistic listening practice produces the complexity of the work from within its depth and does neither abandon nor override the individual element for the production of a total work.

However, for Lyotard the postmodern condition is a cyclical renewal of the modern, which remains at its base and to which it will imminently return. The game-plan is the modern foundation of his postmodern play, which consequently can be marginalized as perverted or decadent, asocial or simply silly and brought back into the fold of reason where the grand narratives validate the work.[32] Composing and listening as an agonistic game with the sensorial material, played not on the board of modernism but up in the air, suspended on the unstable bridge of tendential language, proposes a different view. This practice has left postmodernity, not to return to the modern ground, but to enter the unspeakable, in silence.[33]

Parabolica (1996)

Parabolica sounds power structures of desired places built from personal determination at the intersections of train lines, machine sounds, whistles and voices. Ed Osborn's sound installation is a train set: a set of bendy tracks, suspended in the air, on which, in a darkened room a locomotive and a carriage, laden with one bare loudspeaker cone, make their solitary rounds. The motion of the train, gliding through the dark on ever changing paths, makes the suspended construction swing lightly from side to side. These swaying tracks throw intricate and fragile shadows on the floor that move to the motion of the meandering train. On the many intersections of the track hang black boxes connected to something out of sight by thin black leads that themselves wind their way to the floor and on, to meet their own shadows, creating an intricate net of motion, light and darkness. The locomotive's headlight throws passing shadows on the walls, which mock the scale of the model in their shifting play of light. Tracking the little light I follow the short train coming nearer, going away again, endlessly tracing its trajectories on unstable tracks through a space that disavows its own base.

From the loudspeaker the sound of the train's own mechanism, its warning whistle, the murmuring and humming of social space, and the voice of individuals talking about determination and change produce a vague and transient place. Nothing weighs the installation down.

All is suspended and fragile, hanging from an uncertain ceiling by invisible strings and professing no substantiality, the work is but its swaying and undulating rhythm. The tracks have no ground to stand on. No carefully produced landscape, miniature village and dinky cars give them the purpose of a hobby and the ground of a symbolic engagement. Even the recordings of social spaces sound up in the air, anywhere, connected only in my ears to my own social networking. The voices themselves come at me out of the dark; disembodied they sound ambitions and dreams that are up for grabs rather than lived. The determinations articulated are as much mine as they are theirs, and in their absence I take their seat on my journey around the swaying tracks. But then the size of the model denies me this location. I know that we are all in a different depth, not the depth of the visual signifier but the depth of the work as agonistic complex whose play we experience from within rather than relative to a game plan. This inhabiting is not simple and symbolic, but complex, demanding, changing and shifting. It is agonistic, conflictual and oppositional but playfully so: there is no outcome and no retreat into the foundation of a greater ideology, only the possibility to play on and on. The audio and visual elements conflict and play with each other without cancelling each other out. They are in agonistic relationships: pushing and shoving to produce a multitude of meanings at their sensorial intersections.

The voices are a referent in a game, which includes chance that is however not directed by the material seen and heard but behavioural and strategic, a matter of listening.[34] The voices speak this chance, narrating their determination to change their lives, while the train acts the chance and the shadows and lights all dance this chance playing agonistically with and against the desired trajectory for no purpose at all. And in this futile dance of chance I generate the artwork, the installation, as 'a particular constellation of relations' dependent on my position in relation to the dynamic of the 'intersections' which articulate directions: that of the train and of personal ambitions.[35] These intersections are not given by the construction of the tracks but generated by my own listening as the unexpected moves of the game. The trajectory of my listening practice is closer to the swaying shadows down below rather than to a sense of railway tracks and timetables. Ephemeral and fleeting, not an object and not nothing either, the shadows reflect my sonic sensibility through which I engage in and generate the work as aesthetic flights of fantasy. The legitimacy of the work is my listening practice, the parole of hearing, its competence is gauged at moments of coincidence, understood as aesthetic intersections, where the movement of the train reveals a symbolic quality that is not spoken about but leads into speech as the urgent and individual expression of 'experience by experience' that meets that of others in a shared effort of communication rather than in relation to a social contract.[36]

Building Sonic Bridges and Towns

Sound maps the world not as borders and nations but as dynamic trajectories of individuals moving, being moved and remaining in place. It reveals the world as a timespace arrangement calling for many different entropic maps to be produced. These maps would evidence the dynamics of doubt and of conviction that are the world more faithfully than its borders, mountains and coastlines. Sound gives geography and architecture a new dimension. This is an ephemeral and transient dimension, which demands at least scepticism about the primordial existence of what it is they are mapping and planning, respectively. It proposes an architecture that builds what it builds now, as a place that stands not on the *heimat-ground* but produces in rickety formless shapes its own unstable ground that it stands on; and it suggests a geography that considers the process of place, from within its depth, rather than projecting an aerial view.

Sound casts doubt on whether a town, an architectural site, a room, a spatial landmark and border actually exists as a solid (spatial) fact, however firmly it is established on a map, or evidenced in a slide collection or a photographic tourist brochure. The sonic sensibility understands place through the uncertainty of its dynamic, and assesses belonging through the doubt of perception. It focuses on the inhabitant and his production of a place for him, rather than on the symbolic weight of a collective place or the possibility of visiting it.

On a phonographic field trip I visit a location and walk through its streets. I install myself in rooms and inhabit architecture. Listening through headphones to the place recorded while recording it, it becomes clearer and clearer that neither the town nor the room is really there, I am there. The fleeting voices, my own included, the sounds all around me, create an elaborate and opaque design in the form of a town or a room, but it lacks the assumed opacity of its own architecture, its buildings, its sights, its furniture, in favour of life living now, dense, porous and complex and here. The building seen is but a façade, pretending a permanence that is contradicted by the sounds motion, which proclaims a far more ephemeral presence. The space itself is transitory, produced in the time of my presence and the space of my inhabiting it. In sound the town is stooped in Merleau-Ponty's dark night. It looses its structural shape and function and comes at me; unexpected and unordered, cherry built rickety shapes of broken mappings that invite fantasmic interpretations.

Harmonic Bridge (2006)

Bill Fontana sounds connections that exist as architectural facts but sound as individual trajectories. His installation *Harmonic Bridge* was produced for the Turbine Hall at Tate Modern, and was installed there between 16 June and 28 August 2006. He used the Millennium Bridge on the north side of the Tate Modern to install within its structure a network of vibration sensors, which turned the bridge into a large instrument. The accelerometer microphones picked up the pedestrians and cyclists as they cross the bridge, as well as the wind and weather that resonate its architectural features, and Fontana transformed those recordings into a sound installation which could be heard in the Tate Modern's Turbine Hall and in nearby Southwark

Underground station. The fact that visually the Millennium bridge, with its metal rope construction, vaguely brings to mind a harp does play into the imagination of the piece, which soon leaves the confines of its visual appearance and becomes perceptible beyond what we see however. Since this installation is neither about the bridge, nor about the Turbine Hall or the Tate Modern, it is not about Southwark Underground station, and neither is it about the sounds produced. Instead, it is about the process of inventing a place between those sites, encompassing them all as temporal phenomena. It is a place made up of the time of the motion of the bridge, the time of its recording, the time of my listening, and the time at the Underground station, waiting to hear. Fontana makes visible paths and connections not through the resulting sonic composition itself but through the production of these spaces via the temporality of a conceptual sound. The connections made are not visible but visualized: drawn from the recorded sounds and their imagined relationship to the work as site. This sonic site is generated as an interpretative fantasy by the inhabiting 'I' of the spectator who as listener, *écoutant*, walks the trajectories sounded. He is at the intersections of the work's sites and connects them through the concept rather than the actuality of listening, building the contingent timespace of his auditory imagination.

It is my relationship to this space and my fluidity or fixedness within it that produces the trajectories that is my map of the site as event. And this mapping, heard by myself only, mirrors me in the space thus produced: if I work at the Tate Modern bookshop or as a security guard of the Gallery I am probably held in place by this mirror, fixed on its shiny surface. If however I am a tourist popping by, or leisurely visiting the members' room for a glass of wine, I am a fleeting shadow in its reflection not caught in its space but freed by its time.

Fontana's *Harmonic Bridge* uses sound to produce a complex net of connecting sites, aesthetic plains and hidden ideologies. The sounds heard in the Turbine Hall and at Southwark Underground station do not actually, materially, produce this complexity but act as a sensory concept, a sensibility for the engagement with the work as site. They invite us to listen to hear purposeless connections and playful intersections, where before we stared at functionally fixed architecture. Fontana achieves a sonic sensibility, a sonic knowing of the bridge and its materiality, its environs and their relationships, that is not reached through visual expectations but only generated in a sonic visuality. This is a seeing not supplemented or aided by sound, nor by ignoring the distraction sound can bring to the visual, but a seeing that is informed and produced by the sensibility of timespace: time and space as monistic interactions, which form the sonic dimension of my subjectivity. This perception does not show me *its* place, but grants me insight into the processes of architecture and the urban map through all the traits of a sonic appreciation, and produces a place for me.

Fontana's sound installation gives me the demanding satisfaction of seeing the whole. But this is not a Hegelian totality that has overcome its conflicting elements nor is it de Certeau's godlike view from the World Trade Centre. Rather he invisibly shows me from high above a space that I inhabit in its complex and agonistic contrariness. He makes it senseable through sound, clearer than could have ever been achieved by images. His site specific sound installation produces an '*über-vision*': creating a view beyond the visual totalization and beyond the gnostic drive in a visuality that is on the ground and 'sees' the complexity at once from within its depth. It does not provide a primordial horizon within whose boundary I synthesize its viewpoints but invites me to build an invisible whole of rickety shapes that are my own grounding.

In some ways the work produces a *Gesamtkunstwerk*, connecting pieces to create something that is bigger than the sum of its parts: the bridge, its steel cables, the turbine hall, its speakers, the tube station, the way to the Tate Modern and myself inhabiting this timespace and moving along its trajectories. However, this is not a resolved *Gesammtheit*, this is not a totalizing vision, but a blind vision, generating its own 'view', from within its production. Of course the Millennium Bridge is visible, the Tate Modern and Southwark tube station are visible as architectural facts. But their contingent 'eventness', as well as the subjective connections made and paths taken between, to and away from them, are invisible, rendered perceptible in the conceptualization of the work's sonic processes: Fontana's engagement with the bridge via a sonic sensibility, and my inhabiting of the sonic timespace thus produced. It is the sonic sensibility of the place as agonistic intersections and the playful connections made that produce *Harmonic Bridge* as Chion's 'clump of sensation' understood as a conceptual clump: a clump not of the sensorial material of sound itself, but triggered by it as a sonic sensibility; a sonic appreciation and mapping of place as ephemeral networks.[37] This conceptual clump remains sensorial however, generating my imaginative experience of the work's networked timespace rather than providing an intellectual totalization thereof.

The *Harmonic Bridge* is a sensorial concept. It is the sonic concept of place as ephemeral architecture and transient connectivity made senseable as a clump rather than an outline of relations. Fontana's work embeds me in the depth of my site, which is the passing interconnection of my own trajectories. Those fleeting trajectories, not his sounds, are the work's real sensorial material. Yet it is his sounds that trigger the sonic conceptualization through which these trajectories become a sensorial concept experienced tightly on my body. *Harmonic Bridge* grasps me as I grasp it and it does not attain a certain shape but keeps on flowing and dripping into my ears as I walk along the path that *I* tread. I am honeyed into the architecture and urban infrastructure of the place not through their function and purpose but through the sensorial contemplation of site via a sonic sensibility.

This emphasis on the sonic concept producing a sensorial clump of honeyed intersubjectivity, rather than on the actual sonic materiality of the work, elaborates the signifying practice of listening as a strategy for engaging in and producing work other than sonic compositions. The conceptual sonic allows me to connect, to network and to experience the fragmented spatiality of installation and new media art without synthesizing its dense complexity. The notion of a sonico-conceptual clump of sensation affords me a perceptual complexity that incorporates time in space and space in time and shows me all four sides of a box at once, at the same time as insisting I inhabit this box as it grasps me in its honeyed sticky-ness. I cannot contemplate this conceptual sonic intellectually, but need to obey sound's demand to be heard, even if conceptually. This means to engage in sound as philosophy, not as an observation of the experience but as a phenomenon experienced. The demands for this engagement are those of sound itself: equivalence, intersubjectivity and a signifying practice of perception.

A Sonic Sensibility for New Media Art

Sound, a sonic sensibility, practised as a philosophy of art, allows me to engage with work from within its depth without having to synthesize various viewpoints.[38] Listening, as a conceptual engagement, does not compromise the work's complexity in the summation of different meta-positions; instead it highlights the intersubjective practice through which its fragmented compositions are being produced. Rebentisch's critique of the apparent lack of sensorial engagement in contemporary art's discourse, as elaborated in Noise, finds some response in the articulation of a conceptual sound. Her text argues against efforts at synthesizing the diversity and complexity of installation art into the spectacle of the installation shot or the simplicity of generic description. Instead she promotes the temporality of the work that explores the spatial processes of its own production: 'Denn die Zeitlichkeit, um die es hier geht bezieht sich auf die prozessuale Verfaßtheit des Kunstwerkes selbst, seine Konstitution in den prinzipiell unabschließbaren Prozessen der Ästhetischen Erfahrung.'[39] This temporality is not the limited time of a work's actual, objective duration, and neither is it the objective time of its viewing. Instead it is the timespace of its unfolding in perception; it is the process of producing the work as a timespace phenomenon in the signifying practice of a conceptual listening. This unfolding is generated by my engagement with the work, at the intersections of both our dimensions. Here the work is appreciated in its sensorial complexity rather than distilled into categories, synthesized into a totality or dissolved into an extra artistic discourse. The legitimacy of the work is sought through the fragmented complexity of its own materiality, however virtual, and its competence is measured in the engagement with it as an autonomous practice, rather than in relation to political-, gender-, postcolonial or social studies.

Listening not as an activity of hearing sound but of engaging with sensorial material, plays with the agonistic fragments of a work and innovates its complex temporality in the space of perception. And it is my presence in the depth of the work through which, eventually, out of great doubt an aesthetic interpretation will emerge. The aesthetic fantasy thus produced, however, is as transient as the work, and includes the dimensions of the aesthetic subject *within* its articulation. This agent produces an aesthetic discourse out of language suspended over the chasm between phenomenological experience and its semiotic articulation, that, up in the air, offers itself to communication in moments of coincidence: fleeting instances of understanding in the midst of misunderstandings between those involved in the discussion of the work. These players are not involved in a game with a plan, however. They do not play on the board of modernity, which redeems each solitary or silly move within an overall shared scheme. Instead they play from the physical memory of silence that gives them the fragile positioning of their bodies, which presently, sound, conceptual and real, weighs down on, immerses and fragments.

Digital installations do not necessarily surpass analogue installations in terms of their fragmented complexity, but they call attention to how we inhabit the material to build the work from its fragments. Digital works construct space and time beyond physical objects in the virtual world, whose intersubjectivity is not only suggested and invited but programmed as facets of technological interactivity. In this virtual life-world I generate the site and my trajectory through the site in the time of my surfing in it. I open rooms, unfold them, shed light into them. I close them, it goes dark again, the music stops, it does not exist anymore, at least as far as I am concerned.

The Legible City (1988–1991)

In Jeffrey Shaw's *The Legible City*, a work created between 1988 and 1991, I can cycle through three different cities, deeper and deeper into their architecture, manifest by big looming letters, replacing urban architecture with fictional stories, standing in for them in size and shape, building the city from the notes in its archive. This information I gain from the catalogue rather than the piece itself, which in the context of the Museum looks like a bicycle in front of a projection screen, nothing more nothing less. This description explains the work's outer parameters. It reads like a manual of how to look at this thing and what to expect from it, implicitly acknowledging its awkwardness in the exhibition space. The work itself, as Fontana's *Harmonic Bridge*, is not its immediate self, is not what I see, but is the invisible links made and the trajectories projected. It is neither about the bicycle nor about the letters looming large in front of me, letting me through and drawing me into an urban 'science-fiction' landscape that I build and navigate at the same time. It is not about the screen, a known protagonist in installation art, nor the monitor, another familiar face. It is about invisible relationships: the relationships of the bicycle to the Museum, to the effort of my own tautological cycling, perpetually moving more to move more. It links this space to outside spaces, to real motion, to the city as concept, as a sonic city understood via Michel de Certeau's 'Wandersmänner', who blindly walk the city of their own trajectories, following 'the thicks and thins of an urban 'text' they write without being able to read it.'[40]

The Legible City is not relational but makes relationships available for muscular appropriation. My cycling mimics the playful agonism of listening: *Manhattan*, *Amsterdam* and *Karlsruhe* become sonic cities in the sense that they are produced by my sensory-motor gestures towards the computer programme. Playful pedalling triggers the production of buildings and sites in the contingency of its activity. And in turn the cyclist inhabits these intersubjectively produced timespace places in the process of his perception. The town remains in doubt as a solid architectural fact. It becomes a space of moving through, a timespace, that doubts identity as a stable sense of belonging and focuses on a dynamic inhabiting, contingent and subjective instead.

It is the sonic conceptualization of Shaw's textual city, sensed via Fontana's *Harmonic Bridge* and clarified via de Certeau's 'Wandersmänner', that creates the work's reality as a produced event and allows me to engage in its fragmented and immersive complexity from *within* rather than replace the experience with a summary of its processes or an image of its installation. Sound as concept allows me to understand work, sonic or otherwise, through a sonic sensibility: to grasp and be grasped by sensorial simultaneity; to appreciate its unexpected moves, out of the darkness, and respond to them rather than sublimate them to a visible source; and to engage in the temporospatial complexity that immerses me without seeking an extra artistic discourse to produce a distance between me and the installation from where its elements can be synthesized into the totality of the work. A sonic sensibility transcends the technological pragmatism as well as the visual drive to know the work and invites a more visceral engagement: that we should all sweat to build our cities, which remain forever ephemeral – words only, iterative, fleeting through streets built by those very words.

However, digital interactivity is not intersubjective: the cyclist only pretends true reciprocity. In fact the subject that comes back at him is the technological subject, measured and shaped by the tools of interactivity. The digital life-world is ruled by its programming devices rather than his experiential imagination. It mimics the phenomenological reality of sound, but curtails the imagination to its technological parameters. The work in its technological actuality is limited by the commands of the programme, the screen technology and the actual possibilities of cycling. It most definitively remains an 'actual world' rather than what David Lewis terms a 'possible world': a world that has no indexical link to an actual reality.[41] Listening, by contrast, produces a sonic life-world as a possible world, one not tied to the logic and consequences of the visual world but questioning its supremacy and expanding its logic. Sound creates a proto-digital timespace that allows for the imagination of possible and even impossible worlds beyond the one we pragmatically refer to as the real one. The sonic produces a proto-digital consciousness, realizing a digital virtuality as a real rather than programmed virtuality, well before the first computer was switched on to create a 'second life'. Conceptual sound precedes digital interactivity through generative intersubjectivity and supersedes it in its true virtuality: a virtuality not bound to the parameters of the software or hardware but spun in the generative perception of my interpretative fantasy. Listening as a conceptual practice asserts the iterative force of computer language without being tied to the constraints of its programming.

This is the reason sound, a sonic concept and philosophy, can illuminate the complex timespace of digital works at their networking intersections without limiting them to the parameters of their real, actual virtuality, but opening them up as conceptual virtual constellations: I am not visiting *Manhattan, Amsterdam* or *Karlsruhe*, the place is not there, it is here, where I produce and experience it. The letters produced in my cycling are but another façade, in motion but nevertheless stable and impenetrable. The digital technology that facilitates their generation outlines a permanence, however virtual and fleeting, that is contradicted by the motion of cycling, which confirms the far more transitory presence of the inhabitant on which the concept of place hinges. The place is its movement. It is my moving through it. Temporality and spatiality expand from my body and on my body. I am at the centre of this expansion, timespace myself.

Narrating Temporal Places/Migration

Sound describes my movement not against a permanent landscape but generates a fleeting permanence as the continuity of my production. It evokes the permanence of participation and preserves culture and society as dynamic productions. This emphasis on production rather than on finished artefacts and maps draws attention to the listener as producer rather than consumer of his culture and society, which in turn are understood as invisible and transient assemblages rather than solid and fixed products and contracts.

Since sound is always in its own place, that of its sonic material not that of its source, sound measures migration not in terms of a here and a there, of boundaries and nation-states, but in relation to the presence of the migrant, the inhabitant of sound, wherever he is. It deals with displacement by always being in place, and complexifies the idea of belonging and loss beyond the dialectics of fixity and fluidity in their collaboration on the notion of place as a complex and dynamic timespace.

Linked (2003)

In Graeme Miller's Linked project my walking with a short signal radio receiver activates a level of place that is invisible, hidden in the frozen history of the visual architecture. Linked is a project produced by Miller in 2003 collecting, placing and re-placing voices and sounds that narrate the communal resistance and the nonetheless ensuing destruction of houses and communities for the building of the A12 in East London. The stories are moving, intimate and personal, talking at you from transmitters that are sometimes clearly visible and sometimes remain hidden. These voices are always there, talking now for over five years, narrating their stories and experiences. They let you in to the space behind the façade of what is visible right now, ushering you into a place that was visible once and might still be, if you only come to listen.

This sound walk is equally sad and magical. I listen to the effort of voices re-building houses and gardens, parks and churches that were once on this spot where a big A-road dominates the soundscape now. These voices are like ghosts hanging in the air confronting me with their loss and their memories. They narrate an aural history not archived and dusty, but living on its own land whose present inhabitants will know less and less about it. I wonder what the lady who peered out from behind the net curtains of her 1930s cottage thinks when she sees people in walking boots and with headphones, approaching the light mast outside her house, arms high up in the air clutching a little black box.

'The cat buried under the motor way, the turnip murderer, the tribes at the bottom of the garden, the tree houses, the lollipop shovel, the evictions and Bell's whisky', all come together to build a place in the time of its sound. Sometimes the reception is poor, and the voices fleet in and out, barely audible but still certainly there. This fragility adds to the phenomenological understanding of this place as a sonic timespace. Sometimes sounds of radio signals and disturbances have been composed into the track, deliberately communicating the connection rather than the content, allowing me to sense another space where all these people dwell. In this sense these transmitters do not reveal only one layer of invisibility but hint at many more, if only we had the right receivers to hear them. This understanding is part of a sonic sensibility: understanding the compromise of the visible and participating in the generative multiplicity of sound.

Linked is very particular and local but it is also general and about any locality. It is about place as time and space, inhabited, moved through, away from and into. The geographical location between the Lea Valley and the Wanstead Leisure Centre is articulated through the movement of history heard in my passing, which together produces the place as spatial motions. Sometimes this is a bleak and particular place, as when I walk across Wanstead Green in the rain trying in vain to find a voice to guide me. Sometimes it is joyfully referential, as when I sit in a bus-shelter looking at a half blue painted MOT garage listening to a guitar backing-track. However, any auditory imagination engaged in is pitched against the loud rumble of the A12, which reminds me why I am here and that this here is marked by the road that wiped out all the possible histories that are asserting themselves in these transmissions.

'It is like walking in time', says one voice as I cross Kings Rd. The voice accompanies me a while as I walk on, talking to me about the sorting office and re-tracing daily trajectories of the past. But slowly it fades. These voices have to stay in their dedicated area, re-iterating their stories again and again as I walk on in my own present. However, my perception of this present is different now, it is augmented by the layers of sonic possibilities discovered through these transmissions, which expand and implode the place seen.

The past is not an additional level on the surface of the visual architecture but lodges in its depth from where it generates its shape invisibly. The people who came towards me out of the Tesco's Superstore at the Greenman Roundabout seemed incredulous at my standing around with a black receiver box pointed heaven-wards. The thin layer of our semantic reality allows for the functionality of living. Its quest for purpose hides the complexity of being as motility, always new and now, and pretends, even if temporarily, that all is always as it is: that the A12 is a given fact, an *a priori*. The shoppers are not invited to question the building process but live pragmatically with and against the architecture presented. This relationship is anta-gonistic; each moment is the resolution of a conflict, a higher order ideality immanently dragged into a new conflict soon equally resolved along the trajectories of purpose. *Linked* by contrast sounds absence as much as presence. It constructs a playful agonism of place through movements of chance and exchange without a game plan. That is the place of migration, willing or against my will, moving and being moved, due to visible architectural facts and other less visible struggles.

Chernobyl (2008)

Peter Cusack records dangerous locations to produce a sense of place through sound. The information about where I am and what it is I am hearing is given in the sleeve notes. Each track is carefully explained as to its visual location and event. But when I do not read those notes, when I only listen to the place unfolding it is the absence rather than the presence of the place recorded that becomes most apparent. I am not there, he is. I am in the place of his construction that is not the place either but an interpretative fantasy created between the heard and the seen, in the woods somewhere, far away from what we know.

I know I am in Chernobyl a place that rings in my memory as the epitome of nuclear catastrophe, fuzzy news images and the dread of the nuclear age. The title unlocks and locks the piece. It places it and makes the place invisible. I know where I am but I do not know how to hear it. There are some clear signifiers: the Geigercounter, Russian language, songs and animals, but the place is produced beyond the semantics of the material at the intersections of what I know and what I can never know but only sense through the tendency of humanity to symbolize to each other what we fear for ourselves.

The first track produces an outline, a tentative moving towards the heart of the place, its nuclear 'hot spots'. Cusack is wandering around the periphery, testing the radiation levels, approaching the danger, while protecting himself with a Geigercounter from going too far into its depth. The centre of the recording however is not the radioactive mound but his voice. The regular calling out of radiation counts creates the rhythm of the space as place produced at the intersection between his recording, my listening and the time of the place itself. His counting is the measure of its outline not as numbers but as voice, as presence that pervades all through the work. My movement through this sonic space is dependent on his. He is the guide, invisible and often also inaudible but there, at the core of the material all the same.

The spoken numbers decipher the sounds of the Geigercounter, and the wind, its blustery gust, embalms them both in a place that is not Chernobyl but my imagination of it, produced from somewhere between the facts of its real danger, the memory of the catastrophe and its subsequent cultural production. The Geigercounter dial ensures we do not go too close, and so we hear the periphery, we hear the outline, that frames the centre of danger that makes *Chernobyl* what it is. It is a complex place at the crossroads of all these dimensions; a timespace that expands the notion of the present by insisting on the presence of its past. The Geigercounter is the cricket sound of *Chernobyl* that is always there if you are listening. It is its baseline on which the place is built: an ephemeral, invisible baseline that has the power to determine place.

Cusack measures Chernobyl, measures the invisible layer of radiation that makes it what it is and records that presence as a simultaneous absence. I can hear why it is not anymore what it was. That it is a town deserted apart from those who stayed to tidy up and those who came back nevertheless as there was no reason to be anywhere else. The space between the place as idea, as catastrophe and danger zone, and as home and homestead, but utterly functionless, is audible in sound.

Cusack says the CD should not be listened to sequentially but as independent frames: facets and moments of place. And so I take his advice and listen carefully to individual tracks, out of sequence, producing my chronology of the place. In this way his recordings produce documents of a place, but crucially not a documentary. The work is not textual. It does not offer me to simply read the place, to understand its narrative, but narrates it, shapes and forms it as a formless and complex place in my ears. I gain no geographical bearing or knowledge of the place. But I get a sense of place that is about its fragments moving and moved rather than its map or structure. The work measures absence and presence, existence and non-existence in the paradox of sound that is always there.

Where at first I fill its sounds with cultural references, abundant on the subject of catastrophes, nuclear and otherwise, those get relinquished in a close listening, and all that is left is what I hear. Having curtailed the cultural references I am left with nature, the nature of *Chernobyl*, which is what its culture is increasingly left to be. The act of evacuating cultural references leave the birds sounding odd and different no more like nature recordings but laden with the evacuation that made them audible in the first place. And so when I read about how the power is reversed now and that instead of flowing out of Chernobyl to power other cities and places, the current goes in the opposite direction to help with the cleaning up still in process, I catch a glimpse of an entropic place. The sounds of electricity in an abandoned environment resonate its playful futility: crackling and buzzing to furnish not a nation but to squander resources of function and modernity. These sounds escape assessment in relation to notions of truth and value but find competence in an existence that gets its purpose from a whole other network of legitimation.

Having abandoned the immediate and textual level of place, I am left with a sense of deep and buried networks, fragile connections that intersect unseen as the tendency to live in place. The electricity sounds this tendency, sounding backwards the purposeless play of its being. In that sense Chernobyl is like any other place investigated below its semantic appearance, safe the electricity runs the opposite way, which is what strips it of the semantic layers that hide the purposeless under normal circumstances. The tracks resonate this playful futility as a network of narrations, songs, frogs, chickens and boars, singing out the invisible place that is the town in its own absence as its continual sonic presence.

A lot of these sounds are terribly beautiful, not dangerous at all. Danger does not sound itself, but sounds in its absence what is there when it is too dangerous to be around. And so these sounds do not offer an understanding of an analytical kind but expose the discrepancies, the inability to judge and to know what danger is. It is almost impossible to describe some of the tracks without emptying them out into what they are visually thus taking away the fragile bond between the recording and its sensorial experience. Phonography needs to be talked about not for its sounds, but for the effects its recordings produce.[42] They are affective and emotive: the real danger of the place recorded is the emotional investment made by listening. This affective listening produces knowledge, not however analytical knowledge but the knowing that comes from inhabiting the sensorial material in its depth. *Chernobyl* is a sonic document that questions what knowledge we can have about a place and instead gives us knowledge as a knowing of our own space and time somewhere between the facts of its semantic architecture and the buried networks through which we live in them.[43] Such phonographic documenting invites a radiophonic imagination, in the sense of a 'blind' listening, a listening that has evacuated knowledge and seeks to get to a knowing out of the dark from the unexpected moves of sound.

The Timespace of Radio

La RADIA shall be . . .

7   An art without time or space without yesterday or tomorrow   The possibility of receiving broadcast stations situated in various time zones and the lack of light will destroy the hours of the day and night   The reception and amplification of the light and the voices of the past with thermoionic valves will destroy time.[44]

Radiophonic production has the potential to produce site-specificity not tied to place as architectural fact but as the temporal location of my auditory imagination. It has, as suggested by Filippo Tommaso Marinetti and Pino Masnata, the potential to refute logical, objective space and time, and opt instead to produce a temporality of its very own: dark and honeyed, unfolding through its own material and making us follow its rhythm blindly. Commercial radio however does not work that way. It does not use the potential of its own medium to question objective time, but paralyzes temporality in its strict schedule. It creates an *über-objective* time, the time all clocks can measure themselves by, and it demands of our body to bow to its timetable. And it does not respond to the spatiality of its own medium either, which has the potential to create a possible world rather than insist on relaying the one we see. Radio is not the space of the concert hall or the white rooms of the gallery that frame the work and hold its interpretation. Its signal reaches my car, my bedroom, my walking through town with a portable radio. It is my place wherever I am produced between the timespace of its dissemination and the timespace of my auditory imagination. But that potential freedom is mocked on commercial radio where Classic FM's *School Run* and 5live's *Drive* get you in a very particular spot and resonate its function. The potential remains, however, and late at night, when the purpose of the day has been spent, durational work that knows no operator and no beginning and end can play with what the radio could be in a timespace specificity of its very own making.

Klang;Zeit;Klang (2006)

Benjamin Federer's work *Klang;Zeit;Klang* was produced as part of a series of durational works broadcast through the summer nights of 2006 on Swiss Radio Lora. His piece sounds, by and large, like a sine-wave synthesis, produced principally from sounds that resemble those of a small clock tower in a little mountain chapel and the lapping rhythms of tidal waves. But this source is imagined rather than insisted upon, and in any case it erases itself over the time of its play. The piece makes audible the passing of its time and the rhythm of its site. Not particularly fast nor particularly slow, just passing all on its own. This passing happens in my living room as it emerges from the sightless space of the radio, illuminating my site in its time, composing my timespace in the duration of my listening.

The sounds are not composed, as in synthesized and hand crafted out-of-each sample. They are automated in Max.[45] The sonic processes roll on, hour after hour, within pre-set parameters, filling time through algorithms that extend its space. This automation ensures at least a relative equality between composer and listener. Federer, too, appreciates the work through listening rather than composing. He is here with me listening through the small hours. He allows time to hurry forth rather than hold it in his hands, painfully crafting every second. This is boundless time, quickening my ears. The rudderlessness of its passing provokes the notion of a democratic radio production. It is a time that belongs as much to me as to him or to anyone else listening while always retaining its own space.

The pulse of seconds and minutes turn my radio into a great big grandfather clock. And when I wander through the house at night, up and down the stairs, I can always hear it, faint and far away, or ever louder and distinct, measuring my roaming through the space by the sound of its time. When I am close I can hear the shoreline of the intermittent tidal sounds and the small, insistent, almost irritating rhythms of cymbal like sounds that my body cannot shake off, even when they temporarily hide underneath larger fragments of time. Here, in the unrelenting repetition of these small high-pitched particles the work turns into a dance track for tiny people.

This invitation to occupy its auditory endurance bodily and dance to its temporospatial rhythm all through the night is fostered by the circumstance of its broadcast. It is important that this piece is transmitted in the dark of the night via the radio rather than sold as a CD box-set. Box-sets are a display of abundance, a collecting of sonic material rather than an invitation to listen. This is the work as archive, where the sleeve notes and the cover design determine its appreciation. By contrast, the sensory aspect of the work emerges from a sustained effort of listening. And such a continual signifying practice of listening is more easily engaged in when the work comes at you, unexpectedly, in the middle of the night, without a name or cover, without a beginning or an end, undetected, when it proceeds to take the time it plays rather than the time I planed to listen. In this way the work takes over my space, rendering my circumstance its timespace, and I am quite happy to surrender. It is the playful purposelessness of listening to such a vast quantity of sound broadcast over the airwaves that in the end seduces me into an inhabiting mode, and it is my durational listening that gives the work its contingent purpose.

It is over time that this involvement happens, through the night, as it were. It requires devotion, takes time. I need the duration to sense the dwindling air in Federer's work and focus on the bony timespace provided in its stead. After a while even the grandfather clock that had previously provided a visual referent has gone. Now the work is sheer timespace: I am not listening to anything anymore, but only hear time passing as my space. In a sense I am listening to listening. The line becomes bare and the air rarefied in these small hours. Federer's time is thin and almost static. I experience it beat-by-beat, pulse for pulse. The space has shrunken to its time only. There is nothing left to move: I am only ever now and quite brutally so. Sound offers me only the present moment, which is paradoxically most apparent in durational work. I am kept painfully in the now for a long time. I am caught staring, captivated by the realization of my own time flowing away on the spot of my listening. I am enveloped in my own process of being forever now. It is in this now of durational sound that the notion of timespace becomes perceptible rather than conceived as an abstract concept.

Conclusion: Into the Now of Listening

Durational radioworks give me time to build the space of my listening and to live in this built through the building of it as Heidegger has me do, without his function and purpose however. Instead, the timespace of radio resonates permanently Merleau-Ponty's night that 'starts from nowhere': 'it enwraps me and infiltrates through all my senses, stifling my recollections and almost destroying my personal [visual] identity'.[46] Sound emerges out of the darkness as unexpected moves that are greeted by a vertiginous listening that grasps them as it is grasped in their permanent presence. The radio offers me things from the midst of their thinging, blind and immersive, permanently now. This now is the width of my perception; thick and sensorial, sound illuminates its dark depth.

It is not that sound changes anything on the objective consciousness of time or space, but that it introduces another time and another space that it sounds together as timespace. This is the timespace of the phenomenological subject who performs a reduced listening which does not hear a place but produces its own. This perception is neither idealist nor realist but works on modalities, on possibilities, that remain separate and yet, as concepts of engagement influence and challenge the possibility of the world that we pragmatically refer to as the real one. These are the interpretative fantasies of Adorno's formless empirical subject whose reality is experiential rather than deformed into the functions of a transcendental world. The currency and import of these sonic possibilities is not readily apparent, as it does not fulfil the demands of a visual society. It sneaks in, in the dark of the night, into the now of visual existence, asleep, and bit by bit convinces it of its ambiguous and formless truth that is not its untruth but another truth that is awake in its dark depth. This sonic now is not a moment of intentionality geared towards the form of time and space as functional entities, but an expansion of experience in timespace. It is the present place of the aesthetic moment that is the work tuning on my body, which as its listening subject is central to the production of the here and now condition of the work as place. This timespace place is intimate, produced by the body at the intersections of its dimensions, and these dimensions are not neutral but relative to the dynamic of the world as a network of agencies.

Conceptual and actual listening distinguishes the inhabitant who makes the sound from the commissioner who is in charge of the habitat. In this sense all sound installations are, at least potentially, socio-political echoes that bring to light space as produced between fractions of society, the ones who move in it and the others who commission and determine their movements. By coercing me to inhabit a sonic timespace that builds rather than assumes its built, sound installations orchestrate a socio-political sensibility. Listening to work I am honeyed into the invisible connections of its obvious visual elements and sites as in a conceptual clump of sensation. From within the depth of those correlations I practise rather than synthesize its intersections and come to a view of the work that encompasses its complexity and echoes mine.[47] In this way, sound installations do not document socio-political ideas but incite me to understand the natural attitude of my aesthetic positioning in social and political terms.

It is my intersubjective motility that produces the site as socio-political dynamic, and places me as an aesthetico-political subject within this dynamic. Listening, conceptual and actual, makes me appreciate my own inhabiting on the gradient of power that moves time and space. Thus it is on the level of the aesthetic, the sensorial engagement, that we can discuss the political, not as a pre-existing theory but as a fluid reality generated in the process of listening to sound. And it is in the depth of this sonic sensibility that we encounter the other in our own timespace.

> It is true that the other will never exist for us as we exist for ourselves; he is always a lesser figure, and we never feel in him as we do in ourselves the thrust of temporalization. But two temporalities are not mutually exclusive as are two consciousnesses because each one knows itself only by projecting itself in the present where they can interweave.[48]

Merleau-Ponty's interweaving is my moment of coincidence that is achieved through the effort of exchange and through chance, in the agonistic relationship between listeners. Where he sees a social horizon, a cusp of experience in a collective consciousness, that solves for him the problem of the always already there-ness of the transcendental world for a phenomenological agency within that world as life-world, the sonic life-world knows no such pre-built. Instead it builds, permanently from the doubt in the collective moments of place that can be shared through mutual effort and chance.

The utterances of this exchange play on the ephemeral and transient board of a sonic sensibility. They do not fill the space of expectation and do not speak according to a symbolic lexicon, but build a timespace phenomenon in the articulations of their practical speech. This is language as sound that makes sense through its sensate expression. It does not offer meaning but triggers the effort to produce the meaning of the said at the moment of its encounter and holds the listener to his responsibility in every exchange. It accepts the unexpectedness of each utterance and works from perceived misunderstandings into meanings that are contingent and passing but produce the structure of the place through the temporal spatiality of its perception. This language has no prior function but finds function as a formless garb in the moments of coincidence that are the vertiginous meetings of sound on the silent baseline of its audition. This engagement is affective; it demands an emotional investment in the work and in the subject of exchange. The continual presence of perception is the moment of this emotive engagement. This now is the dynamic of a pathetic encounter, which offers the emotional as a critical faculty of listening. The next chapter *Now* will focus on sound as 'pathetic trigger' that invites perception as an emotional investment and produces the work from this involved subjectivity. In this way the closing part elaborates on the specificity of sound on the basis of its complicit subjectivity via the listener's emotional investment, and from this specificity confirms the relevance of a philosophy of sound art beyond sound and listening.

5
NOW

What I see is always already gone, it engraves itself into my retina as a picture of its past. The visual object is the permanence of melancholia and history. Sound by contrast is the permanence of production that uses the permanence of the monument and discards it by gliding over its form to produce its own formless shape. Like the alphabet the visual invites and enables intellectual reflection of an over-there and of another-time, remote from its own production. It enables thought and engenders the idea of purpose and order by forfeiting the immediate sensibility of its own materiality. Vision captures, orders and disciplines space but it does not see the simultaneity of its time. Visual history is the absence of what is not here anymore as it used to be, or the presence of something that was not here before. But at every moment this absence or presence is certitude, a visual condition, that is unambiguously present or absent. In this sense vision observes Hegel's dialectical history that strives towards an ideal community that has overcome the inner necessity of its conflicting elements in the higher order organization of the present State. Time and progress are the forces of this history, pursuing through reason and logic an objective manifestation of space, defined by the values of sheer presence and sheer absence, and an ideality achieved through their antagonism. There is then no ambiguity of being simultaneously, only causes, consequences and results.

Sound on the other hand *is* its immediate sensibility: unordered and purposeless, always now. The opaque and ambiguous process of living manifests itself in its sounds, and appears in an engaged listening that hears the invisible murmuring at the depth of Hegel's State. It is the unseen but heard simultaneity that develops community not as an ideal manifestation of reason between subjects, but as their coincidental meeting in affection. This is not the history of hegemony and homogeneity but of transient and heterogeneous participation. The sonic location is not the absence of the past but is simultaneously the past and its present manifestation. One does not cancel out the other as both live in the invisible discontinuity of my sonic sensibility now. Sound demands the vis-à-vis and sounds the now as a complex duration of past and present continued together in the action of perception. This now is absence *and* presence in the paradox of sound that is always here. It is not linear or intentional, but extensive and intersubjective: permanently and only here on my body which generates its timespace through the complex effort of my listening, which I extend into my contingent speech as sound again.

Sonic Pasts: An Afterthought

The following contemplations do not constitute a conclusion but merely present an afterthought: a reflection back on the heard, a fleeting thought after much listening. A philosophy of sound art cannot sum up experience but must remain a philosophical experience, proposing a strategy of engagement but not conclude the heard. It is at best a passing theory, constantly present, and careful not to replace the experience of its own subject. But this constant present passing has a past and a future, and thus this final part looks at the other-time and the over-there of sound and the listening subject, to confirm the binding present of sound, while taking care of the place of memory in its production.

The perpetually present sonic subject pursued all through these pages, does not flounder in a solipsistic world without past or future and without an elsewhere of social connection. A philosophy of sound art cannot exist in a vacuum but by sound's very nature experiences its sensorial materiality in its contingent context. The sonic material is not an existential materiality, denying any influence and existence outside its experiential self. But the past of sound is a present past, and the space outside sonic perception is only known as a present knowing. Both are Bergsonian relations, becoming senseable (matter) in a now that is simultaneously perceptual and affective.

Time and Space finished in a moment of now that took in the complexity of its timespace existence and tuned itself on the listener's body. In this way the preceding part did come to suggest the emotional investment that generates the complexity of a timespace moment and declared the emotional as a critical faculty of listening. However, this pathetic remained largely stated rather than explored, and neither its specificity to sound nor to the agency of listening was truly explained. This final chapter *Now* will focus on perception and its relationship to sensation. It will debate sound as 'pathetic trigger' that invites an emotional investment in the work and produces the duration of its aesthetic moment through the agency of memory in its present action of perception. In this way this closing part elaborates the specificity of sound in relation to the extensity of timespace that involves not only the spatiotemporal complexity of every moment, but also that within the depth of every moment: the place of another time and another space of sound. It will consider the duration of the sonic now in order to focus on the process of its form and to illuminate its extensity. As a consequence of this double extensity of sound, as timespace and in timespace, this last part will reconfirm and clarify the centrality of the listener, who echoes these extensities from within, and suggest how affection coincides with perception, and how it eventually drives his practical speech to meet meaning in moments of coincidence that are themselves extensive moments of now.

Since, the sonic sensibility, as I suggested in *Time and Space*, is not bound to an actual materiality but produces a conceptual sensibility, the impact of this critical sentimentality is relevant beyond the deliberation of sound work and the acoustic environment. Conceptual sound allows its consequences to effect aesthetic experience and its philosophy in general terms. It is through the conceptual sound, the sonic sensibility, that the false permanence of the visual is imploded into a complex extensity that includes the objective as the subjective objectivity of every prior sensory encounter, without those becoming an *a priori*. This does not lead to critical theory conventionally understood, but invites the listening engagement of a transitive listener, who builds, from the emotional pull of the sound, the work, not as a transparent totality, but as a passing possibility. This possibility has the temporary authority of his convictions, which lead to theory as the urgent speech of his practice.

Sensation and Perception

Noël Carroll's ideas on art and emotion offer a starting point to debate the relevance of the pathetic for sound art. He laments the lack of critical consideration of how 'works engage the emotions of the audience'.[1] And although his essay on 'Art, Narrative, and Emotion' focuses largely on narrative art, he contests that his observations are 'eschewing an expression theory of art in general'.[2] The reason he theorizes emotions is that he understands them to organize perception, to focus attention and to motivate behaviour. They are according to him, a functional device whose inclusion in art theory helps us to understand how a work influences and manipulates the perception of the audience.[3]

In his view perception and emotion are distinct, separated by the idea of cognition. The thing, or event perceived is a key to the emotional state that is pursued by the work. His emotions are not ambiguous but focused within the direction of the work as text that borrows its emotional charge from a cultural lexicon. These are then decoded and according to him 'elicit broadly predictable responses in standard audiences'.[4] And although he acknowledges that it is our own emotional constitution that we bring to the work, it is nevertheless a lexical and pre-existing constitution that defines us within the terms of a cultural emotionality. 'Within the boundaries of certain cultures, there are certain criteria concerning which emotional responses are normatively correct.'[5] The assumption of homogeneity of author and audience ensures the success of the emotional material in achieving the objective of the work. Ambiguity and the uncontrollable aspect of artistic production and perception are not discussed. It is then not emotions as in feelings and sensations that Carroll is concerned with, but the lexicon of emotions and how it is called upon by the artist to engage and motivate the audience. It is this connection between emotion and cognition that allows him to introduce the emotional into aesthetic discourse without fearing its corrupting force, as Plato did, when he banished art from his 'well-ordered commonwealth', since he feared its emotive charge would pull its inhabitants towards irrationality which could harm the cohesion of the Republic.[6]

Carroll rejects Plato's fear because he takes cultural cohesion and homogeneity as a given. This allows him to understand emotions as elements of a lexicon employed for the manipulation towards the proper meaning of the work. Plato by contrast saw no such homogeneous base, but a fragile attempt at a commonwealth easily destroyed by emotions. For Plato emotions are not cognitive but stimulate and corrupt experience, they undermine reason and logic and threaten his Republic through dissent, vagueness and ambiguity. Carroll's lexical emotions are reasoned, they are rational, do not threaten but enable the production of the work as an objective ideality. They are not sensations but sentiments: thoughts that signify sensations. In this sense his deliberations do not grant us any insight into emotions or subjectivity, and not into communication beyond a structural precept either. Instead they diminish emotions to a means of achieving the right and correct reading of the work, and reduce the work to the propaganda of its content thus produced.

By placing emotions as a trait in the object perceived Carroll separates the object of contemplation from its contemplation. In this way he insures the permanence of the object beyond its moment of perception, and turns sensation into cognition. Similarly he does not consider the perceiving subject in its subjectivity but only in relation to its cultural position: a position, which is not debated but assumed. What I called earlier contingent convictions he calls 'defective beliefs'.[7]

For him emotions serve reason and it is only defective representations that encourage wrong cognitive states that might threaten rationality. In this regard he follows John Ruskin, who, outlining his notion of the 'pathetic fallacy' declared that,

> If you find that a thing which generally 'does so' to other people (as a gentian looks blue to most men), does *not* so to you, on any particular occasion, you will not fall into the impertinence of saying, that the thing is not so, or did not so, but you will say simply (what you will be all the better for speedily finding out), that something is the matter with you.[8]

Carroll shares this assumption of truth independent of perception but triggered by it as its logical and reasoned consequence and through this belief shares Ruskin's romantic aesthetic: articulating the idea of collective emotions he re-introduces a romantic subjectivity and a romantic notion of sentimentality into art discourse, and revisits the notion of a collective sensation, ein Weltschmerz, one universal pain, that directed the dream for the greatest Republic of them all.

The romantic void proffers a visual sentimentality that is anchored in a certain place and describes an unambiguous absence that is substituted imminently by an ideal presence: the collective sensation; a response gleaned from the repertoire of what Carroll terms garden-variety emotions.[9] This sensation is external rather than internal. Guided by a lexicon, it is a learned emotion, always already mediated by knowledge. Never does true feeling, in the sense of unexpected sensations enter the picture. That is where madness lies, the irrational, the unaccountable.[10]

When in *Time and Space*, I discussed Peter Cusack's work *Chernobyl* I acknowledged that there were cultural signifiers: frogs, song, the Russian Language, the Geigercounter, and I also appreciated that when reading the sleeve notes there was a recognition of fear and dread to do with the abstract notion of nuclear catastrophe. However, the sounds themselves did not offer me these ideas.

These are cognitive elements gleaned from the lexicon of fear, sadness and loss, which in their actuality we do not share but only perceive through the physical sensation of our own fear which leads to the action of our generative perception of what it is we fear. The action of my blind perception makes the work more complex, ambiguous and even incomprehensible, but also more real: when the sonic material comes at you, out of the dark, and envelops you in its blind formlessness, no cognitive sense guides you to the right emotion that will promptly deliver the objective totality of the work. Instead, you generate, in your own signifying practice of listening, the sensations that you inhabit as the work plays. Sounds' emotions are not cognitive but generative. They are the coincidence of sensation and perception, involving the body in their simultaneity from which it produces the perceived. Listening that is not causal or musical but truly performs an epoche that focuses on sound as sonic material has no key to its emotional charge, but offers it only a fleshly body that has left the sense of material objectivity to live in the dense ephemerality of sound as itself.

According to Henri Bergson there is between sensation and perception only a matter of degree not of kind. 'There is hardly any perception which may not, by the increase of the action of its object upon our body, become an affection, and, more particularly, pain.'[11] It is the impulse of pain, of a sensation directly on the body that leads to the action of perception that produces the work. When the distance is greater these actions remain virtual, when however this distance is nil then affection and perception are one and the same, and the action of perception becomes its real generative force.

Sound produces this simultaneity. There is no distance between the heard and the listener. I can perceive a distance but that distance is heard in the location of my listening. The distance *is* the heard: it is the separation as perceived phenomenon. This coincidence of the sonic material and the listener was made particularly apparent in *Noise*, where I argued for the way the weight and exclusivity of a noisy-life world bears down on us. I conveyed how Merzbow's sounds assault our senses until we have submitted ourselves totally to his world of noise. His album *1930* makes the intersubjective 'I' contract into its sound: it renders any sensory-motor action of listening an action on our own body, which is held in a tight reciprocity by the vertical charge of his noise. Likewise I discussed the way in which Otomo Yoshihide's noise contorts our ears: his noise induces pain as a concrete rather than a cognitive sensation, and acts directly on the body.

> Suppose the distance reduced to zero, that is to say that the object to be perceived coincides with our body, that is to say again, that our body is the object to be perceived. Then it is no longer virtual action, but real action, that this specialized perception will express, and this is exactly what affection is.[12]

And so at this zero point of noise, affection drives and defines the perception that engenders it, which makes listening simultaneously an affection and a perception and defines hearing as a real action, generating the work. However I also noted that noise is not different from other sounds, it simply amplifies the lack of distance between the listener and the heard. In this sense noise makes the simultaneity of perception and its object more apparent, and thus it serves to demonstrate the coincidence between affection and perception in sound in general. All sounds that come at us, out of the darkness of listening, vertiginous, as unexpected moves, bind the fleshly body into its materiality and generate the work in this sensate encounter, close up and real. This presents the importance of the affective for sound art, and it confirms the need, articulated in *Silence*, for the critic to be embedded in the material: to come to an understanding of the work from *within*; to generate in his contingent inhabiting the work from the affections of its perception, and for those two to meet on his body which thereby becomes the body of his perceptual action; 'the object to be perceived'.[13]

In relation to this I discussed Cristof Migone's *Quieting* whose silence is realized as the aesthetic context of my listening. The piece stages my place within its silence, where I build the work from its coincidence with my body. And so, it is my body that is the real object of my generative action of perception; Migone's work is the affective trigger of its production and mirrors it. This embedded parity between the listener and sound in silence is the starting point for any critical listening: it is the action of sound on the listening body, which triggers this body into the action of perception that produces the work and the body itself. This action is affective. Affection in this sense is the agency of perception, which is triggered by the affection of its object on the listener. Such affection does, as Carroll suggests, motivate behaviour, but not towards the ideal objectivity of the work, but towards its contingent production. The process of this contingent production is the signifying practice of listening that produces its sense as non-sense, as sensate sense.

Sound as 'Pathetic Trigger'

> All violent feelings have the same effect. They produce in us
> a falseness in all our impressions of external things, which
> I would generally characterize as the 'Pathetic fallacy'.[14]

I borrow Ruskin's interpretation of the term 'pathetic' denoting strong and even violent feelings, and call the affective action of sound on the listening body a 'pathetic trigger': an affect that initiates the action of perception through which its sensation is realized. However I use his pathetic not to denounce the fantasies thus triggered, but to explicitly stress the imaginative possibility of sound. I am suggesting that it is precisely the pathetic coincidence of sonic perception that triggers the engagement necessary to produce the work in its sensate sense. This generative perception is not an error, it is not irrational and solip- sistic; it is not a fallacy nor is it falsifying but generates the truth as an experiential truth for me. The cognitive that ensures language and cultural cohesion does not come before this pathetic truth, it is not a given, but is triggered by the pull of its affection. Sound triggers knowledge as sensate knowing: passing but concrete, testifying to experience but never concluding it; and thus it does not start in language but searches for it.

This insight recalls my astounded wordlessness discussed in *Noise*: besieged by noise I am concretely the formless body of my sensation, speechless but ecstatically at one with my object of perception. The affective action of noise is 'unsayable' in and of itself, but it urges towards speech as the practical expression of my own experience.[15] Noise triggers the desire to speak not as cognitive trait but as affection, whose action drives the sensate subject to the effort of communication. Since sound happens on the body, this affective action is a real action and will eventually lead to speech: when my body meets your body in the simultaneity of both our perception. The resulting voice does not make sense, but reciprocates the passing body, which in this way is not reduced to preconceptions but produced momentarily and reciprocally in that coincidence. And so emotions do not destroy community, and they also do not lend it their lexical reasoning. Instead, they produce community, not as a Republic, but as a formless and transient meeting of listeners whose bodies momentarily coincide in their effort of speech.

In *Silence* I discussed the emotion of anticipation as the agency of such a practical language: instead of taking external cues, silence mirrors my agency of listening back to myself, and drives me to the action of language through the agency of my emotions that I encounter in my simultaneity with its sounds. It is from the tension of listening to one's own body in silence that the phenomenological encounter searches out language. This tension and anticipation are the affections that drive perception from the parity of myself with the heard towards the generation of its object: the body of my practical speech. However, these tensions are not the gaps that the authority of structural languages assumes. Instead, they form the experiential baseline of a tendential language. No aesthetic replacement and substitution articulates the fleshly encounter of the listener who moves, motivated by sensation, towards his own expression. And this expression is again affective action that meets the body of the listener in the simultaneity of his sensate perception.

The communication thus produced does not transfer meaning but activates the making of sense: it prompts listening and invites engagement with what we do not know. The bridge between the sonic experience and its articulation sways under the weight of passing strangers, who meet without a ground to stand on, in a moment of their simultaneous crossing. The connections produced are tendential, fragile and a matter of my own effort rather than based on the social contract of a lexical semiotico–symbolic relationship. These strangers, in order for their exchange to be a real action, are not insured by the distance of language, but coincide momentarily in the closeness of their affective speech. I considered this coincidence with reference to vocal noise music. In particular I discussed how Keiji Haino's shouts collapse the distance of language and meet my body in the sensation of his utterances. His screams intertwine our bodies beyond structural language in the affective action of our coincidence. It is from this affective coincidence of perception that critical language must find its motivation and direct its action for it to bring about a philosophy of sound art that puts into words the condition of its object without disavowing it.

This insight gives affections, emotions and sensations an important place in sound art's criticism. It highlights the affective action of perception that generates the work, and confirms the sensate and complicit permanence of participation that preserves not artefacts but the access to cultural production. The pathetic does not facilitate easy recognition but compels a contingent production of the heard, and so it confirms the listener as a maker of culture rather than as witness to its monumentality. Emotions thus understood, are not the exclusive pursuit of women, madmen and 'natives', unable to focus on facts and losing themselves in sentimental fictions; and neither can they be distilled into a singular and universal romantic vision. They cannot be passed off as trivial to artistic production but must be debated centrally, since, without this affective engagement we do not *experience* but only *read* work: we will understand the processes of its text, but not its affective perception. And it is the affective perception, produced in our own simultaneity with its material that will get us to the speech that utters rather than replaces the work. Consequently, it is the affective action of listening that criticism has to engage itself with in order to pay justice to the work heard rather than the work as it emerges from a 'correct' reading: according to the knowledge and expectation of its meaning.

We can read kitsch as an aestheticized and ironic version of sentimentality, mocking emotionality and closing the space of its production. Kitsch is the modernist plug to sentimentality and emotions, separating the artwork from feelings and re-investing it in the categories of modernist discourses. In this sense kitsch is a thoroughly modernist practice that exercises its renewal in a postmodern stance. It demonstrates that however heterogeneous and apparently democratic the postmodern, it never allowed for real emotions to enter aesthetic discourse. The pathetic is too unyieldy, too irrational to be let into the modernist city of art without falsifying its ideology and barring its renewal. Because, the affective questions the autonomy of the work and focuses on the autonomy of its aesthetic production instead. This autonomy comes out of *Noise*, which crashes modernist barriers of obliging politeness and re-asserts experience over modernist reserve; and it is confirmed in *Silence*, not as a spatial, a substantial, but an aesthetic autonomy: it is the autonomy of the work as aesthetic moment produced in my sensate perception; and it is this now of sensate perception that is autonomous. This is, then, not the autonomy of categories that relieves the artwork of purpose by way of a certain *a priori*, but the purposelessness of the signifying practice of listening that finds to meaning and collective purpose through the affective effort of its perception. In this way the pathetic foregrounds the responsibility of the listener and thus stresses the ethical dimension of perception.

For Carroll his cognitive emotionality contributes to the discussion of ethics. According to him we learn to understand ethical decisions and frameworks through the emotions triggered in artworks: they are signposts for the recognition of good and bad, fair and unjust, etc. 'Fictions that encourage us to value what is morally valuable are *ceteris paribus*, to be assessed positively from the moral point of view.'[16] In other words, cognitive emotions translate and communicate moral values. However, like his emotions, these values too are assumed to be shared within one culture and normatively deployed. These, then, are not truly felt but reasoned values that do not bring emotions to moral philosophy but further underpin its focus on logic and reason. Without the modernist framework of the nation-state or that of self-regulating market capitalism, however, values cannot be assumed to be collective either, but need to be worked out in an effort of engagement that involves a contingent production rather than cultural projections.

Emotions do contribute to ethics, but their values cannot be assured in a rational code. Instead, affective ethicality is part of the process of my contingent conviction: it is worked out in my emotional investment, my effort of engagement in any exchange. Such ethics is a dimension of the agonism of perception and exchange as I sketched it out in *Time and Space*. It comes out of a non-dialectical and playful conflict, and describes a moveable and generative production rather than a fixed code. In other words the ethical dimension of my emotions, the moral value of my perception, cannot be measured in relation to culturally agreed moral principles, but is worked out in the agonistic moment of my perception.

This identifies ethics as a dynamic of engagement rather than an Idea. It is the dynamic of the agonistic game between the listener and the sensorial material, played out, not on the board of modernism and its metaphysics of morals,[17] but on the ground, from within the blind depth of the material, by the inhabiting subject. The values highlighted by such an ethical practice are those of movement, of engagement, rather than of the moved through. Consequently there are no amoral subversions possible within art, since, every work triggers emotions whose perception is its ethical production and whose values are a matter of chance and exchange without a lexicon to rationalize them. The only amoral stance is non-engagement and the replacement of the work through prior ideas.

In other words, the ethical dimension of art concerns the responsibility of the audience to engage in the work's affective production and to produce their own emotions that reveal to each listener his own ethicality. This clarifies that the ethical dimension of the work, played out in its affective perception, is not to do with what it might represent, but what it produces in terms of an aesthetic sensibility: as affective subjectivities, and in terms of the affective action towards our coincidence with others. It is the listener's own emotions through which he produces the work and in this sensory-motor action gains access to his own ethical convictions to meet those of others in moments of coincidence. In this sense the consideration of a work of art via its affective engagement brings to light the ethical dimension of identity and social exchange. It reconsiders the socio-political dimension of art, which we discussed in *Time and Space*, and clarifies that art's socio-political quality is not to be found in an ethical message, gleaned from a lexicon of cognitive emotions, but that art brings out the social and political through the ethicality of the audience's affective actions of engagement. This confirms the socio-political dimension of an artwork, maintained in the conclusion of the last chapter, not as a socio-political ideology, but as an aesthetico-political sensibility that concerns the ethicality of my affective perception of the work. This contingent sensibility is produced in the extensive duration of the aesthetic moment, in which I am, reciprocally, generated as a momentary subjectivity. As such a passing and intersubjective subject I continually produce and re-assess my ethical convictions through which I find to the social tendency of my experience in the affective action of my speech.

The Duration of Perception

This aesthetic moment is the now in which sensation meets perception. This is a now whose quantity is hard to grasp, as it is fleeting and ephemeral, and yet it has a duration. We inhabit this duration in our sensate perception that produces the work and our subjectivity. However this production is never concluded, no objective totality is ever produced. Instead, the work remains the dense moment of our affective action of perception. We inhabit this moment and from within it we extend it as it extends us. It happens in our timespace place and produces it; at the same time it extends its time and its space by taking account of the other-time and the over-there of its perception. The duration of this affective now of perception verifies the process of listening as it clarifies the centrality of the listening body and explains the extensity of its timespace.

In *Time and Space* I wrote about the complex value similarity between time and space, whose differences are worked out in a signifying practice of listening. This listening practice builds the place it inhabits from the incongruous congruity of time and space as the timespace location of my perception. I discussed how this perception does not show me *a* place, but grants me insight into the process of *my* place through its sonic dimensions: transience, simultaneity and immersivity.

It was the complex simultaneity of an immersed perception that allowed me to gain access to installation and new media work without having to synthesize different viewpoints. And so I grasped Bill Fontana's *Harmonic Bridge* from *within*: from the intersections of the work's sites that I linked in a conceptual practice of listening; to experience the installation from the depth of its complex and interweaving possibilities rather than understand its totality. But I did not at the time consider the past of the bridge, of the Tate Modern, of Southwark Underground Station, of the artist or of the listener, and it is, according to Bergson this past that grants the present perception the duration that gives it its extensity. The past meets the complexity of the present work in the aesthetic moment of our affective perception and implodes its timespace complexity into an extensity that takes account of the 'inside' of timespace: the place of its duration.

Bergson's memory is an affective action of the past in the present that furnishes the duration of its aesthetic moment:[18] 'However brief

we suppose any perception to be, it always occupies a certain duration, and involves, consequently, an effort of memory which prolongs,
one into another, a plurality of moments.'[19] Memory produces the
sensations that trigger the perception through which it enters into a
present moment, which it extends into a plurality of moments into
which it slides.[20] The duration of this moment is the now of present
perception to which it gives its depth. 'Every perception fills a certain
depth of duration, prolongs the past into the present, and thereby
partakes of memory.'[21] This duration is not long in its actuality but
deep in its perceptual extensity. It explains the brutal now of Benjamin
Federer's work *Klang;Zeit;Klang*, which I discussed in the last part,
since it amplifies the duration of its aesthetic moment by going on
and on. This is not a paradox, the long duration of the work increasingly focuses us on the small but extensive now of our perception.
Playing on, hour after hour, Federer's work gradually erases the composition's referential meanings. The recognition of the clock sounds,
the ticking and the tidal waves, steadily fades away in favour of the
sensation of time. The sounds, relieved off prior knowledge, come to
produce an intense now that is the presence in which memory finds
its space to produce a timespace extensity. I need the long playing
nature of the work to get to its real duration which resides in the
moments of perception that do not dwell on the sounds as source but
produce, through the affective trigger of memory the sensation of the
now. That is the real time of Federer's work, a constant now that does
not move but shows us its complex extensity and lets us inhabit its
depth.[22]

This memory is neither functional nor intentional; it is affective.
It produces the actions of our present perception without holding
them to a datum or chronology. And so the bridge, the Tate Modern,
Southwark Underground Station, Fontana and me are all realized
not in reference to a shared past, but through the affective trigger of
my own past, which extends my present perception. This past is not
a collective memory; it does not work according to a cultural or symbolic lexicon. Instead it is my subjective objectivity: the unordered

simultaneity of everything I have ever experienced, which rushes into the present moment in which it finds a contingent priority and sensate sense. In this way my affective memory extends the duration of perception and expands the timespace place of sonic perception by adding the extensity of its time, and thus it elaborates the idea of sound as a Chionian clump of sensation.

Chion's clump of sensation, which I introduced in *Noise* and described in *Time and Space* to be produced by an actual *or* a conceptual listening engagement, renders the reality of a perceived visual object real as a sensate reality: as an object sensed rather than seen. The potency of this sensation is confirmed through the simultaneity of affection and perception in sound, and it is expanded as a result of acknowledging affective memory as part of the listening process. The clump attains a duration, which memory prised open, and within which the subject slides to produce his affective action of perception: deepening the present complexity through the extensity of another time. This extensity is generated by my affective engagement with the work, at the intersections of my dimensions in its depth. The time-space triggered by Fontana's installation is the place of my subjective objectivity that has abandoned the duality and knows it is one in the contingent duration of my present perception. It is from within the depth of this momentary duration that I practise the intersections of Fontana's sites in their extensity rather than assume their correlations. And so I produce the work without synthesizing discrete viewpoints, but by generating the sensorial complexity from my body at the intersections of its dimensions with those of the work. In this way I come to a 'view' of the work that encompasses its extensive complexity *and* mine.

This confirms and develops the potential of actual and conceptual listening to experience the fragmented and multilayered spatio-temporality of installation and new media art without synthesizing its extensive complexity from different viewpoints.

'By allowing us to grasp in a single intuition multiple moments of duration, it frees us from the movement of the flow of things, that is to say, the rhythm of necessity.'[23] And so we grasp from our simultaneous position within the depth of the material the complexity of its timespace *and* the extensity of its timespace that extends us twofold too. This double extension however works not within a network of intentions and neither does it support the chronology of time. It produces not a dialectical presence but the presence of my subjective objectivity, that is to say the subjectivity of my interpretative fantasy that is my participation in the work's narration. My memory drives my agency to act upon the perceived, to extend it and give it the depth of its duration, which is the extensity that my interpretative fantasy furnishes with references from another time and another place, and my body inhabits in the now of its present actions towards the future that takes it as its past. This is the production of the work that meets the production of language in speech, and I am at the centre of both these actions.

From this centre of action I do not synthesize but produce complex extensions on my body, which will meet those of others in moments that form the chance of our exchange. For Bergson the role of my actions 'is solely to prepare the reaction of my body on neighbouring bodies.'[24] His notion of reactions, of body upon body, describes the condition for tendential language, which in sound, due to our simultaneity with the body heard as a close and contingent 'pain', triggers the real actions of speech. These actions of speech produce language as contingent utterances between the unsayable sensations experienced in noise and the whispers of silence. In *Silence* I suggested that noise though unsayable, is not pre-linguistic. That its affective moment of perception is always already in language, but that this language is tendential. It presents the tendency to speak rather than an infrastructure of meaning, and demonstrates the desire to communicate, as yet without words. I also noted that it is silence that triggers the affection of anticipation that creates the condition for the production of language. This language does not produce substitutions, it is not a post-structural renewal of structuralist principles: slipping and sliding on the foundation of its rules. Instead, it utters quiet words afresh, by stepping tentatively over the suspension bridge between the phenomenological experience and its semiotic articulation. Experience is always unsayable, but again and again speech is found and lost and found again but not ever alike. This circle is not a renewal but a refrain that sounds again and again, not to confirm but to erase the meaning of the heard in the duration of its extensity. The extensity of practical speech is not its epistemological structure nor its endless deferral, but the timespace of its sounds, which do not deny references, present or past, but use them as affective memory material that triggers the moment of perception into which, however, they disappear to leave room for new and contingent articulations that have a tendential but not a contractual sociality. This prevents speech from substituting experience with lexical and cultural knowledge, as it insists on its present production, and it confirms the responsibility of the listener, who performs this action of perception from the affection of his sonic memory material, in a present experience. And through this contingent production of experience he meets a neighbouring body, who takes his action to become his own affection.

This recalls Artaud's incoherent whispers that vibrate on our body and resonate our simultaneity without providing a certain understanding. Artaud's voice sounds the pain of his body directly upon mine without the distance that structural language affords. His speech does not get clearer with repeated listening but sounds as refrain that erases the sensate sense once heard in the deep extensity of its present duration. Incomprehensive as words, his voice has to be felt body to body, again and again, and its meanings are to be found in my own extensions that these coincidences affect.

The Refrain of Now

When we come across a refrain in poetry we return, already in possession of what we have read, to the first case which prompted the poet to write the lines originally. The refrain brings us back to our first experience of entering that poetic world, making it immediate and at the same time renewing it. We return as it were to its source.[25]

For Andrei Tarkovsky film sound used as refrain does more than simply prop up the visual expression. It opens up new possibilities of the same material: 'plunging into the musical element which the refrain brings into being, we return again and again to the emotions the film has given us, with our experience deepened each time by new impressions.'[26] The sonic refrain opens the film to the possible worlds at the blind depth of its images. The refrain grants the listener his context, the over-there and the other-time of his perception, but it does not work to confirm this other-time and other-place, but uses them to provide the extensity of the duration of now. The refrain is not an intellectual repeating but the renewed action of the body upon the material perceived. It produces ever-new layers, burying deeper and deeper into what we conventionally perceive as the real world to create it in its possibilities rather than recognize its perceived actuality. These possible worlds are not tied up to the logic of the plot and its visual consequences, but produce the sensate sense of our own film, as the possible world of our interpretative fantasy. The reality and relevance of this possible world is assured in the simultaneity of ourselves with the material: our immersed and equivalent listening position. Feldman's *Piano and String Quartet*, which I discussed in *Silence*, produces such a complex extensity through the taut arrangement of sounds that recur again and again not exactly the same but same enough to invite the past to hear the present in its full expanse. His sounds do not repeat chronologically but drop into my listening space as a complex and tense simultaneity, that extends my timespace place *and* my timespace time with the reference of each audition. These references, that extend the space of audition, do not remain however, but are the affective material that creates the extensity of the present moment into which they disappear to make room for a new and contingent audition of the heard. The now of my listening gets thicker and thicker as the steady refrains increase the density of what I hear. And so Feldman's quiet sounds build an enormous space that takes in all the time that could ever be imagined to produce a possible place for me.

I noted when discussing this piece, how the work needs my effort of engagement for this extensity to be produced: I need to slide into the works extensive duration, to hold its fragments together on my fleshly body for their affection to trigger the action of my perception. It is this very effort of affective listening that is its experience and that needs to find speech that affects experience rather than replaces it. In other words we need to take care not to speak displacements and substitutions, not to produce what in *Silence* I termed an aesthetic stoppage, but to speak from the fleshly bits of our experience to produce an experience whose affections trigger another's action, to speak his experience for himself.

This insistence on experience does not represent a popularizing and dumbing down of critical discourse, but presents a shift from the rigour of writing art theory to the rigour of writing the experience of art. This implies a foregrounding of the ethics of engagement through the responsibility of the writer as listener, and includes the pathetic trigger of memory as a differentiated subjective objectivity that affects the production of the work in the extensive duration of its perception, always now.

The sonic 'I' is not totally left to his own devices, in the sense of indeterminate, but generates the context that shapes him, through the subjective objectivity of his own perception that is triggered by the affective impact of the other onto the self. It is the effort of this perception that produces the ethicality of the sonic subject and designs the values of a sonic community thus produced. This is not Hegel's ideal community produced from our ability to reason, through logic and argument between the self and the values or responsibilities of the collective. As sonic subjectivities we meet not in reason but in affection, and that meeting is not dialectical, it does not progress towards an ideal community, but produces simultaneity and coincidence. The sonic meeting is agonistic rather than antagonistic: it generates the community, as contingency, in the playful chance of exchange.

Notes

Introduction

1   Theodor Adorno, *Minima Moralia, Reflections on a Damaged Life*, trans. E. F. N. Jephcott, London and New York: Verso, 2005, pp. 70–1.

2   In the *Primacy of Perception* Merleau-Ponty describes the world as a 'life-world', which one creates through ones being in it, and which in turn creates one's self as an intersubjective subject continually at the moment of this inter-action. Merleau-Ponty talks about the concrete and abstract, sensory-motor, movements and gestures with which we approach the world and through which we construct and are constructed in that world. In this 'life-world' we grasp space through our bodily, intersubjective, situation.

> I grasp myself not as a constituting subject which is transparent to itself, and which constitutes the totality of every possible object of thought and experience, but as a particular thought, as a thought engaged with certain objects, as thought in act. Maurice Merleau-Ponty, *Primacy of Perception*, trans. James M. Edie, Illinois: Northwestern University Press, 1964, p. 22.

3   Adorno, *Minima Moralia, Reflections on a Damaged Life*, p. 71.

4   Theodor Adorno, 'The Essay as Form', in *The Adorno Reader*, edited by Brian O'Connor, Oxford: Blackwell, 2000, p. 93.

5   This term is loosely borrowed from Donald Davidson, who in his essay 'A Nice Derangement of Epitaphs' discusses the notion of a 'passing theory' of language, in which the meaning is created on the spot in the meeting of both interlocutors building their own contingent and transient ideas. He suggests that what

> A passing theory really is like a theory at least in this, that it is derived by wit, luck and wisdom from a private vocabulary and grammar, knowl-edge of the ways people get their point across, and rules of thumb for figuring out what deviations from the dictionary are most likely. There is no more chance of regularizing, or teaching, this process than there is of regularizing or teaching the process of creating new theories to cope with new data in any field. Donald Davidson, 'A Nice Derangement of Epitaphs', in *Truth and Interpretation*, edited by Ernest LePore, Oxford: Basil Blackwell, 1986, p. 446.

Listening

1   Theodor Adorno, 'The Actuality of Philosophy', in *The Adorno Reader*, edited by Brian O'Connor, Oxford: Blackwell, 2000, p. 37.

2   Vis-à-vis this practical *fantasy* of Adorno's philosophical interpretation sits Maurice Merleau-Ponty's explanation of the *dream* of science to absolute truth:

> The physics of relativity confirms that absolute and final objectivity is a mere dream by showing how each particular observation is strictly linked to the location of the observer and cannot be abstracted from this particular situation; but also rejects the notion of an absolute observer. We can no longer flatter ourselves with the idea that, in science, the exercise of a pure and unsituated intellect can allow us to gain access to an object free of all human traces, just as God would see it. Maurice Merleau-Ponty, *The World of Perception*, trans. Oliver Davis, London and New York: Routledge, 2008, p. 36.

The dream is an unconscious longing, evoking passivity and the unattainable, whereas fantasy gives rise to itself. Paradoxically in the abandonment of the dream, its total and objective outcome, lies the discovery of its process: the concrete contingency of individual perception.

3   De Certeau's essay 'Walking in the City' from *The Practice of Everyday Life* first published in French as *l'Invention du Quotidien* in 1980, discusses New York from the top of the World Trade Centre and on street level. He juxtaposes the viewing of the total urban text from above with its production by the 'Wandersmänner' 'down below', 'whose bodies follow the thicks and thins of an urban "text" they write without being able to read it.' Michel de Certeau, 'Walking in the City', in *The Practice of Everyday Life*, trans. Steven Randall, London: University of California Press, 1988, p. 93. De Certeau's city on the ground level is created by these blind practitioners, who by association hear rather than see its text, 'make use of space that cannot be seen' and produce with their footsteps the city as a heard phenomenon. (Ibid. p. 93)

4   These radio broadcasts were first published in French as *Causeries 1948* by Editions de Seuil in 2002. The first English translation of that text entitled *The World of Perception* was produced in 2004 by Routledge, the one I am referring to is the 2008 edition.

5   Maurice Merleau-Ponty, *The World of Perception*, trans. Oliver Davis, London and New York: Routledge, 2008, p. 41.

6   Ibid., p. 41.

7   Ibid., p. 39.

8   The modernist painter deals in doubt in order to present a more complex certainty to his viewer who remains apart from his questioning processes. Being motivated by on the one hand the desire to avoid the subjectivism of the romantic era and on the other not to fall into the objectivist camp, both Cézanne and Merleau-Ponty rely on the authority of the painter to communicate doubt and the resultant complexity of appearance rather than make the audience doubt the work. By contrast, listening is to take part in the processes of doubt neither without trying to find a positivist explanation nor by succumbing to a simple subjectivism. Instead listening struggles with the singular position of hearing and the sensorial complexity of the material heard.

9   Ibid., p. 46.

10   Merleau-Ponty never overtly deals with sound, if at all then he mentions music and treats it within its conventions. It is only in his very last writing,

collected together under the title *The Visible and the Invisible*, published posthumously in 1964 from his manuscripts, that he deals with silence and mentions sounds in the conclusion of the last chapter: 'The Intertwining – The Chasm'. I can only assume that this silence would have brought him to a lot more noise had he lived longer, as I understand sound to realize Merleau-Ponty's theoretical phenomenology in practice. 'We shall have to follow more closely this transition from the mute world to the speaking world.' Maurice Merleau-Ponty, *The Visible and the Invisible*, trans. Alphonso Lingis, edited by Claude Lefort, Illinois: Northwestern University Press, 1968, p. 154.

11   This intersubjective 'I', is not known to itself as a rational subject, identified in reference to a pre-existing category, and hence cannot discover the other through his self-certainty. The 'I' in this intersubjective motor-operation produces the certainty of itself and its environment, the life-world, through continuous production in uncertainty. In the reciprocal relationship between the life-world and the 'I', doubt implies self doubt as well as doubt about the world.

The doubt that Merleau-Ponty understands to drive Cézanne to paint, is the doubt through which subjectivity as well as objectivity is produced provisionally and continually in an intersubjective life-world: 'Only one emotion is possible for this painter – the feeling of strangeness – and only one lyricism – that of the continual rebirth of existence.' Maurice Merleau-Ponty, 'Cézanne's Doubt', in *The Merleau-Ponty Aesthetic Reader*, trans. Michael B. Smith, edited by Galen A. Johnson, 2nd edition, Illinois: Northwestern University Press, 1996, p. 68.

12   The closest we can get to divorcing the visual mass from its sonic stampede is by plugging ourselves into the sound bubble of our I-pod, and even then all we do is give the visual mass another sonic shape.

13   In his 1975 essay 'Aural Objects' [originally entitled 'le perçu et le nommé' ('the perceived and the named'), Metz discusses the preference for the substantial, the visible and tactile, which he identifies as primary senses above smell and sound, which are thus qualified as secondary and attribual. Metz correlates this hierarchical order with a capitalist orientation in the West. He talks about a 'primitive substantialism', which according to him, reflects the Western philosophical tradition since Descartes and Spinoza. This tradition, to him, is apparent in the subject–predicate structure particular to Indo-European languages, where the noun of the sentence orientates and determines the predicate, which is thus sublimated to this noun. He comments on the identification of the visual as the stable and primary, the noun, while the sonic is its changing attribute.

The original title of this essay, 'le perçu et le nommé', foregrounds the distinction between a semiotic account of the visual and an experiential engagement stressed by sound. The differentiation between 'the perceived' and 'the named' clearly points to a distinction between a culturally coded, named, understanding of the (visual) thing as sign, and a contingent production (of the sonic) in a perceptual process.

14   Merleau-Ponty, *The World of Perception*, 49.

15   Adorno points out that the empirical subject who is more real in his being a living, concrete subject, is less real in a society in which an individual's function is abstracted to rational social relations.

The more individuals are really degraded to functions of the social totality as it becomes more systematized, the more will man pure and simple, man as a principle with the attributes of creativity and absolute domination, be consoled by exaltation of his mind. [. . .] They (the transcendental subjects) are deformed before hand (before even experiencing an empirical reality) by the mechanism that has been philosophically transfigured as transcendental. Adorno, 'Subject and Object', in *The Adorno Reader*, p. 141.

16   Adorno, 'Subject and Object', in *The Adorno Reader*, p. 143.

17   What appears to us as natural is probably only the habitual of a long-standing habit, which has forgotten the unfamiliar from which it came. That unfamiliar had once, however, attacked the human as an alienating thing, and had astonished thinking. Martin Heidegger, *Der Ursprung des Kunstwerkes*, Stuttgart: Philip Reclam jun., 2008, p. 16. (own translation)

18   Ibid., p. 15.

In *Sein und Zeit* (1927), Heidegger specifies *Bodenlosigkeit*, groundlessness, as a lack of foundation of the felt and said. The idea that one 'sieht den Grund nicht mehr . . .' which, according to him, leads to a separation of experience from its originary sensate moment, which is replaced by an inauthentic sense of reality. Martin Heidegger, *Sein und Zeit*, Max Niemeyer, Tübingen, 1986, p. 177. He tries to re-invest in this 'ground' with his existential phenomenology and the question of the Thing.

19   Martin Heidegger, *Der Ursprung des Kunstwerkes*, Stuttgart: Philip Reclam jun., 2008, pp. 11–19.

20   Ibid., p. 16.

21   'How do the Things show themselves?' Martin Heidegger, *Die Frage nach dem Ding: zu Kants Lehre von den transzendentalen Grundsätzen*, Tübingen: Max Niemeyer Verlag, 1962, p. 25. (own translation)

22   'The thing is thinging.' Martin Heidegger, 'Das Ding', in *Vorträge und Aufsätze*, Prullingen, Germany: Verlag Günther 1959, p. 172. (own translation)

23   Ibid., pp. 32–4.

24   'Das Kunstwerk eröffnet auf seine Weise das Sein im Seienden.' (The artwork unfolds the thinging of the Thing.) Ibid., p. 34.

25   In a collection of his essays brought together in the book *Sense and Non-Sense* published in 1964, Merleau-Ponty articulates 'non-sense' not in reference to rational sense, as its nonsensical opposite, but rather describes with it a sense that comes out of 'sensation'. Non-sense, then, is sense produced by a phenomenological subject, who exists in the world produced continually through his sensorial existence in it, outlining a 'life world' and 'intersubjectivity'. In this life-world the intersubjective subject produces sense as non-sense through sensory-motor actions towards this world. According to Merleau-Ponty, these motions are motivated by doubt, rather than certainty, sensation rather than rationality.

26   In the *Phenomenology of Spirit*, Georg Wilhelm Friedrich Hegel talks about the knowledge 'pure apprehension' as the knowledge of the immediate appearance of the thing. G. F. W. Hegel, *Phenomenology of Spirit*, trans. A. V. Miller, Oxford: Clarendon Press, 1977, p. 55. Hegel's apprehensional knowledge does not practice but meets the object, phenomenon as transcendental *a priori*, immediately. Sound, when it is not musical or subsumed to a visual source is not knowable in this way.

27   Theodor Adorno, *Minima Moralia, Reflections on a Damaged Life*, trans. E. F. N. Jephcott, London and New York: Verso, 2005, p. 69.

28   Ibid., p. 54.

29   These wars are visual wars, paradoxically set off or at least intensified with the destruction of de Certeau's location of the visual, gnostic drive for total knowledge: the World Trade Centres. The fight largely takes place at a distance, reported by travelling newsreaders from their Baghdad and Kabul hotel rooms. After the embedded experiment in the second gulf war, reporters are now kept well away from any fighting and report from their own distance.

30   Ibid., p. 55.

31   In the first signifying practice of the 'narrative', 'material discontinuity is reduced to correlations between opposites (high/low, good/bad, inside/outside) which delineate narrative's geography, temporality, plot, etc.' Julia Kristeva, *Revolution in Poetic Language*, trans. Margaret Waller, New York: Columbia University Press, 1984, p. 90. This signifying practice may include various materialities and sensations, however, these are ultimately 'poured into the rigid molds of a nondisjunctive structure' (ibid., p. 90). Kristeva's 'narrative' is a weak signifying process as it centers on an axial position of the symbolic, and weakens the potential to roam in new meaning. Her second practice, 'metalanguage', is the guarantor for the symbolic system. It places the subject as a fixed subject outside the text: 'he hovers above it' and is 'absent from it' (ibid., p. 95). This symbolic systematicity eliminates heterogeneity and forges omnivalence. Conversely, the fixed position of the subject is the only guarantee for the symbolic to work: The symbolic demands as well as constructs the subject as a fixed subject. This subject is confined to the socio-historical context of his symbolic register and reads the text from this 'meta-'position.

It is in relation to the third signifying practice, contemplation, that Kristeva employs Hegel's notion of *Aufhebung*, sublimation. The problem of sublimation lies in the very conception of the symbolic. Kristeva writes 'this *Aufhebung* of the instinctual *chora* is always already inevitably and inseparably symbolic. The *chora's* closure within contemplation condemns contemplation to meaning, disarticulating it, only to return to it, disenchanted' (ibid., p. 96). This sketches contemplation as a dialectic activity; negation continually arriving at a positive, thesis and antithesis. Any particularity of expression is 'swallowed' continually in this circular dynamic, which she calls a 'ring': 'eternally returning, perpetually trapped' (ibid., p. 95). The material is secondary to this dynamic, sublimated by its symbolic totality. Contemplation, according to Kristeva, is responsible for producing and keeping the ideological, hierarchical status quo of the state, or any other ideological apparatus. She concedes that the signifying play within contemplation shifts and changes, drifting (*dérive*), without however, ever breaking the 'communicative function'.

32   Julia Kristeva, *Revolution in Poetic Language*, trans. Margaret Waller, New York: Columbia University Press, 1984, p. 102.

33   'It (the text) does not instigate the "process-of-becoming-a-subject" of the masses' (Ibid., p. 102). The text is a subjective/singular rather than an objective/collective process, producing a 'subjective ideality', which is realized in what I termed an innovative listening.

34   Ibid., p. 101.

35   Ibid., p. 101.

36   Ibid., p. 102.

37   In the late 1960s, R. Murray Schafer, Canadian composer and founder of the World Soundscape Project, called for acoustic awareness and sought to

establish a pedagogy of listening to the soundscape. His 1977 written text, *The Tuning of the World*, outlines ideas on listening and the soundscape, which embody the foundation of a now international movement of acoustic ecology that seeks to preserve endangered sounds and to produce an awareness of our acoustic environment in order to fight sound pollution and to eventually get to design better soundscapes.

38   Pierre Schaeffer's acousmatic project outlined in his *Traité des objets musicaux: essai interdisciplines* written in 1966, seeks, to produce 'objets sonores' (sonic objects) whose source remains unheard. This technological reduction of recorded sound finds its equivalent in the idea of 'reduced listening': a listening that focuses on the sound as sound itself rather than as musical element or as referent of a visual phenomenon. It is with this acousmatic material and its reduced sensibility that Schaeffer produces acousmatic compositions or musique concrète. (Pierre Henry and Schaeffer found the groupe de recherche de musique concrète in 1951)

39   In his inaugural lectures on pure phenomenology at the University of Freiburg in 1916, Edmund Husserl explains the strategy of bracketing, what he calls epoche, as a reduction that does not seek to diminish perception to the empirical data of things, but to suspend all assumptions of an external world in order to get to the pure phenomenon as it presents itself to consciousness. He brackets all knowledge of context and truth and simply describes the contents of consciousness in order to establish a theoretical insight into the essential nature of the phenomenon and of the perceiving ego. Edmund Husserl, *Ideas: General Introduction to Pure Phenomenology*, trans. W. R. B. Gibson, Australia: Allen and Unwin, 1931.

40   The intersubjective, bodily, being in the world as phenomenological life-world does not prevent solitariness. I am constituted intersubjectively through my interactions with the world and through my awareness of the existence of the other, without however presupposing an *a priori* communication between the self and that other. To the contrary, it is because of the knowledge of the existence of the other that the self struggles with his doubt of the perceived, and it is through this doubt that he might reach a passing understanding with the other rather than through an assumed communication. What we might share then is an understanding of our subjectivity as intersubjectively constituted, and the intention to communicate, not however the code of communication.

41   Kristeva, *Revolution in Poetic Language*, 104.

42   Julia Kristeva, 'The Imaginary Sense of Forms' in *Arts Magazine*, September (1991): 30.
    In this essay Kristeva describes and discusses a particular viewing of sculptures by Alain Kirili's which she views 'in the midst of the (first) Gulf War' at *Commandement XI*, in Paris. Rather than insisting on making her perception coincide with an art-historically verified reading, she understands the material 'lends its geometry to our projections, body and soul' (Ibid., pp. 29–30). I take measure on her method of viewing an artwork, and understand sonic material to demand just such a contingent projection, 'body and soul' as one move rather than a dualistic constellation. However, I am aware that this sensorial engagement is framed by and thus made 'sayable', in the sense of determined, within the rigour of the gallery context. It is corporeal but not floundering.

43   Adorno, 'Subject and Object', in *The Adorno Reader*, p. 140.

Noise

1   In 1913, Italian Futurist composer Luigi Russolo produced a manifesto on noise (*L'arte dei rumori*) and built a whole orchestra of noise machines (*intonarumori*) with which he performed his own noise music. His text and work celebrates the machine age and hails the industrial revolution as symbol of progress: allowing man to assert himself over a 'silent' nature whose sounds he perceives as monotonous and unable to arouse any emotion. By contrast the power of machine noise he understands to usher in a time of greater sonic complexity: embracing dissonance and polyphony to expand musical conventions.

2   The term ideal is used here in the sense of the Hegelian notion of *Idealität* of an 'ideal objectivity'. In his Berlin Aesthetic Lectures of the 1820s Hegel sketches out the notion of an ideal state of beauty at the moment where art has overcome in sublimation (*Aufhebung*) the *'Widersprüchlichkeit'* (the antagonistic contradiction) between inner necessity and outer appearance, and has resolved the Idea, the content and form, its configuration of sensuous material in one total expression. Hegel's aesthetic judgement outlines a progressive dialectic. According to him, art has to overcome inner necessity, our animal nature: eating, shitting, fornicating, etc., in a higher order manifestation: in ideal spirituality that leaves behind the bodily burden of want and need. Georg Wilhelm Friedrich Hegel, *Vorlesungen über die Ästhetik I–III*, Germany: Suhrkamp Verlag, 1980.

3   Masami Akita aka Merzbow is a 1979 initiated Japanese experimental music project recognized as one of the earliest elements of the Japanese noise scene. Here his name stands in for the variety of noise and noise-related work produced since the late 1970s.

4   In an article on 'Audio Sensitisation and Participation in the Soundscape' printed in the *Journal of Electroacoustic Music* in 1999, I considered the world as an interactive sound sculpture whose inhabitants, animate as well as inanimate, (following Aristotle's notion of sound, as the potential and actual fourth dimension of objects [*deAnima Book II*]), were discussed in relation to their position within the sounding environment. The argument made considered the soundscape as a multilayered macrocosm of activity between subjects and objects and suggested that this sonorous macrocosm could be read as the composition of a society. This composition makes its economic, political, social, etc. dynamics audible and offers an opportunity to re-listen and re-sound those dynamics to understand and react to their ideologies and power structures beyond the picture offered by a visual anthropology. In many ways the article suggested to take Jacques Attali's *Noise: the Political Economy of Music,* first published in French as *Bruits* in 1977, and apply his method of enquiring after the economic causes of change in musical practice to the entire soundscape.

Noise is one element of this interactive soundsculpture. Its absolute insistence to be heard rather than remain a potential sound, renders it a great tool to assess and interact with issues of social, economic, political, etc., relations understood as dynamic qualities rather than fixed relationships.

5   Rave nights, despite their outward appearance, do not mimic Friedrich Kracauer's *Mass Ornament* (a collection of essays from the 1920s first issued in Germany in 1963), the surface-level expression of mass movement in which people are not individuals but are sublimated as fractions of a figure. In that sense, despite being a frequent target of cultural critics, spotting the symptom of

capitalist production and consumption lines, ravers produce rather than watch their movement, and in this practice they are *in* noise: acutely sonically sensible. What is practiced on the spot of each dancer's feet is his splendid isolation in a world of his own noise. This solitary position is ultimately a critical position, outlining the sensibility of a sonic consciousness.

6   In *Audio-Vision: Sound on Screen,* Michel Chion assigns sound the task not to simply and directly transpose a visual reality, but to render the visual image real and believable beyond the visual perception, as a holistic sensational experience, as a 'clump of sensation'. According to Chion, sound does not translate one order of sensation into another. Rather, it makes it available to sensation as a sensible whole: the weight, the feel, the speed, the materiality, the process, etc. all sorts of experiential information is produced by sound. The scene of a body falling out of a tower block onto the bonnet of a parked car is rendered believable by sound. The image of the body will not make us feel its weight and pain; it will only make us see it. It is sound that is given the task to render the weight of the body, its pain, the impact on the car and the materiality of the bonnet sensible as a whole clump to the viewer. Michel Chion, *Audio-Vision Sound and Screen*, trans. and edited by Michel Gorbman, New York: Columbia University Press, 1994, pp. 112–13.

7   In 2000 Merzbow released *Merzbox*, a 50 CD Limited edition, Box-set of noise music. Neatly packed in a black custom designed box with a metal nameplate, the *Merzbox* also includes a book, CD-ROM, a medallion, a T-shirt, a poster and postcards as well as stickers.

8   In many ways the really loud and painful sounds of Yoshihide and noise music in general are not the dialectical opposite of quiet sounds and silence. Rather they achieve a similar sense of quiet by deafening you to anything but themselves.

9   In *The Visible and the Invisible* (1964) Merleau-Ponty wrestles with the visual body perceiving and perceived. Due to the dialectical reality of the visual and its complementary relationship to touch, Merleau-Ponty discusses the assemblage of the body at once as phenomenal body and as objective body, as sentient and sensible, as two segments intertwined in 'one sole circular course [. . .] which is but one sole movement in its two phases'. Maurice Merleau-Ponty, trans. Alphonso Lingis, edited by Claude Lefort, Illinois: Northwestern University Press, 1968, p.138. In sound the sentient and the sensible are not circular but simultaneous, as one, intertwined without an abyss from which to turn to and from each other. Extreme noise makes this non-dialectical union abundantly clear: stunned in noise I am a clump of sensation; sensing myself sensed through the vertical downpour of sound. The exclusivity of this noise reveals my phenomenal body to me *as* my subjective objectivity.

10   The piano is the über-instrument that rises out above the orchestra while demarcating the shift from the more homely sounds of chamber music to the public sounds of the concert hall. The piano is loud and substantial, announcing the modernist sublimation of nature by louder and more heroic sounds even before Russolo's intonarumori. The pianoforte presents within the nineteenth century soundscape a dominant and authoritarian voice, manifesting musically the development towards an imperial charge in the space of music. It seems therefore no coincidence at all that it is this, rather than any other instrument, that Palestine makes noise with.

11   Georg Wilhelm Friedrich Hegel, *Phenomenology of Spirit,* trans. A. V Miller, Oxford: Clarendon Press, 1977, p. 55.
Hegel juxtaposes this 'pure apprehensional' knowledge a 'moment of true experience' when the heard is produced in practice. However his idea of experience remains within the idea of dialectical totality. It does not generate subjective knowledge but pursues absolute knowledge through an ideal objectivity. Listening as the generative experience of sound, must remain non-ideal in that it is subjectively ideal, non-progressive and provisional.
12   There is a difficult paradox implicit in this observation for the artist working with sound outside the musical paradigm, which clarifies the need for an aesthetics and philosophy of sound art and explains why it cannot resemble musicological theorizations: if there is no context or critical infrastructure to discuss his work, if there is no sense of how it could be listened to for its sounds rather than its music, it wont be heard. Instead, as suggested earlier, the headphones, the plinth, the visual aspects of the show or anything vaguely musical will override the sonic experience.
Another paradox is that of course over time any critical listening advocated by such a philosophy and first anxiously invited, might develop its own histories and canons, categories and judgements, to rival those of music and the visual arts. This process is well underway. I have no interest in facilitating the building of canons, but only wish to encourage a listening practice, which in its essence is anti-canonical and remains forever an encouragement to listen rather than a theory of the heard. I understand a philosophy of sound art as a lose infrastructure for listening: some fleeting possibilities and suggestions to practise at home.
13   Robert Pasnau, 'What is Sound?', in *The Philosophical Quarterly,* vol. 49, no. 196 (1999): 311.
14   Ibid., p. 314.
15   Pasnau writes contemporaneously and an expectation would be to identify him with post-modern ideas rather than within modernist discourse. However, his quest for rational reason affiliates him within a high modernist ideal and assigns to him Adorno's sobriquet of the Late comer: 'Late comers and newcomers have an alarming affinity to positivism.' Theodor Adorno, *Minima Moralia, Reflections on a Damaged Life*, trans. E. F. N. Jephcott, London and New York: Verso, 2005, p. 52.
16   Jean-François Lyotard, *The Postmodern Condition: A Report on Knowledge,* trans. Geoff Bennington and Brian Massumi, Manchester: Manchester University Press, 1994, p. 74.
17   Terry Eagleton in David Harvey, *The Condition of Postmodernity: An Enquiry into the Origins of Cultural Change*, Cambridge, Mass and Oxford: Basil Blackwell, 1990, p. 11.
18   Michel de Certeau, 'Walking in the City', in *The Practice of Everyday Life,* trans. Steven Randall, London: University of California Press, 1988, p. 93.
19   This of course is a reciprocal position; Zola too is immutable, heavy and fixed in a modernist framework of class, values and judgment. He is not freer just because he observes it. In fact his observations only bind him more closely into the eternal fixity thus created.
20   Clement, Greenberg, *The Collected Essays and Criticism, Vol. 4, Modernism with a Vengeance, 1957–1969,* edited by J. O'Brian, Chicago: University of Chicago Press, 1995, pp. 55–6.

21   A danger of some contemporary discourse on sonic arts is that the score is simply replaced by a technological manual. The *Notenbild* has given way to illustrations of Software processes and Hardware interfaces. The ideology of an *a priori* objectivism and the possibility for meta-discourse, however, remain, as the work is identified within these visual processes. What becomes relevant when aesthetically considering a work by its Max patch is whether it fulfils the visual ideality of its own possibilities, whether it answers the positivism of the computer programme. This emphasis gives the sonic artist the role of the instrumentalist as interpreter, and distances the audience from the signifying practice of listening as they start to realize the computational structure of the audible. Such a focus retains sonic arts' discourse within a modernist aesthetic. It avoids a consideration of the experiential status of the work, its auditory content, which would problematize the compositional control, intention and the unified appreciation of the work.

22   'Ohne Schrift keine hochorganisierte Musik; der historische Unterschied von Improvisation und musica composite fällt qualitative mit dem des Laxen und des verbindlichen Artikulierten zusammen.' – 'Without writing there can be no highly organised music; the historic difference between improvisation and musica composite coincides qualitatively with the difference between negligence (the lax) and rigorous articulation.' Theodor Adorno, *Musikalische Schriften I – III*, Frankfurt: Suhrkamp, 2003, p. 632. (own translation)

23   Ibid., p. 61.

24   If we disregard the demand for manual virtuosity of the musical work and its interpretation, which Adorno seems to judge music by, non-scored music is not lax and lazy but demands a virtuosity of listening. His complexity is the complexity of musical language and its translation into visual tone material. By contrast, the complexity of improvisation is that of listening on the part of the player as well as on the part of the audience.

The non-scored sound of electroacoustic music, particularly in the acousmatic tradition, demands a valuation through hearing as experiential production. I cannot follow the compositional thread but need to continually produce one myself through the focus of a reduced listening, in the dark as it were. Therein also lays lies one value of improvisation and particularly improvisation with unknown devices where not even the instruments can replace and guarantee the visual value of the score. Instead they further confuse and disorientate conventions by opening referential links to extra-musical things and their function within another, non-artistic realm, and their sonic function within the improvisation. Such unknown devices function as Duchampian ready-mades in that they implode the expectation to be able to tie the value of the work to the artistic exclusivity of its materiality and organization. They illuminate the focus of the *Dingheit* of the thing as sonic thing-ness in their avoidance of a distinction between the pure, simple thing and its artistic *Oberbau*.

25   Rosalind E. Kraus, *The Originality of the Avant-Garde and Other Modernist Myths*, Cambridge, Mass and London: MIT Press, 1987, p. 10.

26   Ibid., p. 158.

27   I have no firm opinion as to whether graphic scores further and cement this position of the score as the arbiter of aesthetic value or whether they succeed to open the *Notenbild* for true improvisation, and in doing so undermine and critique the traditional score's insistence on value and authorship. On the one hand

I understand graphic scores as an effort of democratization, empowering the performer out of his role as the interpreter into that of a producer. On the other hand however, and almost paradoxically, due to the variability of the actual sounds produced the graphic score might attain even more status vis-à-vis its fleeting performance, and a critic might feel legitimated in ignoring the performance altogether and instead focus exclusively on the score. Trying to meet the audible in his vision, he might not even need to thread along the compositional lines with his fingers anymore but simply summarize the seen.

28   Russolo's noise is modernist in its concept of progress and anti-nature pro machine ideology. His manifesto *The Art of Noise*, written in 1913, serves as the score or grid of what in listening becomes again just noisy non-sense, individual, contingent and messy. The call to universal celebration of the machine only works on paper, in listening it becomes a more frightening, intrusive and uncontrollable act.

29   Rudolph Arnheim in his 1936 essay *In Praise of Blindness* commends a sightless radio. He demands of broadcasts not to simply relay football games and musical performances but to engender a truly sonic, blind, production. It is easy to follow his suggestion as to what such a blind radio should *not* be, much harder however is it to imagine what it should be instead. There also remains the suspicion that within his own modernism Arnheim had an ideal blindness in mind. However, and ignoring his notion of ideality, one thing this blind radio could be is noise. Noise-radio in the sense that the sounds coming from the box next to my bed, in my car, or on the kitchen table would have nothing to do with the visual world around me. Noise in this sense is sound that is truly not, and never was, related to any visual source and might lead the listener to invent a 'visuality' beyond his visual imagination.

Understood not as a quest for modernist immanence of the positivist reality of the sonic object, such a blind noise-radio surpasses and stretches the visual perception into a generative production: intensively always now, gripped in a continuous present, nothing else and nowhere else, its meaning only ever the listener's. In this context, noise's principle is truly Jean-François Lyotard's postmodern principle of the 'inventor's parology', understood not just as an exception or opposition to a modernist meaning, but as an infinite field of innovation. Lyotard, *The Postmodern Condition: A Report on Knowledge*, xxv. Noise is sound practised: listening to invent and produce rather than to recognize and know. It always demands my participation. And if such a noise-radio is not genuinely achievable it unquestionably articulates an important challenge for sound arts production.

30   Lyotard's *coups inattendus* are the unexpected moves within the language game. Every utterance is thought of as a move in the game, 'new statements' are the unexpected moves. Lyotard, *The Postmodern Condition: A Report on Knowledge*, p. 16.

31   To lead this briefly back to Adorno's criticism of the lax and lazy improvisers: much of what he would term primitive music or disapprove of in relation to Jazz and improvisation has very complex rhythms that might not usefully be grasped within the written score. Their complexity comes out of the material in performance, in practice, rather than from an *a priory* objectivism. This demonstrates that the complexity of the sonic work might not be the complexity of the musical work and to try and use the vocabulary and value system of one to

understand and judge the experience of the other might simply not account for that which it really is, sonically. Additionally, that which really is sonic in the musical work, the body producing the sensory material in all its contingent complexity, might of course also be denied by its own discourse.

32   Jean-François Lyotard, 'The Sublime and the Avant-Garde', in *The Lyotard Reader*, edited by Andrew Benjamin, Oxford: Basil Blackwell, 1989, p. 203.

According to Lyotard, the sublime alludes to something that is not there to be shown but that is conspicuous in its absence. For him, this absence forces a theoretical presence, a presence of theory and judgement. The possibility of an absence, of nothing happening, induces too much anxiety and fear to remain undiscussed. The theoretical discussion, however, renders it at once happening but also defines the scope of nothingness in representation. Lyotard understands that it is from this apparent absence and nothingness that aesthetics asserted its critical right over art, and it is in that aesthetic of absence that romanticism and thus modernity is characterized. In other words, the modern is characterized by absence, made present in aesthetic criticism from a distance. By inference the postmodern must celebrate this absence and push the critic right in, to experience it.

In sound there never is such an absence, the absence heard *is* the sound. The object, using Kristeva's terminology, 'is never posited as lost'. Julia Kristeva, *Revolution in Poetic Language*, trans. Margaret Waller, New York: Columbia University Press, 1984, p. 99. In sound the sublime is an experiential sublime, an individual and solitary absence in the midst of noisy presences. It is the absence of shared signifiers where no other sound infringes on the ecstasy of absentmindedness, which is a sonic state most apparent in noise. To celebrate this absence simply means to engage in the signifying practice of sound's noisy non-sense.

33   Lyotard, *The Postmodern Condition: A Report on Knowledge*, p. 79.

34   Ibid., p. xxv.

35   In the French original *La condition postmoderne: Rapport sur le savoir*, Paris: Les Éditions Minuit, 1979, Lyotard uses the term *'petit récit'* which for the English edition is translated by Geoff Bennington and Brian Massumi, as 'little narrative'. However, to emphasis the practical aspect of this little narrative and refrain from using this interpretation: a *récit* is quite particularly an oral account, a one off live event, an (aesthetic) moment. It is a narration rather than a narrative. To call it a little narrative takes away the clarity of this expression. I will use the term narration since I would like to keep in mind *récit's* live character of narrating rather than the idea of a narrative.

36   The 'grand narrative' validates and legitimizes knowledge in accordance with historical, scientific, political, etc., discourses. Its narrator is a meta-subject, its narrative affirms, through meta-discourse, the power base of empirical science and institutional knowledge. By contrast the 'little narration' is an act of narrating that produces and legitimizes knowledge through its practical performance, or what Lyotard terms a paralogical invention. Lyotard, *The Postmodern Condition: A Report on Knowledge*, xxv. This narrating does not produce a meta-discourse but *is* the practice of discourse.

The grand narratives (symbolic, scientific, historical, ideological, etc.) enable a shared 'narrative sense', while the little narration (the local and contingent paralogy) produces individual and temporal 'narrative sense making processes'.

The different senses thus produced, however, are not entirely divorced from each other but interact in the contingent production of meaning.

37 'The postmodern would be that which, in the modern, puts forward the unpresentable in presentation itself; that which denies itself the solace of good forms, consensus of taste which would make it possible to share collectively the nostalgia for the unattainable.' Lyotard, *The Postmodern Condition: A Report on Knowledge*, p. 81.

38 Nicholas Bourriaud's *Relational Aesthetics* from 2002, is just one point in case. Rather than letting the various strings of a work loose into experience, opening a tight network of production for sensorial perusal, they are garnered up, and neatly pleated together, destroying that in the work which did not *constitute* but *produce* a critical engagement. Now I know the work, I know its references and the social relations it brings together within the sphere of art, but his relational discourse avoids the physicality of these relationships and thus their visceral complexity and instead explains their rational simplicity.

39 The postmodern keyword Collage goes some way to illustrate this suggestion. Collage replaces the modernist term Montage, which established a formalist aesthetic, particularly in relation to photography and film. For Sergej Eisenstein montage is the very essence of film as art. Montage in his sense is the conflictual juxtaposition of the individual cells or frames of a film which persuades or attracts the audience towards the realization of its meaning through the dialectical sublimation of its conflict in a higher order synthesis. Sergej Eisenstein, 'A Dialectic Approach to Film Form', in *Film Theory and Criticism*, edited by Gerald Mast, Marshall Cohen and Leo Braudy, 4th edition, Oxford: Oxford University Press, 1992, p. 140.

The emphasis is on the conflict between two elements embedded in the formal arrangement of the film. This conflict is ultimately redeemed in relation to the totality it is embedded in. Montage is the quintessential modernist moment of closure, which delineates and orders the components in relation to the work as a whole. By contrast, the term collage denotes the cutting and pasting of diverse fragments. It encompasses a simultaneous complexity that negates the effort of a dialectical sublimation and challenges the totalizing dynamic of the montage principle. It implies heterogeneity of materiality and the possibility of different readings. However, collage still functions within the greater game plan of modernity: the diverse fragments are brought together relatively to the underlying rules, embodied by the recognition of the form of the collage as artwork and embedded in discourse. Postmodern collage complexifies the material relationship of montage but depends on the clarity of artistic identity and context to be matched back together again.

For the postmodern listener, Marclay's work is a collage of sounds, cut and pasted into the format of the CD or its performance. I can talk about it in that way and this description immediately relieves me from having to listen to anything else but the seams that bring together the totality of the work. The homogenizing presumptions that are imploded by the listening experience are stitched back together in the term collage and its linguistic comfort.

40 Lyotard, *The Postmodern Condition: A Report on Knowledge*, p. 81.

41 This picks up on Lyotard's argument that the postmodern has 'no taste', 'no good forms' (Ibid., p. 81). For him taste and good form imply a collective judgement, which is suspended in the game of postmodernism. The implication

is that we will get it back when we stop playing. So there is always already the notion of an after the event, when taste can choose good form out of the mass of tasteless, decadent, silly, perverted, expressions produced during its run. This alludes to the idea that the postmodern is a phase, much like an adolescent abandonment of parental guidance, useful only in developing a new set of rules to be passed on to one's own children.

42   By upsetting the conventions of modernist formation, installations actualize, focus and concentrate problems central to the modern aesthetic discourse. In this way they especially provoke another approach to the philosophical reflexion of the term Art and its experience, which, as will become apparent, is decidedly post-metaphysical. Juliane Rebentisch, *Ästhetik der Installation*, Germany: Edition Suhrkamp, 2003, p. 15. (my translation)

43   This aesthetic autonomy is not the modernist autonomy of the profession or the category but is the autonomy of an autonomous experience of the work. It is the autonomous hearing of Yoshihide's noise when I am ecstatically the heard and together we are the formless aesthetic moment of the work's subjective realization. This aesthetic autonomy is the moment of Merleau-Ponty's sensible sentient, which in sound is as one.

44   Modernist formalism considers such centrifugality decadent: 'It is only in periods of decadence in the arts that this *centripetal movement* changes to a *centrifugal movement*, hurling apart all unifying tendencies – tendencies that are incompatible with an epoch that places an over-emphasis on individualism.' Sergej Eisenstein, 'Synchronization of Senses', in *Film Sense,* trans. and edited by Jay Leyda, London: Faber 1958, p. 84. Eisenstein's outrage echoes with Hegel's idea that the refusal of the objective would inevitably lead to 'the form of subjective-selfishness and corruption in the unbound passions and egotistic interests of men.' G. F. W. Hegel, *Reason in History*, trans. Robert S. Hartman, New York: Library Arts Press, 1953, p. 93. Centrifugality of sound, far from being decadent and egotistic, places its emphasis on individual responsibility to generate rather than assume sociality, language and communication. The assumed objective cohesion of modernist aesthetic leads to exclusion, terror and war. It sublimates the subject into the concept of social and national belonging and identity. A sonic sensibility rather than assuming such principles has to generate, on the spot again and again a sonic subjectivity in doubt and astonishment at any temporary belonging and communicative sociality thus produced.

45   Maurice Merleau-Ponty, 'Cézanne's Doubt', in *The Merleau-Ponty Aesthetic Reader*, trans. Michael B. Smith, edited by Galen A. Johnson, 2nd edition, Illinois: Northwestern University Press, 1996, p. 66.

46   The noisy voice, in contrast to the instrumental noise of Palestine, retains its actual, material power in performance. It does not become a spectacular or rhetorical noise. The body is the material of the noisy voice. It fragments its own body and we witness it while we too are being witnessed as bodies fragmented in the fragments of this body. There is no spot from which to hold on to the scene as spectacle, or divorce its sensate materiality off into rhetoric. The implication of my own body is importunate. Observed by other bodies, my body becomes a co-performer, noisy in its unfamiliar and uncomfortable public fragmentation.

Without the visual performance Haino's voice retains its noisy power also. In the dark, alone, his screaming body can become anything. It changes beyond the physically possible into the body of my imagination, enrolling me in the production of symbiotes of my own fear and fantasy: erotic and monstrous.

47   David Harvey, *The Condition of Postmodernity: An Enquiry into the Origins of Cultural Change*, Cambridge, Mass and Oxford: Basil Blackwell, 1990, p. 48.

48   Nicholas Bourriaud in his *Altermodern Manifesto* written in conjunction with his curation of the fourth Tate Triennale at Tate Britain in 2009, declares post-modernism dead. Instead he calls the newly emerging practice altermodernity and suggests that this term serves better to encompass a globalized perception and practice of art. Nicholas Bourriaud, *Altermodern Manifesto*, http://www.tate.org.uk/britain/exhibitions/altermodern/manifesto.shtm

49   Maurice Merleau-Ponty, *The Visible and the Invisible*, trans. Alphonso Lingis, edited by Claude Lefort, Illinois: Northwestern University Press, 1968, p. 130.

Silence

1   In 1952 John Cage's *4'33"* was presented for the first time by David Tudor in Woodstock New York. He comes on stage, sits at the piano, lifts the lid and marks the time of three different movements while not playing a key for 4 minutes and 33 seconds, then he closes the lid, gets up and leaves the stage again.

2   In his book *Noise, Water, Meat* Douglas Kahn connects Cage and Duchamp via the idea of the 'ready made' also. However his focus is on the *canned silence* of Cage's work *Silent Prayer* (1948) produced four years prior to *4'33"* to be played on the Muzak CO. It is the canned nature of this silence, a quasi found object, which he understands as a musical version of Duchamp's 'ready mades' such as his *Air de France* (1919), a bottle of canned air. However, the similarities between Duchamp's *Fountain* and Cage's *4'33"* are more ideological and strategical than actual. It is the general inclusion of new processes and materials into the artistic and musical practice that connects them and makes them both so pertinent for the development and expansion of art and music respectively rather than the notion of the found. Douglas Kahn, *Noise Water Meat, A History of Sound in the Arts*, Cambridge, Mass and London: MIT Press, 2001, p. 178.

3   W. H. Auden, 'Light Prose', in *The English Auden, Poems, Essays & Dramatic Writings, 1927–1939*, edited by Edward Mendelson, London: Faber, 1977, p. 363.

4   In 1951 Cage visited the anechoic chamber at Harvard University, an experience, which influenced his work with silence and about which he said:

> I heard two sounds, one high and one low. Afterwards I asked the engi-
> neer in charge why, if the room was so silent, I had heard two sounds.
> He said, 'Describe them.' I did. He said, 'the high on was your nervous
> system in operation. The low one was your blood in circulation.'

John Cage, *A Year From Monday: New Lectures and Writings*, London: Calder and Boyars, 1968, p. 134.

5   Meditation is one way to deal with this tension between my own murmurs and the tiny sounds of silence, to be able to stay with it and become listening.

Another is to switch on Brian Eno's *Apollo* (1983). His ambient music provides an escape into a different listening to silence. It allows the listener to hear silence and fend of the bustle of a populated and busy soundscape without himself being implicated in its solitude. *Apollo* breaks the silence in silence. The sonic arrangement of Eno's ambient tracks take you out of the phenomenological tension of silence into a recognizable structure that lifts the burden of listening to nothing and enables you to hear without being captured by a musical expectation. I still am always now I hear rather than recognize that over-there but there is safety in his tracks, safety of structure and a certain rhythm that holds absolute silence at bay.

6   The work was commissioned by Ferdinand Pouey, the director of dramatic and literary broadcasts for French National Radio. It was recorded at the end of 1947 and scheduled for broadcast on the 2. February 1948. However, it was cancelled at the last minute by the director of French Radio, Vladimir Porche, on the grounds of being Anti-American and Anti-Catholic. Allen S. Weiss, 'From Schizophrenia to Schizophonica: Antonin Artaud's *To Have Done with the Judgment of God*', in *Phantasmic Radio*, Durham and London: Duke University Press, 1995, pp. 11–12.

7   The power of this agency is, as I will discuss in the next chapter, neither equal nor democratic. However, it serves to hear those who do not speak the dominant discourse by their sounds rather than by their language, in their bodily silence rather than their detached words. It affords us a fleshly hearing of subjectivities that does not sustain old habits of perception but astonishes us in an intertwined and present encounter.

8   In his text 'Écrivains et écrivant' (1960), Roland Barthes identifies the writer as author, the *écrivain*, and the person who is writing, the *écrivant*. While the first is a recognized authority of writing that uses as well as confirms the orthodoxies and conventions of literature, the second is a subject who is at this moment involved in the process of writing. The *écrivant* writes as he speaks, continually in the present without being self-consciously limited by the authority of traditions and conventions. His language is a device rather than an assured and critically ratified material in and of itself. I elaborate on this distinction in relation to the listener as *écouteur* and *écoutant*.

Barthe, Roland. 'Écrivains et écrivants', in *Essais Critiques*, Paris: Éditions Du Seuil, 1964, pp. 148–51.

9   Ibid., p. 152.

10   We might not see the same either but are pretending very well that we do. This sameness however is the ideological and cultural that has conspired as natural attitudes, as habits that impede the curiosity of perception to produce something new. The need to understand follows an ideology of pragmatism that sees us survive but also hinders a more complex perception.

11   In *The Rise of the Network Society*, Manuel Castells, writes about the Greek invention of the alphabet as a conceptual technology. Via Eric Havelock, he discusses how this technology enables a separation of the speaker and what is being said, distancing the subject and the object of discourse. Havelock, Eric A., *The Literate Revolution in Greece and its Cultural Consequences,* Princeton University Press, US, 1982, [orig. *Preface to Plato*, 1963]. He states that this distance enables conceptual discourse. The alphabet gives the thing articulated a security in that it fixes and positions it in letters and words. The object in writing is

spatialized as a material thing. In this state it becomes thinkable, conceptualizable. According to Castells 'it was the alphabet that, in the West, provided the mental infrastructure for cumulative, knowledge based communication'. Manuel Castells, *The Rise of the Network Society, the Information Age; Economy, Society and Culture Vol. 1*, Cambridge, MA: Blackwell Publishers, 1997, p. 356. This implies that conceptualization does not come out of what Castells understands as the insecurity and temporality of spaceless orality. Rather, it is a framework of (alphabetical) representation that grounds the object, which can then be moved and extended in conceptual discourse.

12   The tape recorded of course does allow us to store and replay any sonic moment too, but it only ever produces new sonic moments in my reciprocal listening.

13   'From our lazy hardware equipment we recommend the tap that stops dripping when we stop listening.' (own translation) This is one of the verbal puns on Duchamps 1926 version of *Anémic Cinéma* a dada film of a black and white rotating spiral, moving verbal puns seemingly forward and backward, inwards and outwards, slowly and fast all at the same time.

14   According to Kristeva the symbolic positions the subject, and depends on a socio-historically fixed subjectivity. Meanwhile, the semiotic is the pre-thetic. It precedes this positioning of the subject and breaks the symbolic order and thus moves it on to ultimately re-stage a new symbolic 'reality' to be breached imminently again. Kristeva explains this peculiar relationship between the semiotic and the symbolic in the terms of a poetic practice in which '. . . the semiotic – the precondition of the symbolic – is revealed as that which also destroys the symbolic'. Julia Kristeva, *Revolution in Poetic Language*, trans. Margaret Waller, New York: Columbia University Press, 1984, p. 50.

15   Kristeva states that all enunciation is thetic. The thetic phase 'contains the object as well as the proposition, and the complicity between them' (Ibid., p. 44). In other words, the thetic enables communication by offering the basic ingredients for signification and by giving a 'space' for its coming together. The thetic is the space within which enunciation happens and thus it is the realm of signification. The thetic phase marks the threshold between the semiotic and the symbolic, respective between language and its lexical register.

16   For Kristeva the fetish 'is a displacement of the thetic on the realm of drives' and 'fetishism is a telescoping of the symbolic's characteristic thetic moment and of one of those instinctually invested stases (bodies, parts of bodies, orifices, containing objects and so forth). This stasis thus becomes the ersatz of the sign. Fetishism is a stasis that acts as a thesis' (Ibid., p. 64). In relation to art practice the fetish is the replacement of that which is destroyed in poetic practice. 'Aesthetic fetishism' consolidates the by the artwork contested thetic. The fetish replaces the innovative perception of the sensorial material, and consolidates it within the artwork and in relation to the art world as a whole. The language of the art critic is fetishistic when it puts forward a replacement for the unspeakable experience.

17   Ibid., p. 69.

18   Ibid., p. 65.

19   Maurice Merleau-Ponty, *The Visible and the Invisible*, trans. Alphonso Lingis, edited by Claude Lefort, Illinois: Northwestern University Press, 1968, p. 155.

20   This conviction is the temporal and contingent certainty achieved from doubt in an *a priori* reality through the effort of suspending one's habitual attitudes.

21   Maurice Merleau-Ponty, *Phenomenology of Perception*, trans. Colin Smith, London and New York: Routledge, 2002, 207.

22   Maurice Merleau-Ponty, *The Visible and the Invisible*, trans. Alphonso Lingis, edited by Claude Lefort, Illinois: Northwestern University Press, 1968, p. 14.

Merleau-Ponty's split of the world and perception into the sphere of the visible and the invisible sets up a dialectical relationship between inner and outer world, as the individual and the collective world and brings with it the double issue of sublimation and reflection separate from experience. When the invisible is understood as sonic rather than not visible, it is not the negative to the idea of a visible world but rather produces the visible world continually from the conviction of one's contingent perception.

23   Lévi-Strauss, in his book *The Savage Mind*, employs *bricolage* in relation to mythical thought: 'the "bricoleur" is adept at performing a large number of diverse tasks; but, unlike the engineer he does not subordinate each of them to the availability of raw materials and tools conceived and procured for the purpose of the project.' Rather the process of *bricolage* is contingent, the *bricoleur* makes do with 'whatever is at hand'. Claude Lévi-Strauss, *The Savage Mind*, London: Weidenfeld and Nicholson, 1972, p. 17. This sense of *bricolage* also evokes Jaques Derrida's conception of it as criticality. In *Writing and Difference,* commenting on Lévi-Strauss' notion of *bricolage*, Derrida articulates the idea 'that bricolage is critical language itself.' Jacques Derrida, *Writing and Difference*, trans. Alan Bass, London: Routledge and Kegan Paul, 1978, p. 285.

I am employing the sense of a contingent and individual production of the artwork as *bricoler* to stress the process of production rather than the outcome, the *bricolage*, and the myth thus built; and use it as a critical activity not in reference to the 'building' of a myth, the production of a poetic meaning, but in terms of its processes of critical engagement. *Bricoler*, as verb denotes a critical practice in perception. The interest is not to produce an object, but to continually produce, from parts but not in relation to a whole, my language from the symbolic tendency of the material towards speech.

24   Shimon Levy, *Samuel Beckett's Self-referential Drama: The Sensitive Chaos,* Sussex: Sussex Academic Press, 2002, p. 79.

25   This sonico-social sensibility of the analogue radio is removed in the digital. Digital radio mutes the airwaves and creates an aesthetic stoppage: it arrests the mobility of critical language in the certainty of its dial. No tuning buzz reminds the listener of the fragility of the heard and of the invisible network of hearing that his own audition is part of. The tendential sociality of these sounds will be missed on the backdrop of zapping perfection and download precision.

26   Of course 24-hour radio has no night to sound its silence, but that does not mean it is not there. It maintains at least the concept of silence and affords me glimpses of it, hovering in the background, as I move from station to station.

27   KAB Antonio Bay radio DJ Stevie Wane in the *The Fog*, DVD, written by John Carpenter and Debra Hill, directed by John Carpenter, 1980, MGM/United Artists Video, 2002.

28   This relationship between silence and listening might explain why, according the forum for acoustic ecology the ability to listen is deteriorating. The lack of silence leads to an inability to hear, not in the obvious but in the philosophical sense of negotiating the heard rather than simply acknowledging its presence.

29   This notion of a 'desired collectivity' does in no way assume that this will and effort towards consensual sense indeed exists, that it is unmitigated by means and position, nor that it cannot be used to manipulate and oppress, marginalize and exclude. It certainly does not suggest a naive utopia of democratic consensuality. Rather, the notion of willingness invokes the idea that the artwork as aesthetic moment is shared to the extent that the individual subject is participating in a shared sense produced contingently, rather than a sense shared contractually, assuming a pre-existing order to its collectivity. This also implies that the manner in which the sense is not shared produces itself a sense of social relations. Indeed it is the very fact that a sonic sociality depends on will and effort rather than on a pre-existent contract, which could take care of the marginal and the excluded, that reveals the dynamic of exclusion.

30   Space and time do not prepare and stage this encounter but are produced as equally fragile things thinging that exchange.

Time and Space

1   In many ways sound builds Martin Heidegger's *Hütte*, a cabin built for him in the Black Forest, but crucially without aim or purpose. Sound is the cell of inhabiting, it is the relationship between being and environment, it is dwelling. However, Heidegger's relation between being and dwelling (*wohnen*) is transcendental: the function of his hut is already there in the symbolism of dwelling, which is realized by building, by grounding dwelling in a location. By contrast in sound I am only ever building unstable and fleeting houses out of time. The sonic symbolism is tendential rather than lexical and so I build on horizontal tendencies rather than vertical lines into the ground. Sound has no visual purpose, it does not suffer visual functionalism. It does not offer a meaningful order to temporality and spatiality but produces them fleetingly as passing suggestions. And so it does not build to inhabit but inhabits the built of its own transience.

2   Space and time arise out of perception as immaterial complex. This is an ephemeral, heterogeneous and permanently incongruous amalgamation that is contingently produced by the subject perceiving it and whose ideality is a subjective ideality, and always fleetingly so.

3   Hegel's dialectical time is negated by space, which is its container; a vessel that time bestows its spatial content on. For Hegel the characteristic of time and space is their inner necessity, to become rather than to be, and they are defined, reciprocally, in the dynamic of their dialectical identification. They exist in perpetual '*Widersprüchlichkeit*' (antagonistic contradiction), whereby 'space is negated time' and time sublated space. G. W. F. Hegel, 'Space and Time', in *Philosophy of Nature Vol. 1*, London: Routledge, 2002, p. 233. By contrast Jean-François Lyotard's notion of agonistic playfulness expresses the amicable adversariness through which time and space produce each other in subjective

perception without insisting on a dialectical identification. Jean-François Lyotard, *The Postmodern Condition: A Report on Knowledge*, trans. Geoff Bennington and Brian Massumi, Manchester: Manchester University Press, 1994, p.10. The individual elements, time and space, might fight, push and shove each other, but these are just play-fights, games to test and expand the sense of one and the other without the desire to overcome the difference in an absolute ideality. Rather, the differences present themselves to perception as distinct elements, which are played with to complexify the perception of either and in whose playful competition I am implicated as listener.

4   Sergej Eisenstein, 'The Unexpected', in *Film Form Essays in Film Theory,* trans. and edited by Jay Leyda, London: Dennis Dobson LTD, 1949, p. 20.

5   It is very interesting to note that Eisenstein's monistic ensemble of sound and image is in the end used towards the production of the total film. This totality is achieved through the ideal synthesis of the individual audio and visual frames or cells in a counterpuntal strategy. And so while the first stage of his montage principle, the efforts of non-synchronisation of cells of monistic value similarity is interesting in relation to timespace conceptualized as monistic ensemble, his second step, which views these cells in relation to the ideality of the total film erodes the discrete quality of sound and image and sublimates their distinction for the purpose of the film as *Gesammtkunstwerk*.

6   'Warum bleiben wir in der Provinz?' In der Alemanne, 7 March 1934.

7   Martin Heidegger, in Adam Sharr, *Heidegger's Hut*, Cambridge, Mass: MIT Press, 2006, p. 64.

8   While some of Heidegger's notions of local community, sustainability and the idea of living in concordance with nature regain some credibility within the current context of the ecological crisis of global warming, his leaning towards German romanticism and the mythology of nature together with his alignment with Nazi Germany at the time, makes his hut and the concomitant trends of *Heimat* and folklore deeply disturbing. The dialectics of his space demarcates a distinct engagement with inside and outside, function and order, and portrays a great anxiety towards the new, the other, the flux of being outside the safety of authenticity, rootedness, identity, *Heimat* and language as mother tongue. This espousal of a transcendent nature haunts his hut.

9   *Silence* revealed the murmur of a sonic life-world, which binds the listening subject into its hum: to hear himself murmuring while listening to the hum of his acoustic environment through which he hears himself. From inside this murmuring world the listening subject plugs any apparent gap between being, space and time that the visual might propose and use for their juxtaposition and eventual synthesis. He disables their separation or negation and makes them one on the body of his interpretative fantasy. Thus listening diffuses the functional becoming of time and space in a formless and concrete being.

10   Maurice Merleau-Ponty, *Phenomenology of Perception*, trans. Colin Smith, London and New York: Routledge, 2002, pp. 295–9.

11   Ibid., pp. 330–1.

12   What Merleau-Ponty, in his in 1964 posthumously published book *The Visible and the Invisible*, terms 'The Invisible' particularly with reference to the chapter 'The intertwining – the Chasm', is not so much invisible as it is sounding. It is by moving away from the opposition of visible and invisible, day and night, that a sonic sensibility can be articulated.

13   Merleau-Ponty's differentiation between the functional and ordered field of vision and the erratic and distressed field of sound is particularly apparent in a footnote of this text where he points to the errors of hearing and how these errors find correction through the image, since 'the placing of sound by hearing alone remains incorrect to the end'. Merleau-Ponty, *Phenomenology of Perception*, trans. Colin Smith, London and New York: Routledge, 2002, p. 292.

14   For Merleau-Ponty 'time is nothing but the transition from one present to another' and while this transition does not form a line it nevertheless retains the shape of a sequence, or a linearity of intention, that is achieved in the (transition-) synthesis of present perception, which expresses its objective (Ibid., p. 495).

15   Merleau-Ponty arrives at his continuity of time via Husserl's *Abschattung*, a notion of retention through which I hold the immediate past which I reach in its recent 'thisness' as I proceed to the next immediate now. In this sense the present comes in stages, slithers of a past that overshadow in neat chronology the present moment. *Abschattung* is an idea which Merleau-Ponty develops away from in his own articulation of temporality but from which he retains the significance of his own time as a 'network of intentionalities' (Ibid., p. 484).

16   Ibid., p. 483.

17   The purposeful listening of Merleau-Ponty's 'un-broken continuity' is musical listening, listening that adapts the heard to a visual framework for the correction of its formlessness (Ibid., p. 485). The listening of the signifying practice of non-sense however, is listening as an endless mobility that cannot rely on a primordial river to give it the direction and function of its flow but that *is* its flow in all its purposeless multiplicity.

18   Ibid., p. 503.

19   The transcendental subject, which is according to Adorno always already deformed to the rationality and abstraction of a current (visual) society relates to space and time not through its contingent experience but through the function and purpose which allocate it its place in the social totality. Theodor Adorno, 'Subject and Object', in *The Adorno Reader*, edited by Brian O'Connor, Oxford: Blackwell, 2000, p. 141. In turn it is this functional identity that deforms its experience to transcendental givens.

20   Timespace is time and space as verb, as thing thinging. It does not describe a place and neither is it a place, it is neither adjective nor noun. Instead, it is the site of production of the sound that sounds its motion as an invisible dynamic through which I hear place. In this sense timespace is the site of sound as verb that produces geography from the mapping of our auditory imagination and grants it a provisional authority in the conviction of our urgent perception.

21   David Harvey, 'From Space to Place and Back Again: Reflections on the Condition of Postmodernity', in *Mapping the Futures, Local Cultures, Global Change*, edited by Jon Bird et al., London: Routledge, 1996, p. 6.

Harvey's networking angst is based on a Hegelian idea of time as the annihilation of space and of 'space as negated time'. Hegel, "Space and time" *in Philosophy of Nature Vol. 1*, 233.

22   Harvey, 'From Space to Place and Back Again', in *Mapping the Futures, Local Cultures, Global Change*, p. 4.

23   Ibid., p. 11.

24   The 1999 Film the Matrix directed by the Wachowski brothers, illustrates the understanding of the virtual world as a Hegelian space: a vessel for time

in motion. When Keanu Reeve's character, the computer programmer Neo, decides to enter the Matrix of the virtual world he enters a white space of nothing that is yet to be filled through his actions within it. *The Matrix*, DVD, written and directed by Andy Wachowski and Larry Wachowski, 1999, UK: Warner Home Video, 1999.

25 The notion of conviction in this sense is an individual and practical ideology. It produces one's position and trajectory in the world, and thus it produces one's world, rather than positioning one within a pre-existent world. This position is temporal, continually contingent, producing perpetually my time-space now.

26 Doreen Massey, 'Power-geometry and a Progressive Sense of Place', in *Mapping The Futures, Local Cultures, Global Change*, edited by Jon Bird et al., London: Routledge, 1996, p. 61.

27 It is here that it becomes apparent that simply and theoretically granting the subject agency over the universal power of space to connect things as place, as Merleau-Ponty does, does not take account of political and social powers that define the individual subject's relationship to the dimension of time and space. Merleau-Ponty is right to suggest that the subject is at the intersection of time and space those dimensions himself; to push the visceral body into Heidegger's functional hut. However, not everybody shares the power and control over these dimensions in equal measure. Being for him is 'being situated', it is a 'being-for-the-gaze'. Merleau-Ponty, *Phenomenology of Perception*, pp. 294–5. Being in sound by contrast is an effort of situating oneself, which is fraught with the struggle for belonging and identity.

28 Massey, 'Power-geometry and a Progressive Sense of Place', in *Mapping The Futures, Local Cultures, Global Change*, p. 67.

29 This report was produced in 1979 by Lyotard for the Conseil des Universitiés of the government of Quebec at the request of its president and aimed to reflect on the 'condition of knowledge in the most highly developed societies'. It does so by using the term the postmodern, which was current at the time in America only. Lyotard, *The Postmodern Condition: A Report on Knowledge*, xxiii.

30 Ibid., p. 10.

31 Ibid., p. 10.

32 This goes back to Lyotard's argument that taste and good form are suspended in the postmodern language game, and by implication his suggestion that we will get back to the base of taste and good form, modernism, when we stop playing; when the grand narratives of science and history re-enter the scene to evaluate and chose from the small narrations of local expression. *The Postmodern Condition*, p. 81. This suggests that for Lyotard the postmodern is but a renewal of the modern, which it imminently reaffirms. However, modernism is a thoroughly Western concept that cannot hold the complexity of a current global consciousness without reducing it to its own viewpoint, and thus does not offer a base to which we can return. And so, 30 years later, it is the modern rather than its changeable prefix that needs to be revised.

33 In *Silence* I outlined the relationship of listening to language and meaning not in the sense of a lexical semiotico-symbolic organization but as tendential speech, whose exclamations are not unsaid or indirect, but whose practice works on the fragile and unstable connections between the sensorial

experience and its articulation as experience. This is language as tendency towards rather than as a means of sense. It is not bad taste, frivolous and marginalizable, but finds its legitimation in the sincerity of my practical speech and the moments of coincidence that is belonging as a spatiotemporal event. Such transient belonging denotes society not in relation to its grand narratives and not in relation to self-regulatory small narrations either, but from the bottom up as it where, in a non-renewable effort of the temporality of place.

34   Ibid., p. 57.

35   Massey, 'Power-geometry and a Progressive Sense of Place', in *Mapping The Futures, Local Cultures, Global Change*, p. 66.

36   Merleau-Ponty, *The Visible and the Invisible*, trans. Alphonso Lingis, edited by Claude Lefort, Illinois: Northwestern University Press, 1968, p. 155.

37   Michel Chion, *Audio-Vision Sound and Screen*, trans. and edited by Michel Gorbman, New York: Columbia University Press, 1994, p. 112.

Fontana's *Harmonic Bridge* pushes Chion's clump of sensation, that is sound rendering real the reality of a perceived visual event as a sensory reality, into a conceptual arena. Fontana's work focuses not on the sonic material but on the sonic process, and in this way extends Chion's sensorial clump into the idea of a conceptual clump of sonic sensibility.

38   Merleau-Ponty comes to the depth of the visual world by shifting positions. He suggests that a quasi-synthesis is needed that does not synthesize discrete terms from one viewpoint, but is achieved from multiplicities positions against the background of stable things. It is the viewpoints rather than the objects that are synthesized in his conception and this quasi-synthesis is temporal and subjective but the subject 'in order to arrive at a uniform space, must [nevertheless] leave his place, abandon his point of view on the world, and think himself into a sort of ubiquity.' Merleau-Ponty, *Phenomenology of Perception*, p. 299. By contrast, sound is the invisible depth of the visual spectacle, it is not grasped through a deduction of multiple viewpoints but through inhabiting my own mobile place within them all.

39   'Because the temporality, which is discussed here, relates to the processes of the artwork itself, and its constitution in the essentially infinite processes of aesthetic experience' Juliane Rebentisch, *Ästhetik der Installation*, Germany: Edition Suhrkamp, 2003, p. 152. (own translation)

40   Michel de Certeau, 'Walking in the City', in *The Practice of Everyday Life*, trans. Steven Randall, London: University of California Press, 1988, p. 93.

41   'The (possible) worlds are something like remote planets; except that most of them are much bigger than mere planets, and they are not remote. Neither are they nearby. They are not at any spatial distance whatever from here. They are not far in the past or future, nor for that matter near; they are not at a spatial distance whatever from now.' David Lewis, *On the Plurality of Worlds*, Oxford: Basil Blackwell, 1986, p. 2.

42   If phonography is to bring to us a different understanding from that achieved by photographic documentation, then it has to find a truth in its own material, in sound, that offers us an affective and immersive knowing of places and things, rather than a detached reading of its textual quality or source.

43   Lyotard's report on knowledge, written in 1979, foresaw many things accurately while others got superseded by the consequences of their own logic: the *petit récit* of local and transient competence and legitimation turned out to be

less democratic and heterogeneous and more corrupt and dangerous than pre-dicted. The deregulation and abandonment of state control did not achieve a freedom of the people, but an anti-humanist drive of enslavery to work and money. Subjectivity not measured on the nation-state got replaced by subjectivity meas-ured not by the freedom of locality but the globalization of control of business, which incidentally killed the competence of the nation-state of modernism. And so there is no way back, there is no renewal of modernity through the postmodern language as game. There is only now, as a present state, not nascent out of modernity, but vertiginous and suddenly now, out of the darkness of sound. A new report on knowledge needs to be written, one based on knowing as a sonic sensibility that takes account of the complex relationships between space and time, and whose competence and legitimacy lies on the body of the subject at the intersections of these dimensions: in *his* place. This would have to be a report on knowing, and knowledge, as graspable fact, would have to be worked out of this sensibility in moments of coincidence that take account of the fragile and subjective base of their legitimation and proceed in doubt rather than from an *a priori* through the competence of their own contingent production.

44   Filippo Tommaso Marinetti and Pino Masnata, 'La Radia', in Wireless Imagination, edited by Douglas Kahn and Gregory Whitehead, Cambridge, Mass and London; MIT Press, 1994, p. 267.

45   Max is a versatile graphical development environment that allows composers, performers and sound designers to build complex interactive soft-ware systems for real-time audio synthesis and processing, as well as video and data control.

46   Minkowski in Merleau-Ponty, *Phenomenology of Perception*, 330.

47   As such a politico-sensorial inhabitant I experience time and space through the ambiguity of my own belonging rather than as a functional or sym-bolic place.

48   Ibid., p. 503.

Now

1   Noël Carroll, 'Art, Narrative, and Emotion', in *Beyond Aesthetics: Philosophical Essays*, Cambridge: Cambridge University Press, 2001, p. 215.

2   Ibid., p. 217.

3   Ibid., p. 217.

4   Ibid., p. 229.

5   Ibid., p. 230.

6   'So we shall be justified in not admitting him (the artist) into a well-ordered commonwealth, because he stimulates and strengthens an element which threatens to undermine the reason.' Plato. *The Republic*, trans. Francis Macdonald Cornford, Oxford: Clarendon Press, 1961, p. 329.

7   Caroll, 'Art, Narrative, and Emotion', in *Beyond Aesthetics: Philosophical Essays*, p. 222.

8   John Ruskin, "Of the Pathetic Fallacy" in *Modern Painters Vol. III*, London: George Routledge and Sons Ltd., 1903, p. 168.

In this third volume on Modern Painters, Ruskin writes against the 'pathetic fallacy' arguing that an emotional viewing falsifies the artwork. Instead he promotes the idea of pure facts and rationality for the better production and judgment of art. (Ibid., p. 170)

9   Carroll, 'Art, Narrative, and Emotion', in *Beyond Aesthetics: Philosophical Essays*, p. 216.

10   The romantic body of Carroll's cultural audience is the already deformed body of Adorno's transcendental subject. It does not feel and act but responds to the demands of its environment, which deformed it in the first place. Against this cultural audience stands the concrete subject of experience, which threatens the cohesion of Carroll's subject through its irrational formlessness.

11   Henri Bergson, *Matter and Memory,* trans. Nancy Margaret Paul and W. Scott Palmer, New York: Zone Books, 1991, p. 53.

12   Ibid., p. 57.

13   Ibid. p. 57.

14   Ruskin, 'Of the Pathetic Fallacy', in *Modern Painters Vol. III*, p. 170.

15   Julia Kristeva, 'The Imaginary Sense of Forms', in *Arts Magazine*, September (1991): p. 30.

16   Carroll, 'Art, Narrative, and Emotion', in *Beyond Aesthetics: Philosophical Essays*, p. 331.

17   This is a reference to Kant's text *Groundwork for the Metaphysics of Morals*, written in 1785 that chiefly determined the understanding of ethics throughout the modernist period.

18   Merleau-Ponty critiques Bergson's memory and disagrees with his notion of projection of the past into a present perception: 'Now, for empiricism, "cultural" objects and faces owe their distinctive form, their magic power, to transference and projection of memory, so that only by accident has the human world any meaning.' Maurice Merleau-Ponty, *Phenomenology of Perception*, trans. Colin Smith, London and New York: Routledge, 2002, p. 27. It is the details of his disagreement that reveal why, although an important reference throughout this book, Merleau-Ponty is not discussed in this last part. The notion of memory, the relationship of the past to a present action of perception, brings to light the problems of Merleau-Ponty's phenomenology for sound art, as it reveals the visual sensibility of his philosophy. Merleau-Ponty's memory is functional and intentional. It is cognitive as it is the memory of a source not of an action of perception. It happens in space that is simultaneous but nevertheless discrete. And in this way the multiplicity of the temporal moments in that space, can be synthesized as one real thought rather than produced as possible actions. Merleau-Ponty's phenomenology is a transcendental philosophy that contains thought not as a consequence of the action of experience but as its guiding force. His phenomenological experience does not seek language but has it in hand at all times. What he terms inner experience he understands to be meaningless because it is incommunicable (Ibid., 322n). He calls it a 'mental blindness' and suggests that 'the perceived world has lost for him (the sufferer of this blindness) its original structure which ensures that for the normal person its hidden aspects are as indubitable as are its visible ones' (Ibid., p. 29). Vision sees what is in front of it but knows what is at its back, whereas sound immerses me in the darkness of its unexpected moves: no front, no back, and nothing to know, but its sensate material triggers my present knowing through the affective aspect of its past. In this darkness of sound I build the work and myself in my action of perception, which includes reflection but as experienced thought rather than as thought experienced.

Merleau-Ponty pursues a language that exists as a given, that experience uses rather than forms in its own formless transience. Yet it is exactly this formless transience that grants a phenomenology of sound art the phenomenon of its own language as speech, to embrace the dark ambiguity and passing coincidence of its material.

This does not mean that Merleau-Ponty's reflections are of no use for the articulation of a philosophy of sound art. To the contrary, they lead the way towards its thought, but due to his philosophical sensibility they do not reach its materiality.

19   Bergson, *Matter and Memory*, p. 34.

20   This is not the memory of intellectual contemplation, which reaches from the present into the past to retrieve from it mute moments that remain abstract. Rather, this memory *is* the action of perception, it is the body approaching the world through a past the produces the present and hints at a future.

21   Ibid., p. 244.

22   In this sense the duration of memory invites a reduced listening that brackets sound not only from its concurrent visual source but also takes care of the reference of a previous audition. A focused listening to the work as extensive now, gets to the sound as sound that does not deny references but appreciates them as the affective material that produces the moment of perception into which they fade to make room for a new and contingent production of the work, rather than substituting it through pre-existing meanings and opinions or their renewal.

23   Ibid., p. 228.

24   Ibid., p. 229.

25   Andrei Tarkovsky, *Sculpting in Time*, trans. Kitty Hunter-Blair, London and Boston: Faber and Faber, 1989, p. 158.

26   Ibid., p. 158.

Bibliography

Adorno, Theodor. 'The Essay as Form', in *The Adorno Reader*, edited by Brian O
O'Connor, 91–111, Oxford: Blackwell, 2000.
— 'The Actuality of Philosophy', in *The Adorno Reader*, edited by Brian O'Connor,
23–39, Oxford: Blackwell, 2000.
— 'Subject and Object', in *The Adorno Reader*, edited by Brian O'Connor, 137–51,
Oxford: Blackwell, 2000.
— *Musikalische Schriften I – III*, Frankfurt: Suhrkamp, 2003.
— *Minima Moralia, Reflections on a Damaged Life*, trans. E. F. N. Jephcott, London
and New York: Verso, 2005.
Aristotle. *De Anima Book II & III*, trans. D. W. Hamlyn, Oxford: Clarendon, 1968.
Arnheim, Rudolph. 'In Praise of Blindness', in *Radiotext(e)*, edited by Neil Strauss,
20–5, New York: Columbia University Press, 1993.
Attali, Jacques. *Noise: The Political Economy of Music*, trans. Brian Massumi,
Minneapolis: University of Minnesota Press, [1977] 1985.
Auden, Wystan Hugh. 'Light Prose', in *The English Auden, Poems, Essays &
Dramatic Writings, 1927–1939*, edited by Edward Mendelson, 363–8, London:
Faber, 1977.
Bachelard, Gaston. *The Poetics of Space*, trans. Maria Jolas, New York: Orion
Press, [1958] 1964.
Barthes, Roland. 'Écrivains et écrivants', in *Essais Critiques*, 147–54, Paris: Éditions
Du Seuil, 1964.
Bergson, Henri. *Matter and Memory*, trans. Nancy Margaret Paul and W. Scott
Palmer, New York: Zone Books, [1896] 1991.
Bourriaud, Nicholas. *Altermodern Manifesto*, http://www.tate.org.uk/britain/
exhibitions/altermodern/manifesto.shtm
— *Relational Aesthetics*, trans. Simon Pleasance and Fronza Woods with Mathieu
Copeland, France: Les presses du réel, [1998] 2002.
Bruinsman, Max. 'Notes of a Listener', in *Sound by Artists*, edited by Dan Lander
and Micah Lexier, 88–96, Toronto: Art Metropole and Banff: Walter Phillips
Gallery, 1985.
Cage, John. *A Year from Monday: New Lectures and Writings*, London: Calder
and Boyars, 1968.
Carroll, Noël. 'Art, Narrative, and Emotion', in *Beyond Aesthetics: Philosophical
Essays*, 215–35. Cambridge: Cambridge University Press, 2001.
Castells, Manuel. *The Rise of the Network Society, the Information Age; Economy,
Society and Culture Vol. 1*, 2nd edition, Cambridge, Mass: Blackwell Publish-
ers, 1997.
Certeau, Michel de. 'Walking in the City', in *The Practice of Everyday Life*, 91–110,
trans. Steven Randall, London: University of California Press, [1980] 1988.

Chion, Michel, *Audio-Vision Sound and Screen*, trans. and edited by Claudia Gorbman, New York: Columbia University Press, [1990] 1994.

Davidson, Donald. 'A Nice Derangement of Epitaphs', in *Truth and Interpretation*, edited by Ernest LePore, 432–46, Oxford: Basil Blackwell, 1986.

Derrida, Jacques. *Writing and Difference*, trans. Alan Bass, London: Routledge and Kegan Paul, [1967] 1978.

Eisenstein, Sergej. 'The Unexpected', in *Film Form Essays in Film Theory*, trans. and edited by Jay Leda, 18–27, London: Denis Dobson, [1928] 1949.

– 'Synchronization of Senses', in *Film Sense*, trans. and edited by Jay Leyda, 60–91, London: Faber, [1929] 1958.

– 'A Dialectic Approach to Film Form', in *Film Theory and Criticism*, edited by Gerald Mast, Marshall Cohen and Leo Braudy, 4th edition, 138–54, Oxford: Oxford University Press, 1992.

Greenberg, Clement. *The Collected Essays and Criticism, Vol. 4, Modernism with a Vengeance, 1957–1969*, edited by J. O'Brian, Chicago: University of Chicago Press, 1995.

Harvey, David. *The Condition of Postmodernity: An Enquiry into the Origins of Cultural Change*, Cambridge, Mass and Oxford: Basil Blackwell, 1990.

– 'From Space to Place and Back Again: Reflections on the Condition of Post-modernity', in *Mapping the Futures, Local Cultures, Global Change*, edited by Jon Bird, Barry Curtis, Tim Putnam, George Robertson and Lisa Tickner, 3–29, London: Routledge, 1996.

Havelock, Eric A. *The Literate Revolution in Greece and its Cultural Consequences*, Princeton and Guildford: Princeton University Press, 1982.

Hegel, Georg Wilhelm Friedrich. *Reason in History*, trans. Robert S. Hartman, New York: Library Arts Press, [1837] 1953.

– *Phenomenology of Spirit*, trans. A.V. Miller, Oxford: Clarendon Press, [1807] 1977.

– *Introduction to the Berlin Aesthetic Lectures of 1820s*, trans. T.M. Knox, Oxford: Clarendon Press, [orig. 1823–26] 1979.

– *Vorlesungen über die Ästhetik I*, Germany: Suhrkamp Verlag, [orig. 1832–45] 1980.

– *Vorlesungen über die Ästhetik II*, Germany: Suhrkamp Verlag, [orig. 1832–45] 1980.

– *Vorlesungen über die Ästhetik III*, Germany: Suhrkamp Verlag, [orig. 1832–45] 1980.

– 'Space and Time' in *Philosophy of Nature Vol.1*, 223–40, London: Routledge, 2002.

Heidegger, Martin. 'Warum bleiben wir in der Provinz?', in *der Alemanne*, 7 March 1934.

– 'Bauen Wohnen Denken', in *Vorträge und Aufsätze*, 145–81, Prullingen, Germany: Verlag Günther 1959.

– 'Das Ding', in *Vorträge und Aufsätze*, 163–81, Prullingen, Germany: Verlag Günther 1959.

– *Die Frage nach dem Ding: zu Kants Lehre von den transzendentalen Grund-sätzen*, Tübingen: Max Niemeyer Verlag, 1962.

– *Sein und Zeit*, Tübingen: Max Niemeyer, 1986.

– *Der Ursprung des Kunstwerkes*, Stuttgart: Philip Reclam jun., 2008.

Husserl, Edmund. *Ideas: General Introduction to Pure Phenomenology*, trans. W. R. B. Gibson, Australia: Allen and Unwin, 1931.

Kahn, Douglas. *Noise Water Meat, A History of Sound in the Arts*, Cambridge, Mass and London: MIT Press, 2001.

Kant, Immanuel. *Critique of Judgment*, trans. James Creed Meredith, Oxford: Oxford University Press, [1790] 2007.

— *Groundwork for the Metaphysics of Morals*, trans. Arnulf Zweig, edited by Thomas E. Hill and Arnulf Zweig. Oxford: Oxford University Press, [1785] 2002.

King, Steven. *The Shining*, US: Doubleday, 1977.

Kracauer, Siegfried. *The Mass Ornament, Weimar Essays*, trans. and edited by Thomas Y Levin, Cambridge, Mass and London: Harvard University Press, [1963] 1995.

Krauss, Rosalind E. *The Originality of the Avant-Garde and Other Modernist Myths*, Cambridge, Mass and London: MIT Press, 1987.

Kristeva, Julia. *Revolution in Poetic Language*, trans. Margaret Waller with an introduction by Leon S. Roudiez, New York: Columbia University Press, [1974] 1984.

— 'The Imaginary Sense of Forms' in *Arts Magazine*, September (1991): 28–30.

Lévi-Strauss, Claude. *The Savage Mind*, London: Weidenfeld and Nicholson, 1972.

Levy, Shimon. *Samuel Beckett's Self-referential Drama: The Sensitive Chaos*, Sussex: Sussex Academic Press, 2002.

Lewis, David Kellog. *On the Plurality of Worlds*, Oxford: Basil Blackwell, 1986.

Lyotard, Jean-François. *La condition postmoderne: Rapport sur le savoir*, Paris: Les Éditions Minuit, 1979.

— *The Postmodern Condition: A Report on Knowledge*, trans. Geoff Bennington and Brian Massumi, Manchester: Manchester University Press, [1979] 1994.

— 'The Sublime and the Avant-Garde', in *The Lyotard Reader*, edited by Andrew Benjamin, 196–211, Oxford: Basil Blackwell,1989.

Marinetti F.T. and Pino Masnata. 'La Radia', in *Wireless Imagination*, edited by Douglas Kahn and Gregory Whitehead, 265–8, Cambridge, Mass and London; MIT Press, 1994.

Massey, Doreen. 'Power-geometry and a Progressive Sense of Place', in *Mapping the Futures, local Cultures, Global Change*, edited by Jon Bird, Barry Curtis, Tim Putnam, George Robertson and Lisa Tickner, 59–69, London: Routledge, 1996.

Merleau-Ponty, Maurice. *Primacy of Perception*, trans. James M. Edie Illinois: Northwestern University Press, 1964.

— *Sense and Non-Sense*, trans. Hubert L. Dreyfus and Patricia Allen Dreyfus, Illinois: Northwestern University Press, 1964.

— *The Visible and the Invisible*, trans. Alphonso Lingis, edited by Claude Lefort, Illinois: Northwestern University Press, 1968.

— *Phenomenology of Perception*, trans. Colin Smith, London and New York: Routledge, [1945] 2002.

— 'Cézanne's Doubt' in *The Merleau-Ponty Aesthetic Reader*, 3–13, trans. Michael B. Smith, edited by Galen A. Johnson, 2nd edition, Illinois: Northwestern University Press, 1996.

— *The World of Perception*, trans. Oliver Davis, London and New York: Routledge, 2008 [First published in French as *Causeries 1948*, Paris: Editions de Seuil,

2002 from a radio series commissioned by the French national radio and broadcast on its National Programme at the end of 1948].

Metz, Christian. 'Aural Objects', in *Film Theory and Criticism*, 4th edition, edited by Gerald Mast, Marshall Cohen and Leo Braudy, 313–16, Oxford: Oxford University Press, 1992, [orig. from 'le perçu et le nommé' in *Yale French Studies*, vol. 60, (1980): 24–32].

Pasnau, Robert. 'What is Sound?' in *The Philosophical Quarterly*, vol. 49, no. 196 (1999): 309–24.

Plato. *The Republic*, trans. with notes by Francis Macdonald Cornford, Oxford: Clarendon Press, 1961.

Rebentisch, Julia. *Ästhetik der Installation*, Germany: Edition Suhrkamp, 2003.

Ruskin, John. 'Of the Pathetic Fallacy' in *Modern Painters Vol. III*, 166–83, London: George Routledge and Sons Ltd., 1903.

Russolo, Luigi. *The Art of Noise: Futurist Manifesto 1913*, trans. Robert Filliou, New York: Something Else Press, [1916] 1967.

Schaeffer, Pierre. *Traité des objets musicaux: essai interdisciplines*, Paris: Éditions du Seuil , 1966.

Schafer, R. Murray. *The Tuning of the World*. New York: Knopf, 1977.

Sharr, Adam. *Heidegger's Hut*, Cambridge, Mass: MIT Press, 2006.

Tarkovsky, Andrei. *Sculpting in Time*, trans. Kitty Hunter-Blair, London and Boston: Faber and Faber, [1986] 1989.

Voegelin, Salomé, 'Audio Sensitisation and Participation in the Soundscape' in *Journal of Electroacoustic Music*, vol. 12, London: Sonic Arts Network, March (1999): 39–43.

Weiss, Alan S. 'From Schizophrenia to Schizophonica: Antonin Artaud's to Have Done with the Judgment of God', in *Phantasmic Radio*, 9–34, Durham and London: Duke University Press, 1995.

List of Works

Arn, Stini. *microscopic trips,* broadcast on Radio LoRa Zürich, February 2006.

Artaud, Antonin. *To Have Done With the Judgment of God,* 1947, Belgium: Sub Rosa, SR 092 CD, 1996.

Beck, Julian. *Je n'ai pas le droit de voyager sans passport,* 1968, http://www.ubu.com/sound/beck.html

Bochner, Mel. *8″ Measurements,* 1969, Black ink on graph paper, 11″ x 8,5″, in Richardson, Brenda, *Mel Bochner, Number and Shape,* Maryland: The Baltimore Museum of Art, 1976.

Cage, John. *Silent Prayer,* 1948, idea to produce silent piece to sell to the Muzak Co.

— *4'33″,* performance premiered by David Tudor August 29 1952 Woodstock New York.

Cardiff, Janet and George Bures Miller, *The Dark Pool,* installation at Oxford Museum of Modern Art, UK, 2009, orig. 1995.

Curgenven, Robert. 'Silent Landscapes No2', on *Autumn Leaves* online audio compilation, http://www.gruenrekorder.de/?page_id=196, 2008

Cusack, Peter. *Chernobyl,* 2008. This CD will be released shortly.

Duchamp Marcel. *Fountain,* porcelain urinal, 1917, lost.

— *Air de France,* bottled Air, 1919.

— *Anémic Cinéma,* 35 mm Film, B&W, silent, 7 minutes, 1926.

Eno, Brian. *Apollo – Atmospheres & Soundtracks,* Japan: Polydor, Vinyl, LP, 28MM 0298, 1983.

Federer. Benjamin. *Klang;Zeit;Klang,* on Radio LoRa, 2006.

Feldman, Morton. *Piano and String Quartet,* composed 1985, by the Kronos Quartet with Aki Takahashi, Europe: Nonesuch, CD 7559-79320-2, 1993.

The Fog, written by John Carpenter and Debra Hill, directed by John Carpenter, 1979, MGM/United Artists Video, 2002, DVD.

Fontana, Bill. *Harmonic Bridge,* site-specific installation at Tate Modern, 2006.

Gasson, Clare. *Washaway Rd,* installation at Gimpel Fils Gallery London, UK, 2008.

Haino, Keiji. Performance at the Drake Hotel Underground in Toronto, Canada, 2006.

Jeannin, Brice. *Shapes for Statics,* installation at The Royal Saltworks of Arc-et-Senan, Besançon, France, 2008.

Lane, Cathy. 'On the Machair', 2007, on *Autumn Leaves,* online audio compilation, http://www.gruenrekorder.de/?page_id=174, 2008.

Lucier, Alvin. *I Am Sitting in a Room,* 1970, US: Lovely Music, Ltd., LCD 1013, 1993.

The Matrix, written and directed by Andy Wachowski and Larry Wachowski, 1999, UK: Warner Home Video, 1999, VHS.

Marclay, Christian. *Records,* 1981–89, US: Atavisitc ALP062CD, 1997.

Merzbow. *1930,* 1997, New York: Tzadik TZ 7214, 1998.

— *Merzbox*, 50 CD Box-set, limited edition, Australia: Extreme XLTD 003, 2000.

Migone, Christof. *Quieting*, Montreal, Canada: alien8 recordings, 2000.

Miller, Graeme. *Linked,* site-specific installation in East London since 2003, with ArtsAdmin London.

Osborn, Ed. *Parabolica*, installation at Centre for the Arts, at Yerba Buena Gardens, San Francisco, CA, 1996.

Palestine, Charlemagne. Performance at the Queen Elizabeth Hall, London, 1998.

Parmegiani, Bernard. 'matières induites', composed 1975, on *De Natura Sonorum*, France: INA-GRM INA C 3001, 1991.

Samakh, Erik. 'Entre Chiens et Loups', excerpt of installation at Crestet centre d'art, Vaison la Romaine, 1995, on *Murs du son – Murmures*, France: Villa Arson 4 x CD, ISBN 2-905075-82-1, 1995.

Shaw, Jeffrey. *The Legible City,* installation at ZKM Karlsruhe, 2006 (orig. 1988–1991).

Stone, Susan. 'Langue Etude', composed 1985, on *Tellus Casette #11 The Sound of Radio*, 1985, http://www.ubu.com/sound/tellus_11.html

Westerkamp, Hildegard. 'Contours of Silence', on *Radio Rethink – Art Sound and Transmission*, CD and Book, Banff, Canada: Walter Phillips Gallery, The Banff Centre for the Arts, 1994.

— 'Kits Beach', composed 1989, on *Transformations*, Montreal: Empreintes Digitales IMED 9631, 1996.

Whitehead, Gregory. 'If a Voice Like Then What?', composed 1984, on *Tellus Casette #11 The Sound of Radio*, 1985, http://www.ubu.com/sound/whitehead.html

Yoshihide, Otomo with Sachiko M. turntables, electronics, sine waves and empty sampler performance at the Corsica Studios, London, 2005.

Index

Lightning Source UK Ltd.
Milton Keynes UK
UKOW02f1358210816

281121UK00001B/39/P